QUIET CATACLYSM

QUIET CATACLYSM

REFLECTIONS ON
THE RECENT TRANSFORMATION
OF WORLD POLITICS

JOHN MUELLER
University of Rochester

HarperCollins*CollegePublishers*

Editor-in-Chief: Marcus Boggs
Project Coordination: Ruttle, Shaw & Wetherill, Inc.
Text and Cover Designer: Wendy Ann Fredericks
Cover Illustration: Diane Margolin
Electronic Production Manager: Valerie A. Sawyer
Desktop Administrator: Hilda Koparanian
Manufacturing Manager: Helene G. Landers
Electronic Page Makeup: RR Donnelley Barbados
Printer and Binder: RR Donnelley & Sons Company
Cover Printer: RR Donnelley & Sons Company

Quiet Cataclysm: Reflections on the Recent Transformation of World Politics
Copyright © 1995 by John Mueller

Library of Congress Cataloging-in-Publication Data
Mueller, John E.
    Quiet cataclysm : reflections on the recent transformation of world politics / John Mueller.
      p. cm.
    Includes bibliographical references and index.
    ISBN 0-673-99327-2
    1. World politics—1989- I. Title.
D860.M84 1995   94-1948
327'.09'04—dc20   CIP

94 95 96 97   9 8 7 6 5 4 3 2 1

To JAM and ESM,

to Karl, Michelle, Karen,
Erik, Susan, and Kraig,

to Robert and Helen Dick,

and to the memory of Carl Honig

CONTENTS

ACKNOWLEDGMENTS

Portions of the research and writing were supported by the University of Rochester and by a John Simon Guggenheim Fellowship. For helpful comments and suggestions at various points, I would like to thank Richard Betts, William T. Bluhm, Michael Doyle, Stanley Engerman, Robert Jervis, William Hauser, Chaim Kaufmann, Carl Kaysen, MacGregor Knox, Christopher Lasch, Sean Lynn-Jones, David MacGregor, Melanie Manion, Karl Mueller, Kenneth Oye, Robert Pahre, Samuel L. Popkin, William Reader, William H. Riker, Richard Rosecrance, Bruce Russett, Kenneth Shepsle, and the members of the PIPES seminar at the University of Chicago, the national security seminar at UCLA, and the Harvard/MIT Institutions Seminar. I would also like to thank Stanley Engerman, Richard Kaeuper, and William Reader for help in gathering historical data. I am particularly grateful for several long, rambling, and highly productive discussions on these issues with the late Carl Honig.

JOHN MUELLER

INTRODUCTION

A *New Yorker* cartoon published sometime in the midst of the Cold War depicted some Eskimos gazing skyward at two missiles, one labeled "USSR," the other "US," which were hurtling past each other in opposite directions. One Eskimo remarks, "Well, I guess that's the end of the world as they know it."

Recently we did come to the end of the world as we knew it then, but, as it happens, no missiles were ever launched. This book comprises a set of reflections centered around that amazing development, and it builds from a central conceit holding that over a period of less than three years—from major shifts in Soviet foreign policy by 1988 to the collapse of a conservative coup in Moscow in 1991—the world underwent a cataclysm that was something like the functional equivalent of World War III.

The recent pleasantness (as Winston Churchill might have called it) was preceded, like its unpleasant and far noisier predecessors of 1914 and 1939, by a lengthy process in which rival countries jockeyed for position as they proclaimed competitive visions of the way the world ought to be ordered, armed themselves to the earlobes, made threatening noises, and confronted each other in traumatic crises. As with World Wars I and II, a consequence of the recent cataclysm was that a major empire was dismembered, important political boundaries in Europe were reorganized, and several nations were politically transformed. And, as the ancient institution of monarchy met its effective demise in Europe in World War I and as the newer, but dangerous and seemingly virile, ideologies of Nazism and Fascism were destroyed by World War II, so a major political philosophy, Communism, over which a tremendous amount of ink and blood had been spilled, was discredited and apparently expunged in World War III.

Following World Wars I and II it took a few years for the basic political order to be settled, after which it remained substantially stable until revised by the next war (or war-equivalent). A similar process of shaking-out seems to be going on now in eastern Europe and in the former Soviet Union—and perhaps also in China. In addition, the victors of World War III, like their predecessors in 1918 and 1945 (and, for that matter, 1815), have been given to proclaiming a new world order in which former enemies can expect to collaborate in international police work. Moreover, the winners have moved to help the losers reestablish themselves as responsible and cooperative members of the international community—a process that was a spectacular success for the Western victors after World War II, but an equally spectacular failure for them after World War I.

Although there may be some merit in considering the experience of the 1989–91 period to have been the functional equivalent of a world war, there are at least two extremely important respects in which the conceit fails miserably.

First, of course, the recent cataclysm, unlike its bloody predecessors, was astoundingly quiet: It took place with very little violence. Some shooting occurred in a few places, particularly in Romania where there was a brief period of warfare between the old guard and the new. But this was nothing compared to what had happened in World Wars I and II. E. H. Carr once observed, "Normally, the threat of war, tacit or overt, seems a necessary condition of important political changes in the international sphere" (1946, 216). Our remarkable recent experience provides an important counter to that proposition—neither war nor the threat of war necessarily impelled the changes.

So many people so quickly became so blasé about this phenomenon that it is perhaps worth screaming a little: *over the course of a couple of years, virtually all the major problems that plagued big-country (sometimes known as Great Power) international relations for nearly half a century were resolved with scarcely a shot being fired, a person being executed, or a rock being thrown.* Among the issues resolved were the unpopular and often brutal Soviet occupation of eastern Europe; the artificial and deeply troubling division of Germany; the expensive, virulent, crisis-prone, and apparently dangerous military contest between East and West; and the ideological struggle between authoritarian, expansionist, violence-encouraging Communism and reactive, sometimes-panicky capitalist democracy.

During the Cold War—the runup to the quiet cataclysm—many people were deeply concerned (terrified, might be a better word) that these problems would reach resolution only through war or violence. Political scientist Hans J. Morgenthau was far from unusual when he glumly, if authoritatively, concluded in 1979 that "the world is moving ineluctably towards a third world war—a strategic nuclear war. I do not believe that anything can be done to prevent it. The international system is simply too unstable to survive for long" (cited in Boyle 1985, 37).

Moreover, the Cold War often seemed intractable, and the contestants seemed deeply committed to their own irreconcilable and divergent views of the world. Coping with Soviet strength, observed Secretary of State Henry Kissinger in 1976, is a condition that "will not go away. And it will perhaps never be conclusively 'solved.' It will have to be faced by every Administration for the forseeable future" (1977, 304). "This book is based on a central proposition," declared a major policymaker of one of those later Administrations, Zbigniew Brzezinski, in 1986: "The American-Soviet conflict is not some temporary aberration but a historical rivalry that will long endure" (1986, xiii). Although they show great sensitivity to the important changes being brought about by Mikhail Gorbachev at the time, Soviet analysts Seweryn Bialer and Michael Mandelbaum still anticipated in 1988 that "the Soviet Union will continue to be a rival of the United States; indeed, it will continue to be the preeminent rival, and vice versa, far into the twenty-first century" (1988, 5). And in particular the Soviet Union seemed so physically and ideologically committed to its eastern European empire, and even more so to its Russian one, that it would never relax its grip without a fight —that it did so essentially by default was amazingly "contrary to the normal behavior of great powers," as Robert Tucker and David Hendrickson observe (1992, 190). Although he is fully aware of the problems of ethnic violence within parts of the former Soviet Union, Sergo Mikoyan, the son of a former Soviet President, thought it worth stressing in 1992 that Russia "has just completed a miracle: a great empire was dissolved and a totalitarian dictatorship was liquidated absolutely peacefully."

Second, although World War III may have caused great changes in international politics, it did not, unlike World Wars I and II, notably change the world's military balance. Indeed, about the only thing that *had not* changed very much by 1991 was the balance of weaponry, particularly the supposedly crucial nuclear weaponry, arrayed on both sides. A negative arms race between East and West had begun by that time, but little real reduction had yet taken place.

The experience of the quiet cataclysm impressively demonstrates that radical change can sometimes happen with astonishing speed. The central Cold War issues concerning eastern Europe were settled over a matter of a few months in 1989 and 1990—a transformation that is as astounding in retrospect as it was at the time. Even as this was happening, George Kennan, noting that the "problem was tremendous in scope and difficulty," and pointing out how "complex" and "profound in its implications is the task of designing this new Europe," predicted that "we will be lucky if the task is substantially accomplished before the end of the century" (1989). Meanwhile Henry Kissinger anticipated that it would take "three or four years" to see "a de facto unification of Germany," a process that was accomplished, de jure, in one (Gordon 1989). And Soviet Communism received its coup de grâce almost overnight during a failed coup d'état in Russia in 1991.

This book is concerned with how this came about, how it changes our views of the past, and what it suggests about the future. Three themes, derived from these observations about the quiet cataclysm, recur at several points. One theme suggests that big problems are often merely reflections of differences of ideas, and thus can change without big means, and particularly without war. The second suggests that military considerations are often substantially irrelevant to the central issues of international politics—weapons are more likely to be indicators of tensions and difficulties than their causes. And the third, related to the first, suggests that big problems—precisely because they are merely about ideas—can, rather like a new rage in hairstyles or skirt length, change very quickly.

Chapter 1 reflects on the future for war and for peace in the aftermath of the quiet cataclysm. Despite the turmoil in portions of eastern Europe and the former Soviet Union, it is possible to be guardedly optimistic about the prospects for future war in the wake of the quiet cataclysm: not only has the likelihood of major war diminished markedly, but the death of the venerable myth of revolution and the end of the Cold War contest may reduce two factors which tended to exacerbate local conflicts while the rise of democracy and of a concerned collegial international community may help to limit and mitigate (but not completely eliminate) them. However, as with the triumph over smallpox, the quiet cataclysm inspired no victory parades, and the catastrophe quota remains comfortably full: as many of the major problems that have bedeviled the world over the last half-century have been resolved, concerns which would previously have been considered minor have risen in perceived importance. It appears that the character in George Bernard Shaw's 1903 play, *Man and Superman,* was on to something when he observed, "There are two tragedies in life. One is not to get your heart's desire. The other is to get it."

Chapter 2 deals with the impact of the demise of the Cold War on certain concerns and concepts promulgated in the international relations theory literature, particularly that of the "structural realist" persuasion. Some theorists argue that the essential structure of world politics is determined by the way capabilities, particularly military ones, are distributed. The experience of the quiet cataclysm suggests, in contrast, that the structure was determined by ideas and ideologies, particularly by the expansionary notion accepted by Communists that worldwide capitalism ought to be overthrown. When Communist leaders changed their minds about that, the structure of world politics changed profoundly even though "capability" measures changed little, particularly at first. Moreover, contrary to the anticipations of some theorists, it seems entirely possible for massive changes in the world order to take place—for the international system to be fundamentally transformed—without war, indeed almost completely without violence. And the experience also suggests that notions central to the realist perspective, like "power" and "anarchy," might productively be reassessed in the new emerging world where economics, not military structure, substantially determines status and influence relations among the major countries.

Chapter 3 further assesses the relationship between weapons and policy and suggests the dependence of arms on politics (rather than the reverse). As happened between the United States and British Canada after 1870, the demise of the Cold War between the USSR and the United States brought about what might be called a negative arms race, suggesting that when countries no longer deem it necessary to fight they will get rid of their arms. It seems clear, accordingly, that weapons are often indicators of tensions, not their causes. The experience also suggests that formal arms control measures can be unnecessary, even counterproductive.

Chapter 4 reconsiders deterrence in the new era, and it suggests that the concept should be broadened to include nonmilitary, as well as military, considerations. Most wars that never take place are deterred by factors that have little to do with weaponry, as should be obvious when small countries so often live peacefully alongside large ones. A model that prominently incorporates such nonmilitary considerations is proposed and developed.

Chapter 5 reflects on the role nuclear weapons played during the Cold War. Although they are often given credit for having prevented a major war, for making the world bipolar, and for keeping the central contestants cautious, it seems rather that they had little to do either with the carrying out of the contest or its resolution. Essentially, they were irrelevant. A direct war between the risk-averse Cold War opponent was never really in the cards: thus, nuclear weapons may have been sufficient to prevent a major war, but they were not necessary to do so.

Chapter 6 reassesses, in retrospect, the Western policy of containment as a method for dealing with expansionary, threatening international Communism. It argues that the policy may well have been misconceived in some important respects. Rather than containing international Communism, the most expeditious method for crushing it might have been to let it expand until it collapsed of its own increasingly unmanageable weight. Events suggest that the containment theorists of the 1940s had it essentially right when they argued that Communism was fundamentally defective and would eventually self-destruct. They were also right when they prescribed policies designed to harass Communism. However, their notion that it was vital to contain Communism as part of this strategy was flawed: Communism died not so much because it was successfully contained but because it was given enough rope to hang itself. When containment effectively lapsed in the late 1970s and Communism dramatically expanded, its fundamental flaws were heightened and this helped to trigger its collapse.

Chapter 7 reexamines Pearl Harbor and the Pacific War in light of the experience of the postwar era. It makes two arguments. First, it concludes that from a military standpoint, Pearl Harbor was more of an inconvenience than a disaster for the United States—damage was quite limited and the attack had little impact on the pace of the Pacific War. Second, it suggests that it would have been better after the attack to have continued a policy of containment and harassment policy toward Japan, rather than direct war. After Pearl Harbor, Japan was vastly overextended and a highly auspicious target for the kind of strategy applied successfully (with the caveats of Chapter 6 in mind) to the Soviet Union after the war: a firm, patient policy consisting of harassment and containment, economic pressure, arming to deter and to threaten, assistance to antagonistic combatants, and perhaps limited warfare on the peripheries. If the point of the war was to force Japan to retreat from its empire and to encourage it to return to more liberal ways, hindsight suggests that a policy of cold war could well eventually have had the same result as hot war and at far lower cost to all involved.

Chapter 8 looks at the nature of war itself and concludes that, while it is clearly impossible to make war impossible, war is not a requirement of the human condition nor does it fulfill a crucial social function. Thus, although war exploits natural instincts and proclivities, it is neither necessary nor inevitable. Accordingly, war can shrivel up and disappear without losing its fascination, without a notable change or improvement in human nature, and without being replaced by anything else.

Chapter 9 considers the historical movement of ideas and traces the growing acceptance, particularly in the last 100 years, of the idea of war aversion. In my 1989 book, *Retreat from Doomsday: The Obsolescence of Major War,* I concluded, as the subtitle suggests, that major war (war among developed countries) is obsolescent (not obsolete), and since publication the world seems to have retreated so far from doomsday that the word, recently so fashionable in alarmed political discourse, has already taken on a patina of archaic quaintness. Developing some of the themes in that book (and responding to some of its critics), this chapter seeks to explain how ideas develop, prosper, and become accepted. It focuses particularly on the profound way attitudes toward war changed in Europe at the time of World War I. This change came about, it seems, not because of objective economic or social developments or because the war was all that peculiarly destructive, but because the idea of war aversion was successfully promoted before the war and because the war experience helped to confirm the arguments of war opponents.

Chapter 10 deals with one of the most dramatic developments accompanying the quiet cataclysm and the demise of Communism: the remarkable, and remarkably effortless, rise of democracy. This experience suggests that in many ways, some of them unanticipated either by its proponents or by its detractors, democracy is substantially superior to its competitors. It also appears that democracy is really quite a simple idea, that it can come into existence quite naturally, and that even elections are not necessary for it to take effect. In addition, it seems that democracy has been able to become established and accepted because, despite the assertions of many of its advocates, in practice it has little to do with equality— indeed, effectively it relies on, and celebrates, inequality—and because of that it can often deal rather effectively with minority concerns, a quality which may make it especially useful for addressing some notable problems in the aftermath of the quiet cataclysm. Moreover, one of democracy's great strengths is that it does not demand much of people and that it can function quite well with the minimal human being. Thus about the only prerequisite for the establishment of democracy is the more or less general desire—probably only by its elites—to do so. The chapter sketches a model that seeks to account for the remarkable growth in acceptance of democracy over the last 200 years, a model that, as in the case of the rise of war aversion, finds the promotional efforts and activities of idea entrepreneurs to be more important influences than broader social or economic changes. Some speculations about the interrelationship—or lack thereof—between democracy and war aversion are also included.

All the chapters were developed from material previously published in various forms and formats, mostly during or shortly after the quiet cataclysm (respectively: Mueller 1992a and 1994c; 1993; 1989/90; 1991a; 1991c; 1988b; 1989b; 1991/92; 1991e; 1991b; 1992b; 1992c). In all cases, however, the material has been reworked, updated, embellished, and rethought—sometimes extensively. The appendix arrays for leisurely perusal a set of predictions—mostly cataclysmic ones—from the last few centuries about peace, war, and other issues. Some (particularly before World War I) predict the imminence of world peace, while others (particularly after that war) predict the imminence of catastrophic destruction.

Chapter 1

War, Peace, and Trouble in the Aftermath of the Quiet Cataclysm

In his farewell address upon leaving the Presidency in January 1953, Harry Truman looked to the future with confidence. He considered the "menace of Communism" and "our fight against it" to be the "overriding issue of our time." But he had no doubt that "as the free world grows stronger, more united, more attractive to men on both sides of the Iron Curtain—and as the Soviet hopes for easy expansion are blocked—then there will have to come a time of change in the Soviet world."

He also looked forward, and with great pleasure, to the "world we hope to have when the Communist threat is overcome." It would be a "new era," he suggested, "a wonderful golden age—an age when we can use the peaceful tools that science has forged for us to do away with poverty and human misery everywhere on the earth. Think what can be done, once our capital, our skills, our science—most of all atomic energy—can be released from the tasks of defense and turned wholly to peaceful purposes all around the world. There is no end to what can be done." With "peace and safety in the world under the United Nations, the developments will come so fast we will not recognize the world in which we live" (Truman 1966, 378).

We have, it appears, entered that "new era." It took a while, but the Soviet Union underwent the fundamental change Truman predicted, and the Communist threat has not merely been overcome, but essentially extinguished. Although we are free as never before to use capital, skill, and science to do away with poverty and human misery, however, it somehow doesn't really feel too much like "a wonderful golden age."

Truman's phrase is extreme, of course—it even dangerously borders on the poetic. And if it is taken to suggest a trouble-free utopia, it could casually be dismissed as an unattainable dream. But, while Truman may sometimes have been a bit of a dreamer, he was too realistic to expect utter perfection. Some of our difficulty in surrendering to such a vision may be that, because of the way we tend to look at the world, we wouldn't know we were in a wonderful golden age if it came up and kissed us on the left earlobe.

As we venture through this new era in the aftermath of the quiet cataclysm, this chapter speculates about world affairs in the new era and particularly on the prospects that substantial violence can be significantly contained or avoided in the current version of the new world order. It also reflects on the remarkable tendency for perceptions to change. Specifically, as big problems—"overriding issues," in Truman's terms—become resolved, we tend to elevate smaller ones, sometimes by redefinition or by raising standards, to take their place. Golden ages, accordingly, never happen.

THE PROSPECTS FOR MAJOR WAR

In evaluating the present, it may not be completely irrelevant to point out that it was only a few years ago when very many people were consumed by the concern that a major war might break out among developed nations. Remember the sword of Damocles? Remember the two scorpions in a bottle? Remember the ticking doomsday clock on the cover of the *Bulletin of the Atomic Scientists?* "Nuclear war," observed Bruce Russett in 1983, "is the central terror of our time" (1983, 1).

As the doomsday clock kept suggesting, moreover, many thought calamity was imminent, even nearly certain. An array of predictions about the imminence and danger of our demise in nuclear war is included in the appendix. A sampling here will give a feel for the concern. In 1945, H. G. Wells declared that "the end of everything we call life is close at hand and cannot be evaded," and the usually prescient diplomat Joseph Grew concluded, "A future war with the Soviet Union is as certain as anything in this world." In 1950, historian Arnold J. Toynbee wrote, "In our recent Western history war has been following war in an ascending order of intensity; and today it is already apparent that the War of 1939–45 was not the climax of this crescendo movement," and Albert Einstein was certain that "unless we are able, in the near future, to abolish the mutual fear of military aggression, we are doomed." In 1961, strategist and futurist Herman Kahn wrote, "I have a firm belief that unless we have more serious and sober thought on various aspects of the strategic problem . . . we are not going to reach the year 2000—and maybe not even the year 1965—without a cataclysm," and C. P. Snow in the same year assured his listeners that unless nuclear weapons were restricted, it was a "certainty" that within "at the most, ten years, some of those [nuclear] bombs are going off." As noted in the Introduction, realist Hans J. Morgenthau concluded in 1979 that "the world is moving ineluctably towards a third world war—a strategic nuclear war. I do not believe that anything can be done to prevent it. The international system is simply too unstable to survive for long." Three years later William McNeill advocated that a "global sovereign power willing and able to enforce a monopoly of atomic weaponry" be fabricated because the "alternative appears to be sudden and total annihilation of the human species," and in 1982 also Jonathan Schell proclaimed, "One day—and it is hard to believe that it will not be soon— we will make our choice. Either we will sink into the final coma and end it all or, as I trust and believe, we will awaken to the truth of our peril . . . and rise up to cleanse the earth of nuclear weapons."

As will be argued in Chapter 5, these concerns were substantially overdone, but many felt them to be very real. As late as the mid-1980s, polls found that 20 to 37 percent of the American population considered the prospect of war to be the most important problem facing the country (Mueller 1994a, Table 45).

It is surely clear that the prospects of major war became far lower after the quiet cataclysm, whatever the likelihood may have been in the past. As Colin Gray puts it, "the prospect of a nuclear World War III has all but vanished" (1992, 13). And former Central Intelligence Agency chief Robert Gates observes that "the danger of a major war in Europe or global thermonuclear war has diminished nearly to the vanishing point" (1993). Polls find agreement: by 1989, the portion fearing war had dropped to 2 percent.

The most likely way such a major war could have come about was out of the deep rivalries and disagreements between the well-armed Cold War contestants. With the evaporation of that contest, the prospects for major war have substantially diminished, even though the earth has hardly became cleansed of nuclear weapons.

THE RECONCILIATION OF GERMANY AND JAPAN

Another major improvement ought to be celebrated—or at least acknowledged. Western foreign policy after 1945 had not one, but two, major themes. Because of its trauma, vast scope, and dramatic intricacies, the contest with international Communism—the Cold War—has garnered the bulk of the attention, and the Western success at the time of the quiet cataclysm received great notice and comment. The other policy theme focused on Germany and Japan, and the goal was to bring those defeated countries into the responsible family of nations and, of course, to keep them from repeating what they had done in World War II. Although this policy success inspired far less notice than the Cold War, policy *failure* in this case would certainly have been of cosmic concern.

Of necessity, the Japanese and the Germans were the principal charters of their own destinies, but Western efforts to guide, nudge, assist, browbeat, bribe, and encourage them along the path they took deserve some credit as well. In the process Germany and Japan have been converted from violent and intensely destructive enemies into prosperous friends, allies, and peaceful competitors whose perspective on the world is much the same as that of the Western victors. As policies go, this might well be among the greatest triumphs of enlightened self-interest in human history, and it deserves appropriate appreciation.

LOCAL WARS

However, even with these very substantial triumphs—vastly reducing the thermonuclear threat, reconciling former enemies—there is still plenty of conflict in the world. Major war may have evaporated as a central concern, but local war remains a problem. There has been a plethora of these since 1945—although the vast majority of these have been civil wars and almost all of them have been fought in what is still being called the Third World. In the wake of the quiet cataclysm, many still flourish, and there are escalating troubles in other areas, particularly within Yugoslavia and the former Soviet Union, where armed turmoil increased and several civil wars—or expanded blood feuds—erupted. And perhaps the other shoe has yet to drop in China.

There are, however, at least four important developments which may act to reduce the frequency and intensity of at least some local wars.

THE DEATH OF THE MYTH OF REVOLUTION

As Communism died, so did many romantic myths about revolution. Over the last two centuries many pundits, philosophers, and political activists have waxed enthusiastic over the alleged purifying effects of violent revolution and, most specifically, Communism has for decades preached that successful revolutions and wars of liberation in the Third World would be followed by social, political, and economic bliss.

Through the 1970s at least, even many non-Communists were still working up enthusiasm for violent, undemocratic revolution. In her multiple-award-winning book about Vietnam, American journalist Frances Fitzgerald, in consonance with many people around the globe, fairly glowed with anticipation at what successful revolutionaries could bring to Southeast Asia. "When 'individualism' and its attendant corruption gives way to the revolutionary community," she breathlessly anticipated, "the narrow flame of revolution" will "cleanse the lake of Vietnamese society from the corruption and disorder of the American war" (1972, 589–590). But in each of the ten countries that edged or toppled into the Communist camp between 1975 and 1979, successful revolutionaries variously led their societies into civil war, economic collapse, and conditions of severe social injustice. Neither corruption nor disorder was eradicated when revolution's narrow flame sliced through Vietnam, and notable evils were perpetrated.

The disasters that followed the successful revolutions in Vietnam and elsewhere principally cleansed the world of the notion that revolution can be cleansing. In the process, a political construct that has inspired cauldrons of ink and acres of blood over the last two centuries has been unceremoniously abandoned. Increasingly, violent revolutionary movements that continue to linger in places like Peru and the Philippines have come to seem odd and anachronistic.

THE RISE OF DEMOCRACY

As violent revolution has become discredited, peaceful democratic reform has begun to look pretty good by comparison. As a result, the democratic idea has flared up—not unlike, perhaps, a narrow flame—throughout the world. As discussed in Chapter 10, democracy is an imperfect, but often effective, method for resolving local conflicts peacefully. Moreover, contrary to conventional expectations, it often seems to have been remarkably easy to institute.

THE DEMISE OF THE COLD WAR CONTEST

Few wars since 1945 have been directly initiated by the major belligerents in the Cold War, but quite a few local wars were exacerbated by interfering Cold War contestants. As discussed in Chapters 2 and 6, a central tenet of Communist ideology was that violent revolutionary conflict was inevitable, and that the Communist states were duty-bound to help out. Meanwhile, the Western policy of containment often suggested that force would have to be used to oppose this thrust.

At times the big countries in the contest restrained—or tried to restrain—their smaller clients. But more often they jumped in. In addition to Korea, Vietnam, the Dominican Republic, Lebanon (1958), India, Afghanistan, and Grenada where troops from the United States, the Soviet Union, and/or China became directly involved, the Cold War can be said to have exacerbated violent conflict within Thailand, Burma, Guatemala, Nicaragua, El Salvador, Venezuela, Cuba, Greece, Peru, Uruguay, Argentina, Bolivia, Cambodia, Laos, Angola, India, Mozambique, Chile, Congo, Brazil, Ethiopia, Algeria, Iraq, various Yemens, Hungary, Zanzibar, South Africa, Guyana, French Indochina, Malaya, Iran, Indonesia, and the Philippines.

With the demise of the Cold War, it is to be expected that such exacerbation will not take place. To the extent that this means that fewer foreign arms and less aid will now be infiltrated to the local contenders, violence will be lower: indeed, by 1991 arms sales to the Third World had dropped to one-third of their 1985 peak (Wright 1993) and by 1993 they had dropped another 20 percent (Schmitt 1993). However, experience suggests that encouragement and sophisticated arms are not required for local warriors to prosper and to commit mayhem, so the improvement is by no means total.

THE PROSPECTS FOR INTERNATIONAL POLICING

In the wake of the quiet cataclysm, two contradictory, even paradoxical, lessons about the future of East-West cooperation can be drawn. On the one hand, as the Gulf crisis of 1990–91 demonstrated, East-West cooperation has become far easier to arrange than before. On the other hand, the two sides are likely to find few trouble spots worthy of their active cooperative efforts.

During the Cold War, cooperation was extremely difficult to bring about because East and West were locked in an intensely competitive struggle. Now, however, both sides seem to agree that their interests are best served by "a reliable peace" and by "a quiet, normal international situation," as Mikhail Gorbachev put it in 1985 (Colton 1986, 191). Thus, there is now a strong incentive to cooperate to generate peace and stability.

The dynamic of the Cold War contest also caused the two sides to believe that their interests were importantly engaged almost everywhere: the Western policy of containment was based on the notion that any gain for Communism would lead to further Western losses elsewhere, while the Soviets held that they should aid anti-Western forces throughout the globe. As this elemental contest has evaporated, however, most areas of the world have become substantially less important to the two sides. In the 1960s, a civil war in the Congo inspired dedicated meddling by both sides; in the 1990s no one wanted to become involved very much in the civil war in Liberia—or in such intractable conflicts as those in Lebanon or Sri Lanka. Even costly conflicts in such once-important Cold War arenas as Angola and Cambodia mainly elicited hand-wringing from the former contestants—certainly neither offered to send troops to pacify and police the situation.

Thus, although both sides have an interest in peace and stability, they probably will be stirred to significant cooperative action—sending their troops into harm's way—only in those few remaining areas, like the Persian Gulf, where they feel their interests to be importantly engaged. In this respect, the Gulf experience bodes rather well for at least two potential trouble areas: eastern Europe and Korea. Should resurgent nationalism in the one case or persistent division in the other lead to international conflict or to substantial international crisis, the United States and Russia, together with Western Europe and Japan, may well be launched into cooperative action, possibly even into military action, to contain damage and to rectify problems in these important areas.

Cooperation will certainly be an improvement over the hazardous competition of the Cold War. But euphoria about the emergence of a peaceful new world order or of global collective security is hardly justified. Moreover, with respect to the most likely form of violent conflict—civil war—the big countries may not be able to stir themselves into anything like action. For the most part, they are likely to cheer from the sidelines as organizations like the United Nations take over the singularly unglamorous work of peacekeeping and peace enforcing in peripheral areas. A limited number of lives will be lost in such ventures, but if the organizational structure of such operations is arranged so that losses are suffered by comparatively faceless international volunteers, not by identifiable national units, the domestic political impact in individual countries will be attenuated (see Urquhart 1993).

The contrast of the edgy tedium of Cyprus and Northern Ireland with the dramatic catastrophe of Bosnia suggests that the patient police work carried out in Nicosia and Belfast has probably saved thousands of lives over the years. But it tends to be a profoundly thankless job because the people whose lives have been saved do not know who they are, and they are often critical or even contemptuous of their unappreciated saviors.[1] With the demise of the Cold War competition, such ventures become far more possible, however, as East and West find themselves on the same side of many conflicts. Indeed, of the twenty-six peacekeeping missions the UN undertook between 1945 and 1992, fully twelve were begun after 1988, in the wake of the Cold War (Prial 1992), and the UN's peacekeeping budget quadrupled from $700 million in 1991 to $2.8 billion in 1992 (*New York Times,* 12 December 1992, 12).

In addition, with the application of economic sanctions to Iraq in 1990, to Haiti in 1991, and to Serbia in 1992, the big countries may be honing a credible, inexpensive, and potentially potent new weapon for use against small and medium-size aggressors and troublemakers. Essentially, they have been able to demonstrate that the world can get along quite well without the economic participation of such countries, and that, in their new era of comparative harmony, they can inflict enormous pain on such countries at remarkably little cost to themselves. In some respects, economic sanctions require more patience and fortitude than military action, but, if cooperative harmony continues to reign among the major countries, sanctions may prove to be a credible and sometimes effective weapon of control.

THE QUEST FOR TROUBLE
AFTER THE QUIET CATACLYSM

This survey has suggested a few reasons why one might be guardedly optimistic about some (but certainly not all) issues of war and peace in the aftermath of the quiet cataclysm. However, the quest for things to worry about has continued unabated.

For example, the notion quickly took hold that international affairs had somehow become especially tumultuous, unstable, and complex, an idea repeated so often it soon began to sound like a mantra. Thus, Bill Clinton proclaimed in his

---

[1]The mission to Somalia in 1992–1993 helped to bring order to an anarchic and deadly situation that was causing a famine reportedly killing at its peak thousands of people per day. Within a few months that figure had been brought down to two or three a day. Unlike the Gulf War which cost the lives of tens or even hundreds of thousands, however, this spectacularly successful military mission which merely *saved* large numbers of lives brought no calls for celebratory parades, and the troops who pulled it off remember it most for the boredom and for the teenagers who cursed them (in English) and pelted them with stones and fruit (Lorch 1993). Asked if the mission was worth it, one Army specialist responded, "How many Americans did we lose? Seven? Well, not one of those lives was worth it. . . . Heck, a lot of these people didn't even let us help them" (Fineman 1993). *New York Times* columnist William Safire has blandly observed of the venture that "the saving of hundreds of thousands of lives is no small thing" (1993). What, one might wonder, would he consider to be a *large* thing? Perhaps never in human history has so much been done for so many at such little cost.

1993 Presidential inaugural address that "the new world is more free but less stable." And a few days later his nominee to become the head of the Central Intelligence Agency, James Woolsey, testified darkly (and not, perhaps, without a degree of institutional self-interest) that "we have slain a large dragon, but we live now in a jungle filled with a bewildering variety of poisonous snakes." For the skeptical, he helpfully enumerated the snakes: "the proliferation of weapons of mass destruction and the ballistic missiles to carry them; ethnic and national hatreds that can metastasize across large portions of the globe; the international narcotics trade; terrorism; the dangers inherent in the West's dependence on Mideast oil; new economic and environmental challenges." His predecessor at the CIA, Robert Gates, fully agreed: "The events of the last two years have led to a far more unstable, turbulent, unpredictable and violent world" (1993). This theme has also been echoed by some international relation scholars as they try to come to grips with a field undergoing tremendous change, in which old categories no longer work very well and at times there is an apparent decreased interest in the Academy. Thus as Harvard's Stanley Hoffmann puts it, "the problem of order has become even more complex than before" (1992, 37).

To arrive at such conclusions, five techniques have been applied: the past has been simplified, a Eurocentric bias has been introduced, definitions have been changed, standards have been raised, and problems previously considered to be comparatively minor have been elevated in perceived importance.

SIMPLIFYING THE PAST: RECOLLECTIONS OF THE COLD WAR

Conclusions about the comparative complexity of the world in the wake of the quiet cataclysm stem in part from a remarkably simplified recollection of what went on during the Cold War.

This phenomenon is related to the tendency to look backward with misty eyes, to see the past as much more benign, simple, and innocent than it really was (by contrast, see Bettmann 1974). That is, no matter how much better the present gets, the past gets better faster in reflection, and we are, accordingly, always notably worse off than we used to be. Golden ages, thus, do happen, but we are never actually *in* them: they are always back there somewhere in the past (or, sometimes, in the ungraspable future).

For example, those reminiscing about the "happy days" of the 1950s casually forget McCarthyism, a terribly destructive war in Korea, and an intense unease brought about by the apparently credible Communist threat to "bury" the West in a decade or two, something that was bolstered by CIA predictions that the Soviet Union's Gross National Product might be triple that of the United States by the year 2000 (Reeves 1993, 54).

Or there is Woolsey's recollection that the Cold War threat could be characterized "precisely and succinctly" because our adversary was "a single power whose interests fundamentally threatened ours" (1993). Or the belief of the *New York Times*' Thomas Friedman that "all the policy-makers had to do was take out their compasses, point them at any regional conflict in the world, see which side Moscow was on and immediately deduce which side America should take"

(1992a). Or the confident assertion of *Newsweek*'s Meg Greenfield that "conducting the nation's business overseas has become more difficult with the disappearance of a unifying, clearly defined and universally understood threat" (1993).

But the Communist threat was shifting, multifaceted, and extremely complicated. And most of the time there were two central sources of threat, China and the USSR, not one. Indeed, the challenge the Vietnam War was principally designed to counter came from China, not from the Soviet Union (Mueller 1989a, 168–73). Moreover, China and the Soviet Union, while jointly threatening the West, were often intensely at odds with each other—nearly at war a few times— over both strategy and tactics, complicating things further. And it was often extremely difficult to deduce which side to take: the United States supported the Chinese group against the Soviet one in Angola, puzzled for years over whose side Cuba's Fidel Castro was on, joined with the Soviet Union to support the formation of Israel as well as the leftist regime in Tanzania, found that virtually all Communist rebellions were confusingly associated with indigenous ones, and never really did determine whether some countries, like Mozambique, were Communist or not.

Friedman and others may think that the policy of containment—with its overarching theory about confronting Communist expansionism—gave a clear and easily followed guideline and allowed for a great deal of consistency in U.S. foreign policy, but the actual experience of the Cold War surely suggests that there was a great deal of bobbing and weaving in the application of the policy: the policy was inconsistently carried out and dilemmas proliferated. Even as the containment policy was being formulated, the Truman administration was allowing China to fall into the Communist camp. Eisenhower was unwilling to use military measures to prevent a Communist victory in Indochina, but he held fast on the islands of Quemoy and Matsu off the China coast. Kennedy sought to shore up the anti-Communist position in South Vietnam even as he was acquiescing in an agreement that gave the Communists effective control of large portions of neighboring Laos. Containment policy may have been a useful general guide, but it clearly did not make policy easy to formulate.

Indeed, if the post–Cold War world resembles a jungle filled with poisonous snakes, the Cold War was a jungle filled with at least two dragons *and* with poisonous snakes, some of whom were variously, changeably, and often quite ambiguously in devious complicity with the one or the other of the dragons. It seems obvious which jungle is preferable—and less complicated.

In the process, the Cold War added an especially difficult layer of complexity to U.S. relations with a whole host of countries. At one time the United States had to treat Mobutu of Zaire as a dictator who had brought his country to ruin but who was on the right side in the Cold War. After the quiet cataclysm it can treat him merely as a dictator who has brought his country to ruin. In that very important respect, international policy has become far *less* complex than it was during the Cold War.

Greenfield bemoans "the disintegration of order, authority and institutions all over the world" (1993), implying that w e have just emerged from a world where everything was nice and orderly and where authority was unchallenged—a bizarre suggestion. Relatedly, Hoffmann argues that "during the Cold War, the super-powers, driven by the fear of nuclear war, devised by trial and error, a network of rules and restraints aimed at avoiding direct military collision" (1992, 37). This is true, although it is certainly worth noting that those countries still managed to get into quite a few *indirect* military collisions, some of them extremely bloody. And in our new world, however "disorderly" and "complex" it may be, the dangers of a military collision, direct or indirect, between East and West have become so attenuated that it becomes almost absurd to suggest that "a network of rules and restraints" are necessary to avoid it—any more than one would maintain that such a network is necessary to prevent military conflict between the United States and Canada.

EUROCENTRISM AND THE PERSISTENCE OF NATIONALISM

As will be discussed more fully below, most of the poisonous snakes Woolsey specifies were already there in full measure during the Cold War and thus, applying his metaphor, the post–Cold War jungle has snakes whereas the Cold War jungle contained not only snakes but a dragon as well. Some people might consider that a notable improvement and, as jungles go, a notable reduction in the complexities of daily life.

Warfare arising from ethnic and national hatreds, one of Woolsey' snakes, is certainly not new. As Barry Posen has pointed out, "Nationalism was hardly quiescent in the last forty-five years: it played a key role in the decolonization process, fueling both revolutionary and inter-state warfare" (1993, 80). But there are new concerns about this in Europe, and those who find the world more complicated and unstable than during the Cold War tend to focus on conflict on that continent. For a long period after the end of the Greek civil war in 1949 there were no civil wars in Europe, and that remarkable record has now been shattered with the civil wars that have erupted in the former Yugoslavia. In addition, political and economic chaos—some of it violent—has accompanied the disintegration of the Soviet and then the Russian empires in eastern Europe and particularly in Asia.

These problems are, of course, very real. But it is surely worth pointing out again that they have followed a remarkable—and remarkably peaceful—resolution of a host of key international problems centered in Europe. Moreover, although the resolution of the Cold War may sometimes conceivably have had the unintended effect of releasing ethnic, national, and racial forces that had previously been bottled up by the Cold War contest itself, these forces were kept under control by some of the most brutal police methods ever devised and, while the police may have been able to suppress some ethnic and national violence, they were obviously unable to mitigate the supposed underlying hatreds. Moreover, it is not really clear that the Cold War was so instrumental in arresting civil conflict. "Ethnic cleansing" is hardly new—for years Bulgarian Communists had a persecution policy focused on domestic Turks, for example—and fighting between Armenians and Azeris began before the Cold War ended while Yugoslavia's ethnic conflicts derived from an ill-managed effort to confederate the country, something that could have happened almost as well during the Cold War as after it (see Bell-Fiakoff 1993).

In addition, if it is correct in some sense to suggest that post–Cold War Europe now has more armed conflict than during the Cold War, much of the rest of the world was suffering *less* armed conflict than earlier. Specifically, during the Cold War Latin America underwent a long and bloody series of civil wars most of which were inspired or exacerbated by the Cold War contest. After the Cold War this area became far freer of civil war. Even more notable is the experience of East Asia. The Cold War led to, or notably exacerbated, lengthy and costly wars in Korea, Malaya, Thailand, China, Vietnam, and elsewhere, and in Cambodia it led not only to civil war, but a postwar peace that was even worse. Problems remain in East Asia, but surely it became far more stable, peaceful, and economically productive after the Cold War than it had been during it.

It would be difficult to argue that problems of war have changed much one way or the other in the other major non-European areas—South Asia, the Middle East, and Africa. Troubles obviously persist, although it may be worth observing that there has not been a conventional international Arab-Israeli or India-Pakistan war for decades. Amazingly, present-day Hindu-Muslim violence has occasionally been credited to the demise of the Cold War, a perspective that manages blithely to ignore the wars, riots, and massacres that took place between those two communities with a fair amount of regularity during the Cold War.

Thus, even if it is conceded that instability and complexity have increased in Europe in the wake of the Cold War in some sense—a development, however, that has been attended by enormous gains in freedom and in the resolution of some old and very dangerous territorial and political issues—stability, particularly in the sense of freedom from civil war, has been greatly enhanced in two other areas, Latin America and East Asia, and is probably no worse than before in the rest of the world. Unless one adopts a thoroughly Eurocentric perspective, it is simply not true that "conflicts among nations and ethnic groups are escalating" (Huntington 1993a, 71). The world as a whole is no less stable in this sense than it was during the Cold War.

Because nationalism, or hypernationalism, was a cause of World Wars I and II in Europe, a concern about its reappearance there is certainly reasonable (see, for example, Mearsheimer 1990, Van Evera 1990/91). It is not clear, however, that nationalism has grown any less strong in peaceful western Europe. It is certainly true that few national differences there are being expressed in violence, in threats of violence, or in once-fashionable messianic visions about changing the world to reflect the national perspective (Howard 1991, chs. 2, 4). But that does not necessarily mean that western Europeans are less nationalistic than they were in the 1920s or the 1890s. Do the British (many of them distinctly unamused by the prospects of the new Channel tunnel) love the French any more or less than in days of yore? Do Italians think of themselves less as Italians? Closer economic relations in Europe may only suggest that it has finally dawned on those countries that there is benefit in economic cooperation, not that Europeans love each other any more or that they identify themselves more now as Europeans. German unification was a spectacular (and peaceful) triumph of national desire: if German nationalism had been truly dampened, one might have expected two Germanys to have emerged when the Soviets left, but instead the general conclusion was that an independent East Germany made no sense, and the Germans rushed into each other's arms.

Nationalism can lead to war and turmoil, of course, but as the experience in western Europe suggests, it does not have to be eradicated for peace to prevail. France and Germany today do not by any means agree about everything but, shattering the pattern of the century previous to 1945, they no longer even conceive of using war or the threat of war to resolve their disagreements. As F. H. Hinsley has put it, in Europe and North America, once "the cockpit for the world's great wars," states "are coming to terms with the fact that war has ceased to be one of their options" at least in their dealings with one another (1987, 78–79).

As will be discussed more fully in Chapters 8 and 9, there has been a great change in attitude toward war in most of the developed world. A hundred years ago, as Michael Howard has observed, "war was almost universally considered an acceptable, perhaps an inevitable and for many people a desirable way of settling international differences" (1984, 9). Those views, so common then, are remarkably rare today in the developed world, and this may suggest that the appeal of war has diminished markedly, that war is going out of style, on a continent that for centuries was the most warlike in the world. As Robert W. Tucker and David Hendrickson have put it, in our times, "war is no longer a means generally permitted to states for the redress of rights that have been violated. Still less is war considered a legitimate means for changing the status quo." It "no longer serves as an apt and proportionate means for resolving international conflicts" (1992, 133–34).[2]

It will be of great interest to see if that attitude has infected eastern Europe as the countries there chart their destinies after the quiet cataclysm. As noted, they did remarkably well at avoiding violence during their liberation from Soviet rule, and that may lead one to hope that, despite the Yugoslav case, international war, at least, can be avoided in the area and that the apparent surge of militant nationalism will prove to be a momentary historical blip. Indeed, nationalism in some form could well be a constructive force: if Poland survives its current test of trauma and turmoil, Polish nationalism will probably have been an important strength.

SHIFTING DEFINITIONS

To inspire, or justify, worry in the wake of the Cold War, trouble-spotters have ingeniously changed the meanings of several key words.

---

[2]It is interesting in this regard that many people found Saddam Hussein's invasion of Kuwait in August 1990 to be remarkably odd. Although the Iraqis had been building up troops on the border, the director of the U.S. Defense Intelligence Agency "just did not find it conceivable that Saddam would do something so anachronistic as an old-fashioned land grab. Countries didn't go around doing things like that anymore" (Woodward 1991, 217). That perspective may be premature since there have been a number of out-of-the-blue land grab efforts in recent memory—by such countries as India (1961), China (1962), and perhaps Iraq (1980)—but the general notion that that sort of behavior is going out of style may prove to have substance.

STABILITY.   During the Cold War, instability was usually equated with the dangers of a nuclear war between the United States and the Soviet Union. For people with that perspective, stability was enhanced whenever the United States and the USSR seemed to move farther from conflict with each other. Using that still reasonable standard, the world began to wallow in stability after the quiet cataclysm (see pages 59–60).

For Cold War nostalgists, there are two ways out of the dilemma posed by this seemingly desirable development. One is blithely to deny that thermonuclear war was really all that big a deal. Thus, Karen Elliott House of the *Wall Street Journal* has calmly concluded that "the post–Cold War world is less threatening only in the simplistic sense that superpower confrontation, for the time being, is a thing of the past" (1992). Accordingly, decades of Cold War traumas and fears are casually dismissed out of hand.

Or one can deftly finesse the definition and argue that localized blood feuds and border conflicts are now to be considered signs of instability. But to be consistent, one would then have to suggest, as I have above, that the Cold War by that standard was also very unstable because blood feuds and border conflicts happened all over the place and because conflict among the Great Powers was often real or potential in many of them.

MAJOR WAR AND GLOBAL CONFLICT.   In the olden days of the Cold War, major wars or global conflicts were conflagrations in which the big countries—Great Powers, some people called them—became viscerally and directly involved: the kind of thing that happened in World Wars I and II. However, on 14 July 1992, former President Jimmy Carter made a speech about foreign policy at the Democratic National Convention (a distinct rarity at that venue) in which he announced that there were thirty-five "major wars" going on in the world. As he explained it later, he designated a "major war" as any conflict in which at least 1,000 people had been killed.[3] Thus, he took a standard definition for "war" (see Singer and Small 1972, 49) and relabeled it "major war." For Carter, apparently, wars are like olives: they are all at least gigantic.

Similarly, in a review in 1991 in the *New York Times* of a book by Michael Howard that came out before the Gulf War of that year, Herbert Mitgang argued that the following observation of Howard's is "prescient": "The one place in the world today where a global conflict might still conceivably originate is the Persian Gulf" (Howard 1991, 169). The only way that statement could be considered prescient would be if one elevated the Gulf War to the status of "global conflict." Mitgang adds, rather opaquely, that "after two World Wars, it's hard to distinguish local wars from large-scale wars" (Mitgang 1991). One would have thought it would continue to be easy to discriminate: the differences, after all, are not really all that subtle.

---

[3]MacNeil/Lehrer NewsHour, 15 February 1993.

WEAPONS OF MASS DESTRUCTION. A similar sleight of tongue seems to have been carried out on what Woolsey calls "weapons of mass destruction" (see also Krauthammer 1991, 30). At one time, the phrase was taken to refer to nuclear arms, but somewhere along the line it came to refer as well to chemical ones—devices that are far less effective at killing.[4]

This ingenious exercise in redefinition may help to solve a problem for the professional doomsayers who have been beating their breasts about nuclear proliferation for the last several decades. For example, the National Planning Association predicted "a rapid rise in the number of atomic powers . . . by the mid-1960s" (1958, 42). A couple of years later, C. P. Snow sagely predicted that, "within, at the most, six years, China and several other states [will] have a stock of nuclear bombs" (1961, 259). Meanwhile, Britain's sometime defense minister, Denis Healey, remarked that "so far, no country has resisted the temptation to make its own atomic weapons once it has acquired the physical ability to do so" (1960, 3). This was not true even then. Canada could have gone nuclear by that time if it had wanted to, and it is Canada's experience that seems to have been more nearly typical (see Mueller 1967).

As Stephen Meyer has shown, there is no "technological imperative" for countries to obtain nuclear weapons once they have achieved the technical capacity to do so (1984; see also Kaysen, McNamara, and Rathjens 1991, 98). Indeed, one of the most interesting developments in the postwar world has been the slow pace with which nuclear weapons have proliferated. Moreover, several nations— Brazil, Argentina, South Africa, South Korea, Taiwan—have actually backed away from or reversed nuclear weapons programs (Graham 1991).[5] Some of this has no doubt been due to the hostility of the nuclear nations. But much seems as well to be due to the inability of many potential nuclear states to see much value in the possession of the weapons. What problems would such an expensive venture solve? How much more status would Japan have if it possessed nuclear weapons? Would people pay that much more attention to Britain or France if they possessed 50,000 nuclear weapons, or would they pay that much less if they possessed none? Israel's nuclear weapons did not keep the Arabs from attacking in 1973, nor did Britain's possession of them prevent Argentina's seizure of the Falklands in 1982. And the tens of thousands of nuclear weapons in the hands of the enveloping allied forces did not cause Saddam Hussein to order his occupying forces out of Kuwait in 1990.

Thus nuclear proliferation has been disappointingly slow from the pessimists' standpoint. But if we can now embellish the definition by adding other weapons and pretending they are the same as nuclear weapons, there is some hope we can worry afresh and with renewed alarm.

---

[4]On these issues, see McNaugher 1990. McNaugher also observes that a preoccupation with missile proliferation may be misplaced. For most countries, missiles are vastly inferior to aircraft for delivering weaponry. Thus it may be wise to encourage countries to waste their money on these expensive and unreliable weapons systems in preference to having them buy cheaper and more effective airplanes.

[5]A survey of 800 experts conducted in 1977 picked Brazil and South Africa as the countries most likely to have nuclear weapons in the "near future," and only 11 percent were of the (correct) view that there would be no additional nuclear countries by 1982 (Kramer and Russett 1984, 332).

Raising Standards

A caption poised above an old carpet sweeper on display in an exhibit in the Strong Museum in Rochester, New York, nicely illustrates the phenomenon of standard raising. "Labor-saving devices like carpet sweepers helped middle-class people satisfy their desire for cleanliness within the home," observes the caption writer. Lest one conclude that this advance made things better, however, the writer quickly adds, "Unfortunately, each new development raised standards and expectations for cleanliness, making the ideal as hard as ever to achieve." Things, accordingly, never get better.

Hoffmann, for example, suggests that "a policy of world order would require that the many sources of global or regional turbulence be dealt with in ways that would minimize violent conflict among states, reduce injustice among and within states, and prevent dangerous violations of rights within them" (1992, 38). But, as Max Singer and Aaron Wildavsky suggest, Hoffmann sets amazingly high standards for order, "standards never attained in human history," and they aptly characterize his conclusion, "the obstacles to such a policy are formidable," as "the mother of all understatements" (1993, 191).

Similarly Gates argues that we now live in a world "where instability, turbulence and violence are widespread and where no one can predict the shape of things to come" (1993). That is, the standard he seeks is a fantastic one in which instability, turbulence and violence have evaporated and where prediction is perfect. Meanwhile Zbigniew Brzezinski published an alarmist book in which he argued that "global change is out of control" (1993, ix), implying apparently that there was a time when it was notably *in* control. Huntington argues that "wherever one turns, the world is at odds with itself" (1993c, 194), a vague formulation that has always been, and always will be, true in some sense or other. And Norwegian Foreign Minister Johan Jørgen Holst once observed that "a clear and present danger has been replaced by unspecified risks and dangers" (1992). As discussed in Chapter 8, conflict—and therefore trouble, not to mention unspecified risks and dangers—is inevitable because it is impossible for everyone to have exactly the same interests. To yearn for its eradication is essentially absurd.

Relatedly, commentators regularly apply exalted standards to judge the many states of the world that have suddenly become democratic and capitalist. They bemoan the corruption that has attended the development of capitalism in some formerly Communist countries, blithely ignoring the facts that the displaced Communist system had often been monumentally corrupt and that corruption is often rampant even in highly developed capitalist countries like Japan.[6] Or they complain about the inability of some newly democratic countries to get things done even as they forget the presidential campaign of 1992 in democratic America

---

[6]A 1990 survey of Moscow residents about economic issues found in some cases that notably anti-capitalistic notions were held by substantial numbers of people there. As it happens, the same survey was given in the world center of capitalism, New York City; it found attitudes there to be much the same. See Shiller et al. 1991.

which was largely devoted to noisy moans and groans about the "gridlock" that is purportedly endemic in that political system.[7]

ELEVATING SMALLER PROBLEMS

Finally, when big problems (dragons in Woolsey's characterization) go away, small problems (snakes) can be elevated in perceived importance.

As it happens, none of Woolsey's poisonous snakes is new and some of them are actually of less urgent concern than they were during the Cold War. As argued above, nuclear proliferation is no more a new problem—in fact, may well be less of a problem—than it was in 1960 when John Kennedy repeatedly pointed out with alarm that there might be ten, fifteen, or twenty states with a nuclear capacity by 1964 (Kraus 1962, 394). And the international drug trade has obviously been around for quite some time, while the West's supposedly dangerous dependence on Mideast oil has been a matter of pointed concern at least since 1973.

The impact of international terrorism has often been more in the exaggerated hysteria it generates than in its actual physical effects—fewer Americans had been killed by terrorists than had been killed by lightning in the preceding decade (see Figure 1.1). Indeed, although there was a rise in 1991 at the time of the Gulf War, terrorism declined in frequency from late Cold War days—mostly because of enhanced prevention measures and better international policing.[8] Few seem to remember how frequent and fashionable airline hijackings once were, and even fewer remember the enormous concern generated during the Cold War era by the Red Brigades in Italy, the Baader-Meinhoff gang in Germany, the Red Guards in Japan, and the Symbionese Liberation Army in the United States. Despite all this, however, Gates confidently predicts that "there will be a steady increase in the resort to terrorism" (1993).

Economic and environmental challenges are hardly new either, but new alarms can be raised. Some have sighted a dangerously new enemy on the economic front: insidiously peaceful Japan. Those of the FLASH! JAPAN BUYS PEARL HARBOR! school, like Huntington, argue that we must fear not "missile vulnerability" but "semiconductor vulnerability." "Economics," he apparently seriously warns us, "is the continuation of war by other means" (Huntington 1991a, 8, 10),[9] and he admonishes that the issue is whether the United States "can meet the eco-

---

[7]One analyst notes with alarm that a poll has found that 79 percent of the Romanian population feels politicians were "ready to promise anything to get votes" while 65 percent say politicians are more interested in strengthening their own parties than in solving the country's problems (Shafir 1993, 18). The improbable implication, apparently, is that those numbers would be lower in real democracies like the United States.

[8]On successful Spanish and French police work against Basque terrorists, see *New York Times*, 11 March 1993, A5.

[9]The concept of economic war comes close to being oxymoronic. There are times when it may make some sense (as when the world ganged up in 1990 against Iraq), but war is substantially zero or negative sum while economic exchange, although not always fully fair or equal, is generally positive sum—both parties gain. See Jervis 1993, 57–58.

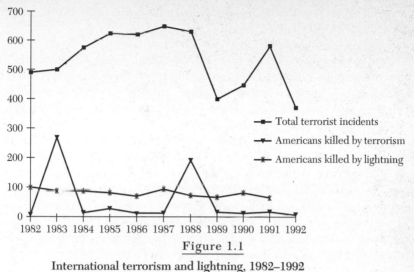

Sources: U.S. Department of State, Patterns of Global Terrorism, January 1988, April 1993; National Safety Council (Chicago), Accident Facts, various issues.

Figure 1.1

International terrorism and lightning, 1982–1992

nomic challenge from Japan as successfully as it did the political and military challenges from the Soviet Union." If not, the U.S. is destined to lose its "primacy in a crucial arena of power" (1991, 8, 10, 16). Danger signals arise because Japan has become the largest provider of foreign aid and because it has shockingly endowed professorships at Harvard and MIT (Huntington 1993a, 77, 80).

By mid-1993, however, the Japanese economy had gone into a slump while the U.S. economy was beginning to look pretty good by comparison. Huntington, ever the most flexible and inventive of doomsayers, now extrapolated from the civil war in Bosnia and proclaimed that, actually, the "fundamental cause of conflict" henceforth will *not* be "primarily ideological or primarily economic." Rather, "The great divisions among humankind and the dominating source of conflict will be cultural" (1993b, 22). There are, it turns out, some seven or eight major civilizations in the world, and these civilizations are destined to "clash" mightily, mostly along "the fault lines separating these civilizations from one another" (1993b, 25).[10] Western "civilization," primarily supported the creation of a state in Bosnia that would be dominated by people from the Islamic "civilization," but this troubles Huntington so little that he ignores the issue entirely (1993b, 37–38), so busy is he assuring us that the Western ideas of "liberalism, constitutionalism, human rights, equality, liberty, the rule of law, democracy, free markets" have "little

---

[10]On the other hand, Huntington also argues that "wars occur most frequently between societies with high levels of interaction" (1993c, 192), so violent clashes presumably are even more likely *within* civilizations.

resonance" in places like liberal, law-abiding, democratic, constitutional capitalistic Japan (1993b, 40).[11]

Or there are other problems. In 1993, historian Paul Kennedy wrote a pessimistic best-seller in which he attempted to peer into the next century and was able to work up quite a bit of concern over pollution, immigration, and robotics. Interestingly enough, war, a central issue in another pessimistic best-seller he wrote in 1987, had apparently vanished from his concerns: the word, *war,* does not even appear in the index of his later book.

Additionally, of course, one can always find domestic issues to worry about. In another 1993 book, Zbigniew Brzezinski found turmoil everywhere and blamed much of it on material wealth, on self-indulgence, and on that perennial recipient of potshots, television. Or we can rediscover hate and racial problems as if they had never existed before, moan about the economic problems caused by the fact that people live too long and medical care has gotten too good,[12] and agonize over whether it has become necessary to raise gasoline taxes or to re-regulate cable TV.

Or we can worry that Americans "are being overwhelmed, even paralyzed" by all the choices that confront them in the marketplace. Thus, David Goslin asserts "As social scientists, we know that with an increase in choices, people tend to become more anxious;" sociologist Todd Gitlin points out that "If you have infinite choice, people are reduced to passivity;" and futurist Alvin Toffler worries about "overchoice—the point at which the advantage of diversity and individualization are canceled by the complexity of the buyer's decision-making process" (Williams 1990). Clearly, if Hamlet was faced by only two alternatives and found himself agonizing over it for five full acts, we must be far, far worse off today. This conundrum seems to be an updated version of the classic Aristotelian puzzle known as "Buridan's ass" in which the animal is placed at an equal distance from two bundles of hay and eventually starves to death in terminal indecision. There seems to be no evidence any ass ever actually underwent this agony, but all the information thus far is merely anecdotal and this might well be one of those many areas crying out for well-funded systematic research.[13]

---

[11]Huntington challenges his (many) critics to produce "a better explanation for what is going on in the world" (1993c, 194). One that suggests itself is Thomas Friedman's observation (1992b) that the world is being divided into forward-looking states like Japan who effortlessly produce superb products like the Lexus automobile and backward-looking ones like Serbia who fight over who owns which cherry tree. While the Lexus-builders of the world are willing to expend money and a small number of lives to help the cherry tree battlers settle their disputes, they are principally determined, failing coherent resolution of these conflicts, to contain and isolate such conflicts while they continue pursuing their primary goal—to become even richer. See also Rosecrance 1986.

[12]In 1993, it was announced that life expectancy at birth for Americans had risen to a record 75.5 years. So boring was this news that the *New York Times* simply reprinted as Associated Press dispatch on the issue and buried it on the thirteenth page of its September 1 issue.

[13]In one area, however, the problem may solve itself. If customers in supermarkets become paralyzed with anxious indecision in front of, for example, the corn flakes, they will block the aisles. This will reduce the profits of the store owner who will then logically be forced to increase the aisle space which will in turn reduce the choice angst confronting the previously hapless customer.

THE CATASTROPHE QUOTA

In all, then, misanthropes can take unaccustomed cheer. Even in a state of considerable peace there will still be plenty to complain and worry about: the catastrophe quota will always remain comfortably full (see also Safire 1991). Even though the chances of a global thermonuclear catastrophe (a humongous war on Carter's scale, presumably) have diminished to the point where remarkably few even worry about it anymore, one can concentrate on more vaporous enemies like trouble, chaos, uncertainty, unpredictability, instability and "unspecified risks and dangers." These are enemies that—like economics, civilization, and choice—will always comfortably be with us.

Howard observes that "each new generation is presented with new problems and new challenges" (1991, 5). That is certainly true, but one can still perhaps pause to celebrate such passing achievements as the eradication of smallpox or the decline of the threat of global thermonuclear war, and it does not seem too much to suggest that a world without such terrors is better than one with them. But for all that, it really does appear that if we ever enter Truman's "wonderful golden age," we will never notice: "Status quo," as Ronald Reagan reportedly liked to put it, is Latin for "the mess we're in."

Chapter 2

REALISM AND THE COLD WAR

Robert Dahl has observed that "because of their concern with rigor and their dissatisfaction with the 'softness' of historical description, generalization, and explanation, most social scientists have turned away from the historical movement of ideas. As a result, their own theories, however 'rigorous' they may be, leave out an important explanatory variable and often lead to naive reductionism." Since beliefs and ideas are often, as Dahl notes, "a major independent variable," to ignore changes in ideas, ideologies, and attitude is to leave something important out of consideration (1971, 182–183, 188).

This chapter traces the impact of ideas on issues concerning international relations theory and international security. Related notions about the importance of changes in ideas appear in Chapters 9 and 10.

First I consider explanations for the late, and occasionally lamented, Cold War. I conclude that the essential shape and history of that conflict was chiefly determined by differences in ideas and ideologies, not by structural differences in the distribution of capabilities as suggested by some theorists.

Then I argue that because of the quiet cataclysm and because of the way major nations have changed their ideas over time about how they ought to comport themselves in the world, it may be useful to reexamine such constructs as "stability," "system transformation," "power," and "anarchy" that have been central to much policy and theoretical discussion in international relations.

THE COLD WAR:
A TEST OF TWO EXPLANATORY MODELS

The changes in relations between the United States and the Soviet Union during the quiet cataclysm make it possible to test two prominent explanatory models for the Cold War. One of these, the classic Cold War model, stresses ideas: it argues that the Cold War, the grand strategies of the major contestants, and the "bipolar" structure of postwar international politics sprang from a contest of ideas, from an ideological conflict. The other, the structural realist model of Kenneth Waltz, seeks to minimize the impact of ideas and ideology as a determining variable: it argues that the contest, the strategies, and the structure emerged from the way military, economic, and political capabilities were distributed at the end of World War II.

THE CLASSIC COLD WAR MODEL

When a band of Bolsheviks formed the Soviet Union in the wake of the revolution of 1917 they came equipped with the essential belief that international capitalism, or imperialism, was a profoundly evil system that must be eradicated from the face of the globe by violence. The acceptance of this central idea profoundly shaped the country's policy and dictated that the country, in the words of Joseph Stalin, serve as a "base for the overthrow of imperialism in all countries" or as a "lever for the further disintegration of imperialism." Stalin would often quote Lenin on such matters: "The existence of the Soviet Republic side by side with the imperialist states for a long time is unthinkable. In the end either one or the other will conquer." Meanwhile, the official Party history proclaimed its "confidence in the final victory of the great cause of the party of Lenin and Stalin, the victory of Communism in the whole world" (Historicus 1949, 198, 200, 203–204). Soviet leader Nikita Khrushchev ebulliently kept the faith in 1961: "The victory of socialism on a world scale, inevitable by virtue of the laws of history, is no longer far off." And he defined what he called "peaceful coexistence" as "a form of intense economic, political and ideological struggle between the proletariat and the aggressive forces of imperialism in the world arena" (Hudson et al. 1961, 214).[1]

Any country designated "imperialist" by the Soviets would naturally tend to find such pronouncements threatening, particularly after they had been hurled thousands—perhaps millions—of times, and it would logically conclude that it was vital to oppose the Soviets as long as they remained imbued by such a per-

---

[1]In his memoirs, Khrushchev puts it this way: "Both history and the future are on the side of the proletariat's ultimate victory. . . . We Communists must hasten this process. . . . There's a battle going on in the world to decide who will prevail over whom. . . . To speak of ideological compromise would be to betray our Party's first principles" (1974, 530–531); and "peaceful coexistence among different systems of government is possible, but peaceful coexistence among different ideologies is not" (1970, 512).

spective. From this contest, according to a classic interpretation, has stemmed the postwar Cold War between East and West. Advocates of the classic Cold War model would subscribe to John Lewis Gaddis' observation: "Moscow's commitment to the overthrow of capitalism throughout the world had been the chief unsettling element in its relations with the West since the Russian revolution" (1974, 388).[2]

The Soviet threat was particularly unsettling to the West after World War II because it was backed up by an exceptional military capacity. However, while this capacity may have concentrated the imperialist mind, it did not determine the essential shape of the contest. A Soviet Union that was militarily less capable might have been less worrisome, but, like Khomeini's Iran in the 1980s (or for that matter like the Soviet Union of the 1930s), it would still have been seen to be an opponent.

Nor, according to this approach, was it disgust with the Soviet domestic system that impelled the Cold War. As the quintessential Cold Warrior, John Foster Dulles, once put it, "The basic change we need to look forward to isn't necessarily a change from Communism to another form of government. The question is whether you can have Communism in one country or whether it has to be for the world. If the Soviets had national Communism we could do business with their government" (Gaddis 1982, 143). Western democracies in fact were able to come to terms, and even ally, with unthreatening countries whose domestic systems they deemed reprehensible: Spain and Portugal, for example.

THE STRUCTURAL REALIST MODEL

In formulating his influential and widely discussed theory of international politics usually called "realism," "structural realism," or "neorealism," Waltz has chosen substantially to downplay attributes such as "ideology, form of government, peacefulness, bellicosity or whatever." What chiefly makes the system tick, according to Waltz, is the "distribution of capabilities." States differ in their capabilities and from these differences springs the structure (1979, 98).

For Waltz, a country's capability includes its "size of population and territory, resource endowment, economic capability, military strength, political stability and competence" (1979, 131). In the postwar period two countries have been far more

---

[2]Another analysis puts it this way: "The prime cause of the conflict opening up between the Russians and the Americans (and their allies) was the ideology of the Soviet leaders, and their consequent incapacity, rather than their reluctance, to make permanent arrangements with the leaders of capitalist states. This was stated by Maxim Litvinov in June 1946, in one of those strange, candid remarks of his: the 'root cause' of the trouble was 'the ideological conception prevailing here that conflict between communist and capitalist worlds is inevitable'. When asked what would happen if the West were to concede to Russia all her aims in foreign policy, Litvinov replied: 'It would lead to the West being faced, in a more or less short time, with the next series of demands'" (Thomas 1987, 548). Aleksandr A. Bessmertnykh, Soviet foreign minister in the late 1980s, characterized the period from 1917 until the end of the Cold War as an era of ideological rivalry (Lewis 1993). See also Gaddis 1987, ch. 2.

"capable" than any others by these more or less objective measures, and from this condition, concludes Waltz, stems the essential conflict: "the United States is the obsessing danger for the Soviet Union, and the Soviet Union for the United States, since each can damage the other to an extent no other state can match" (1979, 170). The Cold War between them, therefore, "is firmly rooted in the structure of postwar international politics, and will last as long as that structure endures" (1988, 628).

A TEST OF THE MODELS

Both Cold War models characterize the postwar world as "bipolar." Waltz sees this as a consequence of the distribution of capabilities, while a classic Cold Warrior would argue that the bipolarity was a consequence of ideology, not capabilities: the United States found the Soviet Union to be an "obsessing danger" not simply because the Soviet regime brandished big weapons or because it occupied so much space on the earth's surface, but because the Soviets espoused an ideology that was threatening.

THE ORIGINS OF THE COLD WAR.   As will be seen, the changes in the Cold War at the time of the quiet cataclysm put these models to their greatest test; but problems with this version of the structural realist approach could have been evident even earlier. For example, consider the following modest thought experiment. Suppose Stalin's Communist regime had been deposed in 1945 by one dominated by someone with the views of Winston Churchill, Thomas Jefferson, Mahatma Gandhi, Alexander Kerensky, or, for that matter, Mikhail Gorbachev. Suppose, in addition, that this hypothetical country would have been just as capable as Stalin's—that is, equally big, well endowed, militarily strong, politically stable and competent. Although it could have damaged the West just as effectively as Stalin's Soviet Union, it seems inconceivable that this imaginary country would have been seen to pose such an "obsessing danger" or that postwar international politics would have taken anything resembling the oppositional, bipolar course that it did.[3] It is entirely possible, in fact, that the United States and a liberal Moscow regime would have joined with Britain and other important democracies to form a consortium to deal jointly with world problems, including a settlement in Europe. In other words, the devices built into the Charter of the United Nations might well have functioned more or less the way they were intended by their idealistic creators.

Capabilities hardly seem to have been the chief causative factor in the other major contest of the Cold War era either—the mutual hostility and fear that flour-

---

[3]Actually, as Carl Kaysen has suggested, since the arms race was importantly impelled by the ideological conflict, an ideologically harmonious U.S. and USSR would probably not have emerged so vastly superior to other countries in military terms.

ished between the United States and China from the late 1940s into the 1970s. During that period China was far less capable of damaging the United States than the wealthy, nuclear-armed Britain, yet Britain was an ally and China an enemy. Conversely, if Britain had been taken over by Communists in, say, 1965, it would have suddenly become an obsessing danger to the United States that would have rivaled or surpassed any posed by China. Ideas and ideology seem chiefly responsible for the dynamics, not capabilities.[4]

THE DEMISE OF THE COLD WAR. The real test of the models, however, came in the late 1980s. There was little change in the capability indices proposed by Waltz: the Soviet Union did not become any smaller; its resource endowment remained the same; however troubled, it continued to have one of the largest economies in the world; its massive military and nuclear strength remained very much in place; and, while shakier than in the past, it continued (until late 1989 or 1990 at least) to be politically stable and competent. Although there was some catching up in the economic sphere by Japan and by the states of western Europe, the United States and the USSR remained far more "capable" by the Waltz criteria than any other countries in the world. In the key area of military capacity the two countries continued to maintain a military—and, in particular, a nuclear—capacity that dwarfed any conceivable rival.[5] Even after the changes in the Soviet empire in 1989–91, the Soviet Union (or, later, Russia) remained a "superpower" in this crucial respect. Waltz argues that the United States and the Soviet Union found each other to be an "obsessing danger . . . since each can damage the other to an extent no other state can match" (1979, 170) and that the Cold War was "firmly rooted" in a structure determined by the distribution of capabilities (1988, 628). If this is so, each side should have continued to "focus its fears on the other, to distrust its motives, and to impute offensive intentions to defensive measures" (1988, 628) as long as each remained suitably capable.

In the late 1980s, however, there was an important change in ideas as the Soviet Union abandoned its threateningly expansionary ideology. Its love affair with revolution in the advanced capitalist world, frustrated for decades, ceased to have even theological relevance, and its venerable and once-visceral attachment to revolution and to "wars of national liberation" in the Third World no longer even inspired much in the way of lip service. As Francis Fukuyama has observed, "the role of ideology in defining Soviet foreign policy objectives and in providing

---

[4]The split that occurred between the Soviet Union and China in the late 1950s and the early 1960s seems also to have been determined far more by a dispute over ideas and ideology than by differences in capability or other power political considerations. From an economic or military perspective, the split made no objective sense, especially for China which lost economic aid and trade as well as military protection. For a discussion, see Mueller 1989a, 133–151, 163–165.

[5]That military capabilities are far more determining than economic ones in the Waltz perspective is suggested by his exclusion of the economically capable, but militarily weak, United States from his list of major players on the international scene in the nineteenth century (1979, 162).

political instruments for expansion has been steadily declining in the postwar period" and Gorbachev "further accelerated that decline" (1987, 12). In 1985 Gorbachev said his country required "not only a reliable peace, but also a quiet, normal international situation" (Colton 1986, 191). In 1986, he began forcefully to undercut Communist ideology about the "class struggle" and about the Soviet Union's "internationalist duty" as the leader of world socialism (Oberdorfer 1992, 158–164). By 1988, the Soviets were admitting the "inadequacy of the thesis that peaceful coexistence is a form of class struggle," and began to refer to the "world socialist system" or the "socialist community of nations" rather than to the "socialist camp" (Binder 1988), and the Kremlin's chief ideologist explicitly rejected the notion that a world struggle is going on between capitalism and Communism (Keller 1988). Then, in a major speech in December 1988, Gorbachev specifically called for "de-ideologizing relations among states" and, while referring to the Communist revolution in Russia as "a most precious spiritual heritage," proclaimed that "today we face a different world, from which we must seek a different road to the future" (New York Times, 8 December 1988, A16; 9 December 1988, A18). Most impressively, in February 1989, Gorbachev matched deeds to words by carrying out his promise to remove Soviet troops from Afghanistan.[6]

With these important changes—which took place *before* the disintegration of the Soviet empire in eastern Europe and long before the crumbling of the Soviet Union itself—the structure of world politics changed profoundly: the Cold War and bipolarity evaporated. The New York Times proclaimed on April 2, 1989 that the Cold War was over, and on May 24, the Wall Street Journal added, "We won!" Later in the year staunchly anti-Communist commentators were concluding the Cold War is indeed "coming to an end. . . . The Soviet leaders have for all intents and purposes given up the ideological struggle . . . [and they] have retreated from the basic doctrine of international class struggle—the doctrine that gave rise to the Cold War in the first place" (Harries 1989, 40).

Far from emphasizing bipolarity and far from continuing to "focus its fears" on the United States, Gorbachev's USSR was proposing as early as 1987 that the United States and the Soviet Union join together in an international consortium along the lines envisioned a half-century earlier in the United Nations Charter (Lewis 1987; Keller 1987; Lewis 1989). It even began to be possible that the United States and the USSR could again become allies as they were during World War II. In 1988, in his last presidential press conference (long before the changes in eastern Europe), Ronald Reagan was specifically asked about this, and, stressing the ideological nature of the contest, he responded essentially in the affirmative: "If it can be definitely established that they no longer are following the expansionary policy that was instituted in the Communist revolution, that their goal

---

[6]For a 1986 analysis tracing the decline in fervor in the Soviet Union for its ideological commitment to the international Communist revolutionary movement and for the suggestions that this decline "could eventually result in the end of the cold war" and that "we may be coming to the end of the world as we know it," see Mueller 1986. On the Gorbachev transformation, see also Garthoff 1992.

must be a one-world Communist state . . . [then] they might want to join the family of nations and join them with the idea of bringing about or establishing peace."[7] Six months later (but still before the eastern European changes) his successor, George Bush, was urging, without Reagan's tentativeness, that Western policy should change, moving "beyond containment" to "seek the integration of the Soviet Union into the community of nations" and to welcome it "back into the world order" (Oberdorfer 1992, 348; Bush 1989). An "evil empire" no more.

Material Effects.   Thus the key element in the demise of the Cold War derived from changes in ideas. As discussed in Chapter 6, material factors may have helped to bring these changes about: the failure of the Soviet economic and administrative system clearly encouraged Gorbachev and others to reexamine their basic ideology. However, as Myron Rush observes, these problems by no means required a doctrinal change: had the Soviet Union done nothing about its problems, "its survival to the end of the century would have been likely," and "by cutting defense spending sharply . . . a prudent conservative leader in 1985 could have improved the Soviet economy markedly" (1993, 21). Material change, therefore, does not consistently impel changes in ideas, ideology, or policy: faced with the same economic strains, a Soviet leader other than Gorbachev might have been unwilling to abandon basic ideology. Indeed, as Daniel Deudney and John Ikenberry have pointed out, many Western experts expected the Soviet Union to respond to its problems in the 1980s "with renewed repression at home and aggression abroad, as it had in the past" (1992, 123).[8] It may be useful in this regard to recall the once-popular "fat Communist" theory in which it was plausibly argued that the Soviet Union would mellow its foreign policy when it became materially *contented;* partisans of this theory feared that an economically strained USSR might be tempted to lash out in desperation.

Economic determinism does have a comforting certainty about it. Economics is seen to be the key explanatory variable whether wealth is followed by contentment (Japan or Germany today) or by arrogant expansion (Germany before either world war), or whether economic strain is followed by capitulation (Gorbachev's USSR) or desperate adventurism (Japan in 1941).

Two more thought experiments may make it clear that it was the change in ideology, not in economics, that was crucial to the demise of the Cold War and to

---

[7]*New York Times,* 9 December 1988, A18. Notably, Reagan tied this development to an end of the Soviet expansionary threat, not to the reform of its domestic system. That is, cooperation, even alliance, was not contingent on the progress of Soviet domestic reform. As long as the Soviet Union, like China in the 1970s or Yugoslavia after 1949, continued to neglect its expansionary and revolutionary ideology, it could be embraced by the West. Illiberal, nonexpansionist Portugal, after all, was a founding member of NATO. On the possibility of East/West alliance, see Mueller 1989/90, Mueller 1991a.

[8]In an analysis of Soviet Third World policy in 1987, Francis Fukuyama noted that over history Soviet policy had repeatedly shifted back and forth between the assertive and the comparatively pliant. He suggests that, while policy was becoming "less ideological," it would remain "expansionist" and might well soon swing back to the assertive mode.

the consequent changes in grand strategies. First, suppose that persistent material failure had caused the Soviet Union to lapse into steady Ottoman-like decline but that its ideological quest to overthrow international capitalism had continued unabated: suppose, in other words, that it took on the characteristics of China in the 1950s or 1960s or of the Soviet Union in the 1920s or 1930s. Something like this could conceivably have come about if the hardline August 1991 coup against Gorbachev (and Boris Yeltsin) had been successful. Under that circumstance, the West might have become somewhat less concerned that a major war would develop from the contest, but its hostility would have continued. That is, the United States would still have considered the USSR to be the "obsessing danger," and the Cold War would have prospered. On the other hand, as a second possibility, suppose that the Soviet Union had *not* lapsed into material stagnation or decline, but that its leaders had undergone an ideological conversion to democratic liberalism or for that matter to Burma-style isolation and xenophobia. In that case the Cold War would have abated.

REEXAMINING CENTRAL CONSTRUCTS

Thus, the Cold War came about because of a clash of ideas, and its demise in the time of the quiet cataclysm principally resulted from an important change in those ideas, not from a major change in the distribution of capabilities. In turn, this extraordinary transformation is helping nations to reshape their ideas about, and approaches to, international affairs. Because of this, it may now be time to consider substantially recasting—or perhaps even retiring—several constructs that have been central to much international relations theorizing, especially that of the "realist" school: stability, system transformation, power, and anarchy.

BIPOLAR STABILITY

According to Waltz, a system is determined to be stable not because war is avoided but rather because "no consequential variation takes place in the number of principal parties that constitute the system" (1979, 162). Bipolarity is more stable than multipolarity, he argues, because it allows for less uncertainty between the major players and because it has been enforced by nuclear fears (1979, ch. 8; Waltz 1988; Waltz 1990). (The comparison is not entirely convincing: as he notes, multipolarity lasted for centuries and therefore was also stable by this definition.)

If ideology has been the dominant force determining the bipolar structure of postwar international politics, however, the system has been quite *unstable* by Waltz's definition. While the distribution of capabilities and therefore the placement of a country in Waltz's international system cannot change very fast, its ideology can alter quickly when new leaders take charge or when old ones change their mindsets.[9] And this can lead bipolarity to give way to some other structural form.

WAR AND SYSTEM TRANSFORMATION

For Kenneth Organski and Jacek Kugler system-transforming or hegemonic wars are started by countries which seek to "redraft the rules by which relations among nations work" (1980, 23). For Robert Gilpin such wars historically have been "the basic mechanism of systemic change in world politics" (1981, 209). They reorder "the basic components of the system," "reestablish an unambiguous hierarchy of prestige," and determine "who will govern the international system and whose interests will be primarily served by the new international order." They lead "to a redistribution of territory among the states in the system, a new set of rules of the system, a revised international division of labor, etc." As a result, "a relatively more stable international order and effective governance of the international system are created based on the new realities of the international distribution of power" (1981, 198). And E. H. Carr has observed, "Normally, the threat of war, tacit or overt, seems a necessary condition of important political changes in the international sphere" (1946, 216).[10]

Bruce Bueno de Mesquita has argued that even very small wars, such as the Seven Weeks War of 1866, can sometimes have such an effect (1990). However, the experience of the quiet cataclysm suggests that, in fact, no war or important war threat is required at all: the system can be transformed by a mere change of ideas. That is, as suggested in the Introduction, it rather appears that between 1988 and 1991 the world experienced something like the functional equivalent of a system-transforming or hegemonic war.

---

[9]An abrupt change came about after 1948 when the once-ideological leaders of Yugoslavia, excommunicated by Stalin from the international Communist movement, abandoned their shrill commitment to worldwide revolution. They were soon embraced by their capitalist ex-enemies, and for a while Yugoslavia was close to becoming an informal participant in NATO (Campbell 1967, 24–27). More spectacular was the shift with respect to China in the 1970s. Once it abandoned its threatening affection for the anticapitalist cause, the United States proved entirely willing to accommodate. Diplomatic contacts were first established for old-fashioned realpolitik reasons: China feared the Soviet military danger to the north, and the United States hoped China could be cajoled into pressuring North Vietnam concerning the ongoing war in Vietnam (see Kissinger 1979, 164, 194, 691). Eventually, however, China abandoned its expansionary ideology and, although Chinese capabilities remained about the same, American-Chinese friendship blossomed. In 1980 there were official discussions between the two about the possible transfer of American defense technology to China and about "limited strategic cooperation in matters of common concern," although these never reached fruition (Pollack 1984, 159; on the potential for alliance, see also Talbott 1981, 81–113). As hardliner Richard Pipes has observed, "Since the death of Mao [in 1976], China has turned inward and ceased being aggressive, and so we are friendly toward China, just as we are toward Yugoslavia. We may deplore their Communist regimes, but these countries are not trying to export their systems and therefore they do not represent a threat to our national security" (*Policy Review* [Winter 1985]: 33).

[10]For Waltz the system can be changed by major war, it seems, or, in the bipolar case, if one country establishes hegemony or manages to "enlarge the circle of great powers by promoting the amalgamation of some of the middle states" like those in Western Europe (1979, 199). See also Gilpin 1981, 242–244.

After the Soviets changed their worldview and abandoned their threateningly expansionary ideology, the patterns of international relations changed enormously. In consonance with Gilpin's catalogue, the basic components of the system have been reordered: there have been important territorial readjustments (especially in Europe), a splintering of alliances, a substantial reordering of prestige and status rankings, a new set of rules and conventions, a revised division of labor, and new procedures for managing the international system, as well as a negative arms race (discussed more fully in Chapter 3).

The change may have been from what Morton Kaplan calls a "loose bipolar system" to (or toward) a "universal international system." In the former, according to Kaplan's rules, the blocs seek to "eliminate the rival bloc," to "increase their capabilities in relation to those of the rival bloc," to fight "rather than to permit the rival bloc to attain a position of preponderant strength," and to "attempt to extend the membership of their bloc." In the latter, major countries "use peaceful means to obtain their objectives," "do not resort to force or the threat of force," and "attempt to increase the resources and productive base of the international system" (1957, 38, 47).

Essentially, the change is from a zero-sum situation to a positive-sum situation for the major countries. As an important Soviet official put it in 1987: "Previously we reasoned: the worse for the adversary, the better for us. . . . But today this is no longer true. . . . The better things are going in the European world economy, the higher the stability and the better the prospects for our development" (Snyder 1987/88, 115). It is a profound transformation, and it came about because ideas changed. No war, as it happens, was required.

POWER

The concept of power has been at the center of a great deal of theorizing about international affairs particularly after realist Hans J. Morgenthau grandly declared in 1948 that "international politics, like all politics, is a struggle for power" (1948, 13).

Morgenthau defines "power" as "man's control over the minds and actions of others" (1948, 13), while Waltz offers "the old and simple notion that an agent is powerful to the extent that he affects others more than they affect him" (1979, 192). Words exist in the English language which more closely and less ambiguously approach what these definitions seem to suggest: "influence" in particular, or "control," "status," "prestige," or "importance." Since these words are more precise, they ought to be preferable: the word *power* is not needed.[11]

More importantly, in the international context the use of the word *power* compellingly tends to imply military strength, and as Samuel Huntington observed, "realist theorists have focused overwhelmingly on military power" (1993a, 72; see also Rothgeb 1993, 18). Indeed, Morgenthau and Waltz make the connec-

---

[11]On this issue, see also Riker 1964. Huntington makes the words "power" and "influence" synonymous: "In international politics power is the ability of one actor, usually but not always a government, to influence the behavior of others" (1993a, 68).

tion quite explicit. "The dependence of national power upon military prepared-ness," declares Morgenthau, "is too obvious to need much elaboration" (1948, 183). Because of the "weight" of American "capabilities," observes Waltz, "American actions have tremendous impact" (1979, 192). The notion that a dis-armed country could possess great "power" is all but inconceivable under these patterns of thought. As Robert Art and Waltz conclude, "the seriousness of a state's fundamental intentions is conveyed fundamentally by its having a credible military posture. Without it, a state's diplomacy generally lacks effectiveness" (1983, 7).[12]

But if "power" essentially means "influence" or "status," contemporary Japan has become a "powerful" state. It happens to have rather substantial "self-defense forces," but it is not respect for these forces which makes Japan's diplomacy effec-tive, gives it weight in world affairs, or allows it to "set the scene of action for oth-ers," in Waltz's expression (1979, 72). If power in the sense of influence, control, status, prestige, or importance can be achieved with very little military capability or preparedness, the word, with its attendant and inevitable military implications, has become misleading or misdirecting at best.[13]

---

[12]The stress on power and on military considerations can also lead to the conclusion that "war is nor-mal" (Waltz 1988, 620). This emerges fairly naturally if one concentrates only on the Great Powers and then proceeds to define a Great Power in considerable part as a country which tends to get into war a lot. That war participation is an important definitional component of greatness is clear from the case of the United States a century ago. Although it was more advanced economically than any Great Power except Britain and had shown in its recent Civil War that it could easily mount an army of over a mil-lion, it was not admitted by analysts into the ranks of the great until it got involved in wars in Europe in the 20th century. Japan could comfortably be considered a Great Power throughout this century until 1945 when it was defeated, occupied, and disarmed, at which point it was dropped from the ranks (see the table in Waltz 1979, 162). This association of greatness with war is recognized by Waltz. But in-stead of arguing that countries are considered by analysts to be great in part because they participate in war, he argues they necessarily participate in war because they are great. Great Powers, he urges, "find ways to use force." Further, "their involvement in wars arises from their position in the international system, not from their national characters. When they are at the top, they fight; as they decline they become peaceful" (1959, 187).

The deft association of war with greatness leads to a puzzle when the two greatest Great Powers, the United States and the USSR, somehow managed to avoid war with each other. Waltz is led to explain this curious condition by concluding that it is the existence of nuclear weapons that has "banished war from the center of international politics" (1988, 627). Bipolarity, he finds, is not enough alone to ex-plain the "long peace"; also needed is "that other great force for peace: nuclear weapons" (1988, 624; see also Waltz 1959, 176; Waltz 1990). The possibility that the two quintessential Great Powers may have gotten the idea from their (nonnuclear) experience in World War II that such enterprises are dis-tinctly painful is not considered since this would suggest they have somehow changed their "national character," a phenomenon specifically eschewed by Waltz (1979, 187n). The anticipation then, is that the United States and the USSR, following normal Great Power instincts, would have been at war by now if the worst they could have feared was merely an exercise of the magnitude of World War II. Great Powers, apparently, are long on instinct, short on brains. (On this issue, see Chapter 5.)

[13]Two analysts who claim to be applying a "realist" approach to the Japanese case come to opposite conclusions. Huntington argues that, even though it has no important military capability, Japan is seek-ing to "maximize its power"—and has become an alarming threat to U.S. "primacy"—by accepting "all the assumptions of realism" but applying "them purely in the economic realm" (1993a, 72). Layne, on the other hand, concludes that Japan cannot today be considered a Great Power because it lacks "the requisite military capabilities, especially strategic nuclear arsenals"; he confidently predicts, however, that Japan will soon "acquire the full spectrum of great power capabilities, including nuclear weapons" (1993, 5n1, 37), a notion that may come as a surprise to many Japanese (see Katzenstein and Okawara 1993; Berger 1993).

Moreover, it is becoming increasingly questionable whether it is wise to place the concept of power—however defined—at the center of any construct that tries to deal with international affairs. There have always been problems with this notion. If all politics is a "struggle for power" or if nations are consumed by a "lust for power," the international behavior of the United States for much of its history defies description. In the period before World War I, and indeed for much of the twenty-year period after it, the United States hardly seems to have been the very model of a modern major power-seeker if that means struggling lustfully for influence in the councils of the big people. In that sense, the United States often adopted a strategy that could best be characterized as power-averse.

In the present post–Cold War era, we may well be moving toward a situation in which classic ideas about power are becoming remarkably anachronistic. In *War and Peace* in 1869, Leo Tolstoy observed that "all historians agree that the external activity of states and nations in their conflicts with one another is expressed in wars, and that as a direct result of greater or less success in war the political strength of states and nations increases or decreases" ([1862–69] 1966, 1145). Today Japan and Germany, the big *losers* in the last war, enjoy great "political strength" and status.[14] As Paul Schroeder has put it, "Not only may conditions change: collective mentalities may also" (1990; see also Luard 1986).

This does not mean that conflict will vanish, but only that war and military force will not be used by important developed countries to resolve their conflicts. For example, the United States and Japan once had a dispute over who should run the territory of Okinawa—exactly the sort of argument that has often led to war in the past. The issue was resolved without war or the threat of it: a deal was cut. Similar discussions have taken place concerning the four northern islands the Japanese feel were unjustly taken from them by the Soviets in 1945: to get the islands back, Japan is using its economic might, not military threats, to pull what might have once been called a "power play." And most spectacularly, during the quiet cataclysm in 1989 and 1990 the major countries of the world resolved their most pressing international disagreements—including the division of Germany— with scarcely a shot being fired.

In fact, to push this point perhaps to an extreme, if we are entering an era in which economic motivations became paramount and in which military force is not accepted as a sensible method for pursuing wealth, not only would "power" with all its military implications become obsolete, but so would "power" in the sense of influence or status. In principle, pure economic actors do not care about influence or prestige. They care about getting rich. (Admittedly, as Japan has found, influence, status, and prestige tend to accompany the accumulation of wealth, but this is just an ancillary effect.) Suppose the president of a company could choose between two stories to tell the stockholders. One message would be, "We enjoy great

---

[14]Increasingly it seems that status, like beauty, lies in the eye of the beholder. China's quest to host the Olympics in the year 2000 stemmed in part from the belief that it would be a "mark of entry into the big league of world powers" (WuDunn 1993). And some Koreans have apparently come to believe that status is achieved when a country has many entries in the *Guinness Book of World Records*: says one, "The more records we have leads to world power" (Darlin 1990).

status, prestige, and influence in the industry. When we talk everybody listens. Our profits are nil." The other would be, "No one in the industry pays the slightest attention to us or ever asks our advice. We are, in fact, the butt of jokes in the trade. We are making money hand over fist." There is no doubt about which story would most thoroughly warm the stockholders' hearts.[15]

ANARCHY

Another concept due for reconsideration is "international anarchy." If major nations now come to accept the idea that economic development is a primary goal, and if they substantially abandon the idea that war is a sensible method for solving problems among themselves, the notion that those countries live in a state of "anarchy" will become misleading and could encourage undesirable policy developments.

Technically, of course, the concept is accurate: there exists no international government that effectively polices the behavior of the nations of the world. It is, as Waltz puts it, a condition of "self help" (1979, 111). The problem with the word *anarchy* lies in its inescapable connotations: it implies chaos, lawlessness, disorder, confusion, and random violence. It would be equally accurate to characterize the international situation as "unregulated," a word with connotations that are far different, and perhaps far more helpful.[16]

Waltz argues that "interdependent states whose relations remain unregulated must experience conflict and will occasionally fall into violence" (1979, 138).[17] And realist John Mearsheimer argues that in a condition of anarchy, "there is little room for trust among states" and "security will often be scarce" (1990, 12, 45; see also Art and Waltz 1983, 3–6). Insofar as this perspective is a useful way to look at international politics, it holds only where the idea is generally accepted that violence is a suitable and useful method for doing business. If that idea no longer prevails, regulation is not required and "anarchy" could become a desirable state.

---

[15]On these issues, see also Rosecrance 1986. The concept of leadership will also be undergoing significant evisceration if the pursuit of wealth—the "lust for prosperity," a Morgenthau revisionist might call it—becomes a dominant motivation in world affairs. Continental Airlines at one time enjoyed "price leadership" in the industry, but registered poor profits—something unlikely to impress stockholders. The United States is still overwhelmingly the world leader by almost any traditional standard. Yet it is often consumed with a jealousy of follower Japan that sometimes approaches paranoia. According to the dictionary, the word *turgid* means bombastic, inflated, pompous, grandiloquent. But most people, responding to the sound of the word and, perhaps confusing it with *tepid,* think it means its near-opposite: dull, dreary, gray, heavy. This confusion is so great that the word has become useless. Unless the author explains what is meant by the word (in which case there is no point in using it in the first place), it is impossible to be sure what is meant when the phrase "turgid prose" is used. Thus both communication and comprehension would be improved if "turgid" were banished from the language. Perhaps it is time to consider a similar fate for the word *power.*

[16]On this issue, see also Milner 1991, but compare Rosecrance 1992.

[17]Or: "With many sovereign states, with no system of law enforceable among them, with each state judging its grievances and ambitions according to the dictates of its own reason or desire—conflict, sometimes leading to war, is bound to occur" (Waltz 1959, 159).

Chapter 3

ARMS RACES:
POSITIVE AND NEGATIVE

Hans J. Morgenthau once proclaimed that "men do not fight because they have arms"; rather "they have arms because they deem it necessary to fight" (1948, 327). If that is so, it follows that when countries no longer deem it necessary to fight they will get rid of their arms.

A country buys arms because its leaders espy a threat or opportunity which, it seems to them, requires them to arm. Thus, during the Cold War the United States and the Soviet Union saw each other as threatening and armed themselves accordingly. The British and the French, on the other hand, did not find each other militarily threatening, and therefore they did not spend great sums on arms designed to counter each other.

As tensions slackened, however, a certain degree of arms relaxation began to take place between the United States and the USSR as the Cold War came to an end, and it accelerated greatly during and after the quiet cataclysm. It was a negative arms race.

THE NEGATIVE ARMS RACE
BETWEEN CANADA AND THE UNITED STATES

There is an interesting and informative precedent for this. Americans and Canadians are so accustomed to living peacefully side by side that it is easy to as-

sume this has always been the case.[1] But once there was enormous hostility
between the United States and British Canada, and it was registered in wars in
1775–1783 and 1812–1814. After the latter war the contestants lapsed into a long
period of wary coexistence—of cold war, in fact—but they nevertheless managed
to agree to one arms control measure.

Impelled as much by economic exhaustion as anything else, the United States
reduced its fleet of warships on the Great Lakes and proposed that the British do
likewise. The British eventually agreed, and the results were formalized in the
Rush-Bagot Agreement of 1817 which placed exact limits on the number, size,
and armament of warships. But there was no provision actually to destroy warships, and both sides kept some in dockyards where they could always be put into
action should the need arise. Furthermore there was quite a bit of evasion and
technical violation over the next half-century, and both built ships that could easily
be converted to military use if necessary. Both sides continued to build forts along
the border, and the British created an extensive and expensive canal system in
Canada as a military supply line.

This arms race was accompanied by a series of conflicts between the two
neighbors. There were border skirmishes in 1837, a crisis in 1839 in disagreement
about the boundary between Maine and New Brunswick, continual war appre-
hension over the Oregon boundary (settled in 1846), substantial tension during
the American Civil War, and sporadic raids by Irish-Americans into British
Canada. Meanwhile many Americans were caught up in the romantic notion that
it was somehow in their "manifest destiny to overspread the continent allotted by
Providence for the free development of our yearly multiplying millions," as a
newspaper manifesto put it.

By the early 1870s, however, most of the claims and controversies had been
settled. Canada was granted independent status in part because British taxpayers
were tired of paying to defend their large, distant colony and, with the Americans
focusing on settling the West and recovering from their calamitous civil war, it
seemed safe to begin to withdraw the British army from Canada (see Preston
1977, 41–43, 57–59; Stuart 1987, 119). Without formal agreement, disarmament
gradually took place between the two countries. Their forts became museums
where obsolete cannon still point accusingly but impotently in the direction
of the nearby former enemy. "Disarmament became a reality," observes a
Canadian student of the era, "not by international agreement, but simply because
there was no longer any serious international disagreement" (Stacey 1955, 12).[2]

---

[1]For a valuable overview of these issues, see Stacey 1955. See also Falk 1961.

[2]Or as Falk puts it, when "points of dissension disappeared, or could be amicably reconciled, the armaments disappeared with them" (1961, 73).

THE NEGATIVE ARMS RACE
BETWEEN THE UNITED STATES AND THE USSR

In a similar manner, the weapons that had been built up by the United States and the Soviet Union during the Cold War began to seem burdensome and even parodic as tensions eased in the late 1980s. Accordingly, the two contestants began to seek arms reductions.

Total disarmament was hardly in the offing, of course. The possible reemergence of a dangerous hostility would have to be guarded against, and there were peripheral concerns that might require military preparedness. Furthermore, neither side would be at all pleased if an arms reduction somehow triggered insecurities that led to the emergence of a vengeful, rearmed Germany or Japan. And both would keep some arms around to aid in their quest for "influence" around the globe insofar as they continued to consider that to be part of their international role.

It was clear, however, that these needs hardly called for ships in the hundreds, for thermonuclear weapons in the tens of thousands, or for standing armies in the millions. And neither side had difficulty envisioning other ways to spend its money. The United States had built up a burdensome deficit, and many argued that its overemphasis on arms expenditures had kept it from being able to compete in international markets. The pressures on the Soviet budget, massively bloated by defense expenditures, were even more severe (see, for example, Pear 1990).

Both sides quickly found, however, that arms reductions would be more difficult if the reductions were accomplished through explicit mutual agreement— that an exquisitely nuanced agreement must be worked out for every abandoned nut and bolt (see also Kaysen, McNamara, and Rathjens 1991, 107). Arms agreements tend to take forever to consummate: the nonproliferation treaty of 1968, a very mild measure that was clearly in everyone's best interest, was argued for five years.[3] Indeed, the existence of arms control talks has often hampered arms reduction in the past. In 1973, for example, a proposal for a unilateral reduction of U.S. troops in western Europe failed in Congress because it was felt that this would undercut upcoming arms control negotiations—which then ran on unproductively for years (Smoke 1987, 195). Similarly, opponents of the MX missile and of Ronald Reagan's Strategic Defense Initiative failed in Congress in part because some of those who considered the weapons systems dangerous or valueless never-

---

[3]Moreover, such agreements often became irrelevant under conditions of arms competition because while one weapons system was being controlled by laborious negotiation, a better one was being invented. Overall, formal arms control measures have had little history of reducing overall defense spending when tensions were high—reductions in one defense area were characteristically compensated for by increases in another (see Berkowitz 1987, especially ch. 2).

theless supported them because the weapons seem to be useful as bargaining chips in arms control talks. Whether those arms reductions were wise or not, they failed in considerable measure because arms control talks existed.[4]

When arms are reduced by agreement under conditions of arms competition, both sides are going to strain to make sure that all dangers and contingencies are covered, and they will naturally try, if at all possible, to come out with the better deal. Reduction is certainly possible under those circumstances, but it is likely to be slow and inflexible. Arms control is essentially a form of centralized regulation and it carries with it the usual defects of that approach. Participants will volunteer for such regulation only with extreme caution because once under regulation they are often unable to adjust subtly to unanticipated changes. Moreover they are often encouraged, perversely, to follow developments that are unwise. For example, the Strategic Arms Agreement of 1972 limited the number of missiles each side could have, but it allowed them to embroider their missiles with multiple warheads and to improve missile accuracy, thereby encouraging them to develop a potentially dangerous first-strike capability.

The alternative was simply just to *do* it. The arms buildup, after all, was not accomplished through written agreement; instead, there was a sort of free market in which each side, keeping a wary eye on the other, sought security by purchasing varying amounts of weapons and troops. As requirements and perspectives changed, so did the force structure of each side.

With the demise of the Cold War a similar reactive arms policy continued between West and East except that now it was focused on arms reduction. Under severe economic pressure to reduce arms expenditures, the Soviet Union's Mikhail Gorbachev dramatically announced in December 1988 that he was going to begin to do so unilaterally. Months before Gorbachev's announcement Lord Carrington, then retiring Secretary General and Chairman of the North Atlantic Treaty Organization, warned about what he called "involuntary or structural disarmament" within NATO where a relaxation of East-West tensions "has made support for defense spending harder to win." This was of concern, he held, because, although Gorbachev clearly "has a real interest in reducing military expenditures," he had apparently not done so yet. However, if the Soviet buildup did begin to swing into reverse, Carrington conceded, NATO's tendency toward "structural" disarmament "would not matter" (1988, 3-5).

As if on cue, press reports were observing within days of Gorbachev's announcement that there was a "new reluctance to spend for defense" within NATO (Shlaes 1988). In a month, there were reports that Gorbachev's pronouncements "make it harder for Western governments to justify large sums for military machines;. . . the Soviet bear seems less threatening to Western publics these days, so that they want to do less on the weapons front. . . . Western perceptions [are]

---

[4]A message of George Bush's 1988 campaign for the presidency seems to have been that a weapons system, no matter how costly, stupid, or redundant, should never be unilaterally abandoned if it could serve as a bargaining chip in arms control negotiations. See, for example, his arguments in debate: *Congressional Quarterly*, 1 October 1988, 2750.

that the Soviet threat is receding and that big armies are expensive and inconvenient—perhaps even irrelevant" (Keatley 1989). A few months later, as more proposals and counterproposals were spun out by both sides, the *Wall Street Journal* was calling the process a "race to demobilize" (31 May, 1989, A1).[5] Some reports at the time suggested, in fact, that some officials, alarmed at the disarmament impetus, were hoping to use the formal arms control mechanism to slow the process.

At first both sides reduced cautiously, in sensible if perhaps overly sensitive concern that a severe arms imbalance could inspire the other to contemplate blackmail. Then, after the failure of the Soviet hardline coup in August 1991, the negative arms race sped ahead. If there was a contest, it was caused by the arms control process trying to catch up with reality. When the U.S. Senate in 1992 ratified a nuclear arms reduction treaty that had been signed in 1990, both sides had already moved to reduce arms even further than required by that treaty (Cushman 1992).

CONCLUSIONS

The two arms-reversal processes discussed here were as chaotic, halting, ambiguous, self-interested, and potentially reversible as the arms race itself, but arms were significantly reduced.[6] As the negative arms race between the United States and the Soviet Union (later Russia) flourished, the Canadian-American experience suggested that arms reduction will happen best if arms negotiators keep out of the way. There could be a role for agreements focused purely on arms *control* measures that cannot be accomplished unilaterally—instances include improved communications links, mechanisms to detect surprise attack preparations, or improved methods to verify the size of the other's military forces. But arms *reduc-*

---

[5]An especially vivid acknowledgment of this tendency was put forward by John Tower in January 1989 in his ill-fated confirmation hearings for Secretary of Defense in the Bush administration. While he foresaw no early reduction in the Soviet armed threat, Tower observed that if that threat *were* to diminish "we could obviously reduce our dedication of resources to defense. If there were no threat we'd be spending enormously less than we spend now. . . . We'd be maintaining the kind of army we had in 1938 [which was] about half the size of what the Marine Corps is now." Significantly, Tower did not insist that such a remarkable reduction would have to come about through formal agreement, but clearly implied it could transpire naturally, even automatically, if the perceived threat diminished. (Confirmation Hearing for John Tower for Secretary of Defense, Senate Armed Services Committee, 25 January 1989)

[6]To reduce Cold War tensions, Charles E. Osgood once proposed something he called GRIT: Graduated Reciprocation in Tension-Reduction (1962, especially ch. 5). He supposed high tension and then proposed a series of explicit unilateral initiatives to reduce arms and tensions. His initiatives had stringent requirements which made them very difficult to engineer in practice. For example, he required that they be diversified, publicly announced, explicitly capable of reciprocation, executed on precise schedule, unambiguous, and susceptible to verification. Although he referred to his approach as an "arms race in reverse," arms races are not so rigorous or formal. They are filled with deception, guesswork, ambiguity, abrupt lurches, whim, panic, and elaborate efforts to evade verification. The negative arms race, by contrast, supposes *low* tension. Since, as Morgenthau suggests, the progress of the arms race has been impelled by high tensions, low tensions, combined with economic pressures, should naturally impel a negative arms race.

tion will proceed most expeditiously if each side feels free to reverse any reduction it later comes to regret. Formal disarmament agreements are likely to slow
and pedantify the process.

And more generally, the experience of the negative arms race suggests that
Winston Churchill had it right when he argued in a House of Commons speech on
July 13, 1934, that "it is the greatest possible mistake to mix up disarmament with
peace. When you have peace, you will have disarmament." With the demise of
fears of another major war, many of the arms that struck such deep fear for so long
are quietly being allowed—as the bumper sticker would have it—to rust in peace.

While it may not be entirely fair to characterize disarmament as an effort to
cure a fever by destroying the thermometer,[7] the analogy is instructive when it is
reversed: when fever subsides, the instrument designed to measure it loses its
usefulness and is often soon misplaced.

---

[7]The image is proposed, but not adopted, in Rappard 1940, 490.

Chapter 4

EXPANDING DETERRENCE

In the aftermath of the quiet cataclysm, it may be time to reconsider deterrence, one of the central concepts developed during the Cold War. The problem is that deterrence has almost always been looked at strictly as a military issue. A typical definition characterizes it as "the threat to use force in response as a way of preventing the first use of force by someone else" (Morgan 1977, 9) or as "altering the behavior of a target by using, or threatening to use, force" (Rothgeb 1993, 139).[1]

Starting with a definition like that, most discussions of deterrence quickly get bound up with analyses of military postures that make war more or less likely to be successful or profitable. As Paul Huth and Bruce Russett have observed, "scholars have tended to concentrate on the question of what types of military capabilities will effectively threaten the attacker with high costs, and what types of diplomatic and military actions strengthen the potential attacker's assessment of the defender's resolve to honor its threat of military retaliation" (1990, 470). Ideally, a classic argument runs, each side should have a secure second-strike capability: it should be able to absorb a surprise attack fully confident that it will be able to respond with a devastatingly effective counterattack. Thus each side, rationally fearing costly and punishing retaliatory consequences, can be expected to refrain from initiating war.

This view of deterrence has inspired quite a bit of criticism. It seems inadequate because it simply does not explain very well how states actually behave.

---

[1]On these issues, see also Snyder 1961, ch. 1; Singer 1962, ch. 2; K. Mueller 1991.

Sometimes countries start wars even when they have little reason to believe they will be victorious; at other times they remain supremely cautious, refraining from war even though they feel threatened and even though they enjoy a substantial military advantage (Jervis 1985, 6; Lebow 1985, 204; see also Rosecrance 1975, 33-35).

But instead of abandoning the notion of deterrence because of these important criticisms, it can easily be recast to deal with them—and perhaps in the process to relate better to realities in the wake of the quiet cataclysm. A broader and more fully pertinent concept would vigorously incorporate nonmilitary considerations as well as military ones into the mix, making direct and central application of the obvious fact that states do not approach the world solely in military terms. As Huth and Russett observe, "Inclusion of positive inducements as a means to deter is not standard practice in academic writing or policy debates, but the lack of theoretical or practical attention cannot be justified on grounds of strict logic." And they label such considerations "a long-neglected and therefore underdeveloped component of deterrence theory" (1990, 471).

When deterrence is recast to include such considerations it becomes clear that the vast majority of wars that never happen are deterred by factors that have little or nothing to do with military concerns. Moreover, it becomes clear that the oft-quoted crack reported by Thucydides, "the strong do what they can and the weak suffer what they must" (1934 ed., 331) is actually quite simplistic. In addition, a recasting of deterrence suggests important modifications in the concept of stability.

DETERRENCE

Specifically, *deterrence* can be defined as a state of being—the absence of war between two countries or alliances. If they are not at war, then it is reasonable to conclude that each is currently being deterred from attacking the other. We observe, for example, that the United States and the Soviet Union never went to war with each other, and we conclude that the United States was deterred (by something or other) from attacking the Soviet Union while the Soviets were similarly deterred from attacking the United States. Then by the same reasoning we can also say that the United States is currently being deterred from attacking Canada, and that Canada is currently being deterred from attacking the United States. And finally, we can observe that Pakistan is currently being deterred from attacking Bolivia even while Bolivia is similarly being deterred from attacking Pakistan.

This unconventional way of looking at deterrence tends to draw attention to nonmilitary forms of deterrence and it immediately highlights an important central consideration, one that has attracted remarkably little attention. If countries are principally deterred by military considerations from attacking one another in our chaotic state of international "anarchy" as so many have suggested ("if you desire peace, prepare for war"), why is it that there are so many cases where a militarily superior country lives contentedly alongside a militarily inferior one?[2]

The United States obviously enjoys a massive military advantage over its northern neighbor and could attack with little concern about punishing military retaliation or about the possibility of losing the war. Clearly something is deterring the United States from attacking Canada—a country, as noted in the previous chapter, with which the United States has been at war in the past and where, not too long ago many war-eager Americans felt their "manifest destiny" lay. But obviously this spectacularly successful deterrent has little to do with the Canadians' military might. Similar cases can be found elsewhere. Despite an overwhelming military superiority, the USSR was never anxious to attack such troublesome neighbors as Poland and Romania. To be complete, a concept of deterrence ought to be able to explain common instances like these, as well as those in which military elements are presumably dominant such as the considerations which deter Syria from attacking Israel (see also Rosecrance 1975, 35).

The Components of the Deterrence Calculation

In contemplating an attack, it can be said, a would-be aggressor considers two central conditions and compares them: what its world is likely to be like if it goes to war, and what that world is likely to be like if it remains at peace. If, after making this assessment, the aggressor decides the war condition is preferable to the status quo—that is, if it feels it can profit from war— it will go to war. If it finds the status quo preferable to war, it will remain at peace—that is, it will be deterred from starting a war.

I will assume here that someone contemplating war does at least a modicum of thinking about it before taking the plunge. Although it would be foolish to suggest that decision makers go through an exquisite and precise numerical process, there does seem to be a fair amount of rationality in the way wars begin. As military historian Michael Howard concludes, after a lifelong study of the subject, "Wars begin by conscious and reasoned decisions based on the calculation, made by *both* parties, that they can achieve more by going to war than by remaining at peace" (1984, 133).[3]

The would-be aggressor's calculations about what war is likely to be like can be broken down into three components. One is the net value it would achieve by winning the war: the benefits gained from victory minus the costs entailed in achieving it. Another is its net value should it lose the war: the benefits gained in losing (sometimes there are benefits) minus the costs (usually considerable and

[2]On this issue, see also Levy 1989b, 100–101. On the issue of "anarchy" in international politics, see Chapter 2.

[3]Political scientist Bruce Bueno de Mesquita argues that "for all the emotion of the battlefield, the premeditation of war is a rational process consisting of careful, deliberate calculation"; and he notes "one clear indication of the rational planning that precedes war is that only 10 percent of the wars fought since the defeat of Napoleon have been quickly and decisively lost by the nation that attacked first" (1981, 19). On this issue, see also pp. 114–115 and Blainey 1973, ch. 9; Luard 1986, ch. 5; Mueller 1989a, 227–232.

unpleasant) entailed in losing. Finally, it must make some effort to calculate its chances of winning. These three considerations are blended together and the result is a general conclusion about what war would probably bring, and this is then compared to the value placed on remaining at peace—the status quo.

There is likely to be a great deal of guesswork in these calculations but something like them will normally be made. In general, a would-be aggressor is likely to be deterred when it finds (1) the status quo to be pleasant, (2) the net value of winning a war to be rather low, (3) the net value of losing to be very low—penalizing, in fact—and (4) the probability of winning to be low.

Each of these four components can vary over time and each can be manipulated by other countries. A *policy of deterrence* involves a conscious effort by one country to manipulate another country's incentives to go to war so that the potential aggressor, in thinking things over, finds the virtues of peace to be, on balance, substantially greater than those of starting a war. But of course two countries may very well be deterred from attacking each other even if neither has anything like a policy of deterrence toward the other: Bolivia and Pakistan enjoy a firm deterrence relationship though neither, it seems reasonable to presume, gives much thought to the issue one way or the other.

And, more importantly for present considerations, the absence of war—successful deterrence—does not necessarily prove that a *policy* of deterrence has been successful. The United States had a clear and costly policy in which it tried to deter the Soviet Union by threatening nuclear punishment for any major Soviet aggression. But the fact that the Soviet Union did not start a major war cannot necessarily be credited to American policy; indeed, as will be argued in the next chapter, the USSR seems to have had little interest in getting into any sort of major war, no matter how the United States chose to array its nuclear arsenal.[4]

THE NET VALUE OF THE STATUS QUO.   To consider now the four components of a would-be aggressor's calculations, it is useful, if unconventional, to begin with the value it places on the status quo, on not going to war. Peace is most secure when a potential aggressor finds the status quo to be substantially preferable to the value it places on victory. In other words, if the blessings of peace seem to be even greater than those of going to war and winning (much less losing), the potential aggressor will surely be deterred even if it has a high probability of winning. The persistent American unwillingness to attack Canada is surely principally explained by such reasoning. The United States finds the independent existence of its huge northern neighbor to be highly congenial. Although there may be disagreement on various issues from time to time, on the whole Canada contributes very significantly to the American sense of economic, political, and military well-being and, since there is little hankering in the United

---

[4]Vasquez suggests the example of the boy in Brooklyn who runs out of his house once a day waving his arms in order to "keep the elephants away." When someone points out that there are no elephants in Brooklyn, the boy triumphantly observes, "See? It works!" (1991, 207). The boy does have a policy of deterrence toward the encroachment of elephants, but the apparent success of the policy hardly demonstrates that the policy has been a necessary cause of the success.

States for a fifty-first state anyway, cheer, contentment, and peace prevail between these militarily unequal countries. To get invaded, Canada would probably have to do something to dramatically lower its neighbor's pleasure with the status quo. Agreeing to become an outpost for hostile missiles—as Cuba did in the early 1960s—might do the trick.

A would-be aggressor's sense of the value of the status quo includes estimations of the future—a country may be basically content at present but, fearing a future attack by its opponent, may be led to preempt while in a position of comparative strength. The perceived value of the status quo also varies over time, and it is a quality that can be manipulated by a country trying to deter war. Canada, of course, does plenty of things that encourage the United States to prefer the status quo over aggression—for example, establishing a beneficial trading relationship that war would painfully disrupt. While Canada's actions are probably not conscious enough to be considered a policy of deterrence, they do have the effect of lowering the American incentive to invade by raising the value of the status quo— that is, they help to deter war.

There was a conscious effort to deter by manipulating a would-be aggressor's estimate of the value of the status quo during the Cuban missile crisis. The United States loudly let it be known that its satisfaction with the status quo had just fallen precipitously: it had a severe grievance—the pending implantation of offensive nuclear arms by the Soviet Union in Cuba—and it was apparently prepared to go to war to rectify this grievance. It was deterred from carrying out its threat when the USSR agreed to improve the American evaluation of the status quo by removing the offending arms. Similarly, the United States has sought to deter Egypt from attacking Israel by raising Egypt's evaluation of the status quo though extensive aid which war would terminate. And it seems likely that the Poles in 1956— and perhaps also in 1981—deterred a Soviet invasion in part by putting forward political leaders who were to the liking of their large and threatening neighbor.

In fact, except in the cases where a country goes to war for the sheer fun of it, *all* wars can be prevented by raising the potential aggressor's estimation of the status quo. Pearl Harbor could have been prevented by letting the Japanese have Asia, Hitler's aggression might have been deterred simply by giving him the territory he wanted, and Israel could send Syria into peaceful contentment at most any time by ceasing to exist. As these examples suggest, a policy of deterring war by raising a would-be aggressor's estimate of the status quo closely resembles what is commonly known as "appeasement," a word that has picked up extremely negative connotations. More neutrally, it can also be called "deterrence by reward," "positive deterrence," or "reassurance" (Milburn 1959; see also Baldwin 1971; Jervis 1979, especially 294–296, 304–305; Stern et al. 1989, 21–22; K. Mueller 1991).

But however labeled, such a policy contains both dangers and appeals. Clearly, if the aggressor's price is higher than the deterrer is willing to pay, appeasement is simply not feasible: in 1991, Iraq's Saddam Hussein could have deterred the war against his country by withdrawing from Kuwait, but he apparently was convinced that such a humiliating backdown would result in his elimination from office (and perhaps from life), a price he was unwilling to bear (Mueller 1994a, 21). Furthermore, to apply the central lesson usually drawn from the

Munich crisis of 1938, even if the price is bearable, serving the demands of an aggressor may be unwise and ultimately counterproductive because the aggressor's appetite may grow with the feeding, and thus it may be enticed to escalate its demands on the next round, ultimately demanding a price too high to pay. However, the discredit heaped upon appeasement as a result of its apparent misapplication in the 1930s does not mean that the policy is always invalid. Obviously the policy worked in 1962: the Soviet withdrawal of offensive forces in Cuba satiated the American appetite for concession, it did not whet it.

THE NET VALUE OF VICTORY.   Against its estimates of the value of the status quo—the value it finds in remaining at peace—the potential aggressor balances its estimates of what war would most probably bring. For present purposes its thinking about war has been broken down into three components: its estimates of the net value of victory, of the net value of defeat, and of the probability of winning. All three of these qualities can change with time, and all are potentially manipulable by a country which is pursuing a policy of deterrence.

The first of these, the net value of victory, is rarely discussed, yet it is probably the most important of the three, and a close examination of it in juxtaposition to the value of the status quo helps to explain why there is so much peace in so much of the world. For, simply put, many countries much of the time prefer the status quo to fighting a war and *winning*, and thus they are comfortably deterred no matter how big their military advantage. Spectacular cases in point, again, are the noninvasions by the United States of Canada and by the USSR of Romania or Poland: the big countries believed, probably quite accurately, that they would be *worse* off after the war even if (as seems highly likely) they were to win handily.

There are quite a few policies a country—even a comparatively weak one—can adopt to deflate a would-be aggressor's anticipated value of victory. It can make threats which either reduce the benefits the aggressor would gain upon victory or increase its costs for achieving victory.

Presumably an aggressor will see some sort of gains—territorial, economic, or whatever—in a victory. The deterrer could announce a scorched earth policy, in which it pledges to burn everything as it retreats, and thus significantly lower the potential aggressor's anticipated gains. The Dutch have threatened from time to time to greet invasion by destroying their dikes, inundating the victor's newly acquired territory. The Swiss have mined their railway bridges to suggest that a successful aggressor would occupy a country with plenty of Alps, but no transportation system. Fearing encroachment by the United States during the petroleum crisis of the 1970s, some poorly armed Arab states pledged to blow up their oil wells if invaded (see Rosecrance 1986, 11). Another device, promoted by pacifists, is to organize to be able credibly to threaten passive, nonviolent resistance after losing the war. If an invader is interested in taking over a country because it seeks the productive capacity of the people of that country, it will be deterred if it becomes convinced its invasion would cause the country to become unproductive (Holmes 1989, ch. 8; Brown 1987, 127–131; Sharp 1973; Johnson 1987, 248-253). As with all deterrent threats, policies like scorched earth, economy destruction, and passive resistance will be effective only if they are believed by the would-be aggressor. Since these threats involve a certain amount of self-destruction by the deterring country, there is an inherent problem with credibility. The Dutch never did blow up their dikes in World War II, and aggressors who are sufficiently bloody-minded may feel confident they can break down passive resisters.

A country can also seek to increase a victor's costs. As war becomes more destructive in general, the pain suffered even by the victor increases. If the war is sufficiently terrible, victory can quickly become Pyrrhic with the costs outweighing the gains. In the age of long range bombing, a losing country can often embellish the usual costs of war by threatening to visit destruction upon a victor's cities far behind the lines of battle. If the bombers carry nuclear weapons, this threat becomes highly dramatic indeed. This approach—often called deterrence by punishment—was more difficult to carry out before the advent of airpower, though punitive raids could be conducted (Schelling 1966, 178–180). One analogous earlier procedure was for kings who were potential combatants to have their heirs brought up at each other's court, making them hostages against an outbreak of hostilities.

There are policies even small countries can adopt to increase a victor's costs considerably and thus to enhance deterrence. Switzerland is surrounded by countries that have at various times been militarily strong and aggressively inclined; yet its last battle was fought in 1798. In considerable part this is because the Swiss have a large, dedicated, well-trained civilian army: "Switzerland does not have an army," Metternich is reported to have said, "It is an army" (Perry 1986). The country does not threaten so much to defeat an invader as to make the costs of invasion, even a successful invasion, very high—and this threat has apparently been effective even against such devoted aggressors as Adolf Hitler (K. Mueller 1991). If defeated in initial battles, the Swiss army has been trained to fall back into a network of secluded bases and installations in the Alps; from this bastion it would foray out to harass and obstruct the occupiers (Quester 1977, 174; Perry 1986). Moreover, were the Swiss to fight as tenaciously as they threaten, an invader could conquer the country only by destroying it as a productive society, thus lowering the gains of victory (unless, of course, the aggressor wanted to control the country solely for its scenery).

Other small countries have used similar threats in an attempt to deter. At various points in its postwar history, Yugoslavia had reason to fear a Soviet invasion. At those times, Yugoslav officials were quick to let the potential invader know that, if attacked, they would revert to the kind of costly guerrilla warfare they used so effectively against the German invaders during World War II (Quester 1977, 174–175). Fearing an attack by the United States, the Sandinistas in Nicaragua made similar threats, as did Castro in Cuba.

A victor's costs may be substantially and importantly raised by factors other than those developed by the invaded country. The Soviet Union doubtless noticed that its surrogate invasion of South Korea in 1950 caused great alarm in the West and set in motion a substantial anti-Soviet military buildup worldwide; it surely could anticipate similar undesirable, costly developments were it to seek to conquer Yugoslavia or Finland or Iran. The Soviet invasion of Afghanistan in 1979 was met not only with an enervating guerrilla campaign in the country itself but also with trade boycotts, and the Soviets suffered costly reductions in credibility, trust, and prestige in important Muslim areas. In the wake of the quiet cataclysm, as noted in Chapter 1, the big countries of the world are now of such similarity of mind that they can gang up to impose, with little cost to themselves (and consequently with considerable credibility), devastating economic embargoes against small and medium-size countries they deem guilty of aggression—a form of deterrence by punishment. A winner could also become so weakened by victory that it might become tempting prey to other states.

Furthermore, a victor has to live with itself after success has been achieved. If its victory is treated by its population as a productive achievement, a thing of glory, a symbol of virility, an economic or political gain, then the victory will presumably add up on the plus side of the ledger for the leaders. But if the victory were to engender a domestic political upheaval—of the sort, for example, that the British suffered after their brief, successful war against Egypt in 1956—that could be a considerable cost. An adventurous American victory over Canada would likely cause just such a domestic crisis because it would be seen as an outrage by those Americans who would hold such an intervention to be unjust and unwise.

In fact, as Michael Doyle (1983, 1986), Bruce Russett (1990), and others (Streit 1939) have argued, Immanuel Kant's assertion in his 1795 essay, *Perpetual Peace*, that liberal regimes are disinclined to go to war has held up—at least insofar as war among liberal countries is concerned. For the 200 years during which there have been liberal countries, no constitutionally secure liberal states have ever gone to war with each other.[5] Liberal states tend to regard each other as legitimate and unthreatening (Britain, after all, has long had the ability to destroy American cities with nuclear weapons, yet the United States has never seemed to worry much about that prospect). And since the population in a liberal state can directly affect the government, an invasion of one liberal state by another will be effectively protested by many in the population of the victorious country, thus raising—perhaps devastatingly—the costs of victory to the victor. For this subset of countries, one which has increased markedly in number over the last two centuries, deterrence has held firm. And it is extremely unlikely that military factors have had much to do with the peculiar peace that liberal countries so far have worked out among themselves.

It also appears that the psychic costs of war have increased dramatically over the last 200 years or so, at least in the developed world. Where people once saw great glory and honor in war—and particularly in victory—they are now often inclined to see degradation in it instead as war has increasingly come to be regarded as an enterprise that is immoral, repulsive, and uncivilized (see Chapters 8 and 9). In deterrence terms, this change means the value of victory has been sharply reduced.

THE NET VALUE OF DEFEAT.   A would-be aggressor will also be deterred if in its estimation the net value of defeat is sufficiently low—very

---

[5]For some caveats about this relationship, however, see the discussion at the end of Chapter 10.

negative, one might say. Sometimes an aggressor might envision gains in defeat: a well-fought, but unsuccessful, war might recoup lost prestige or self-respect for a country, or the test of war might have beneficial domestic consequences. German General Friedrich von Bernhardi argued before World War I that "even defeat may bear a rich harvest" because often "it leads to healthy revival, and lays the foundation of a new and vigorous constitution," giving the gains the Boers found in defeat in the Boer War as an example (1914, 28, 43–45). Or perhaps the loser can anticipate a generous postwar aid program from the victor: there are Japanese who argue that losing World War II was the best thing that ever happened to their country. Perceived gains like these will be reduced and war deterred if the would-be aggressor can be credibly assured that such benefits will not accompany its defeat.

The main method for reducing the net value of defeat is to raise the costs of defeat—that is, to make war as painful as possible. A would-be aggressor is less likely to be deterred if it concludes that the costs of defeat will be unpleasant but bearable—the loss of a bit of unimportant land, perhaps, or the payment of some not-terribly-expensive reparations—than if it anticipates the kind of total loss legendarily suffered by ancient Carthage at the hands of the Romans.

War is more likely to be deterred if prohibitively high costs are the likely consequence of war itself rather than simply something tacked on at the end as they were at Carthage: the total destruction of the state, the execution of the men, the sale of women and children into slavery, and the salting of the earth so that nothing would grow there again. While it might make sense from a deterrence standpoint to lower a would-be aggressor's value of defeat by threatening it before the war with a Carthaginian "peace" should it be defeated, the threat will be successful only if the potential aggressor believes the deterring country will actually carry out its threat. However, an army that anticipates extermination after defeat has every incentive to fight to the last, thereby raising the costs to the victor and giving the winning country a strong incentive to cut a deal before the war is over. If the aggressor understands this before the war, a Carthaginian threat will not be credible. This dilemma reaches its ultimate in the age of the "doomsday machine"—the threat to blow up the entire world should the aggressor start a war. Even if the technology exists, the aggressor may well refuse to believe the deterring power will ever carry out such a self-destructive policy. Similar credibility problems arise with lesser nuclear retaliatory threats. In general, threats that require massive costs to be borne by the threatener—whether trade boycotts or suicidal destruction—are not likely to be very believable, and if they are not believable they may not be effective.

If, however, tremendous costs are a necessary consequence of any war—if extremely destructive warfare is the only kind likely to develop no matter what policy either side adopts—then the would-be aggressor can anticipate with some certainty that its costs will be very high, and it is therefore more likely to be deterred. Furthermore while Carthaginian costs are paid only by the loser of the war, costs that arise out of warfare itself accrue to both loser *and* winner; that is, *both* the aggressor's cost of winning and its cost of losing are raised. Thus the "nuclear winter" thesis—the notion that even a fairly "small" nuclear war could trigger a catastrophic climatic change because of the lofted smoke and soot from fires (see

Sagan 1983/84)—would be, if accepted as valid, an example of a credible dooms-day machine since unacceptable destruction to both sides would inevitably attend any nuclear war.

It is important to note that this factor is more a matter of escalation than of technology. Countries armed with nuclear weapons could still fight restrained and inexpensive wars with each other (Mueller 1989a, 237–238)—thermonuclear weapons are destructive only if they actually go off. However, if a would-be aggressor anticipates that a war is likely to escalate until it becomes intolerably costly (in all, or virtually all cases, this would be well below the nuclear level), it will be deterred. As discussed in the next chapter, insofar as World War III has been prevented by military considerations, it is this fear that conflict will escalate that has been crucial.

Raised psychic costs lower the value of defeat as well as the value of victory, and unlike the physical costs, they suffer no problem of credibility. If war is no longer held to be an honorable and invigorating test of manliness but is considered instead to be repulsive and uncivilized, one can only engage in it—win or lose—with a distinctly unpleasant sense of repugnance, and therefore at high cost.

THE PROBABILITY OF WINNING.   Finally, the would-be aggressor must reflect upon its chances of winning the war. Normally it will be more likely to be deterred if its chances of winning seem low.[6] By increasing its armed strength, a country with a policy of deterrence can seek to manipulate the calculations of a would-be aggressor in a favorable direction since better arms will lower the aggressor's probability of victory (while perhaps also usefully raising its anticipated costs of war).

As with appeasement, this policy could be counterproductive. If the country one is trying to deter misreads the signal and sees the arms buildup not as deter-

---

[6]This proposition assumes, of course, that the aggressor prefers victory to defeat, certainly a reasonable assumption under most circumstances. There may be a few instances, however, where it does not hold true. In 1898 many Spaniards welcomed a war with the United States over Cuba because a defeat there would allow them honorably to withdraw from that highly troublesome colony (see Lebow 1985, 222-223; Small 1980, 20 and ch. 3.) (Unfortunately for them, however, the victors went on to take over more valued Spanish colonies—Puerto Rico and the Philippines—which caused a revolution at home, exactly what Spanish politicians had sought to avoid with their Cuban policy which was, as it turned out, insufficiently fine-tuned.) Another instance is a fictional one. In the 1959 film, *The Mouse That Roared*, the impoverished Duchy of Grand Fenwick, a tiny country in Europe that somehow managed to miss getting involved in World War II, decides to invade the United States so that it can then enjoy the generous aid that Americans give to countries they defeat in war. Unfortunately the Fenwickians accidentally win; had they suspected their fate in advance they would have been deterred from their aggression. Though they never actually started a war, some Grenadians and Panamanians may be real life Grand Fenwickians: in the view of many grateful Panamanians and Grenadians, the American invasion of their countries threw out bad governments that had somehow gained control over their lives, and replaced them with better ones and with a degree of U.S. largesse. Some French Communist leaders said that they would fight for the Soviet Union in a war with France, thus suggesting that, as Frenchmen, they would prefer defeat to victory in this case (Shulman 1963, 58-61); however, they might be considered, from the French perspective, to be traitors or enemy agents and therefore not really speaking as true Frenchmen. During the Cold War, the Soviet Union had reason to believe that many of its Polish allies might find defeat in a war with the West to be preferable to victory.

rence, but as preparation for an armed attack, then it might actually be tempted to launch an attack before its opponent can do so—the nightmare of arms races and arms buildup that rightfully haunts so many discussions of military matters particularly since the advent of nuclear weapons and that has been labelled the "security dilemma."

DETERRENCE AS EXPECTED UTILITY

The four deterrence variables discussed—the net values of the status quo, of victory, and of defeat, and the probability of victory—can be neatly and simply interrelated by means of an expected utility formulation. The exercise leads to some nonobvious conclusions—for example, that countries with little chance of winning might still want to go to war.

FOOTBALL.   Expected utility can productively be illustrated with an example from football. After scoring a touchdown in the college version of the sport, a team is given an opportunity to do one of two things: to placekick the ball through the goalposts, garnering one point if successful, or to move the ball past the goal line by passing it or running with it, in which case two points will be awarded. Now, what a football team wants is well known: to get more points than the other team. And since virtually all football players are aware that two is greater than one, one might suppose that teams would invariably go for the two-point play. But in fact they do not: they almost always kick.

This happens because the desirability of an option is not determined only by its value, but also by the probability one will be successful in obtaining it. Kicking is far more likely to be successful than running or passing, and thus, all things considered, kicking is a better deal. What the team is trying to maximize is not points, but expected utility. If one assumes that the kick has a probability of .9 of being successful, the expected utility for the kick option is calculated as follows: the value of success (1 point) is multiplied by its probability (.9), and to this quantity is added the value of failure (0 points) multiplied by its probability (.1). Thus, the expected utility for a kick is $1 \times .9 + 0 \times .1 = .9$. If a running or passing play has a .4 probability of success, its expected utility is the value of success (2 points) multiplied by its probability (.4) to which is added the value of failure (0 points) multiplied by its probability (.6). Thus the expected utility for running or passing comes out to be $2 \times .4 + 0 \times .6 = .8$. If those probabilities are reasonable real-life estimates, it is wise to kick, and football coaches are doing the sensible thing when they pursue the less valuable but more probable option. They may not call it that, but they are seeking to maximize expected utility.

WAR.   It is true that war is not the same as a football game, but the same logic can be used to sort through the decision making process. Using the deterrence variables already discussed, a would-be aggressor's expected utility for war is the value it places on victory multiplied by its estimate of the probability of winning, to which is added its value of defeat multiplied by its estimated probability of losing (1 minus its probability of winning). This expected utility for war is then compared to the expected utility for nonwar, or the status quo, which is the value the would-be aggressor places on the status quo (multiplied by its probability, which is 1). If the aggressor finds the expected utility of war to be higher than that of the status quo, it will go to war, and vice versa.

The usefulness of this approach is that it is comprehensive. It makes room for all the considerations discussed earlier—cost and benefit, reward and punishment, concerns about warfare, morality, trade boycotts, domestic political turmoil—and then interrelates them. It also allows one to sort through some of the puzzles deterrence critics have brought up.

For example, some analysts have suggested that the decision of the Egyptians to go to war against Israel in 1973 made no sense from a deterrence standpoint because the Egyptians knew they were likely to lose (for a discussion, see Stein 1985). But a country goes to war, not because it feels it can *win,* but because it feels it can *profit*—that is, emerge better off.

This can work either way. On the one hand, the United States refrains from attacking Canada because the United States could not profit from the encounter even though it could surely win militarily. On the other, the Egyptians seem to have felt, on balance, that they could profit from a war against Israel in 1973 even if they stood little chance of winning it: they had come to feel that the status quo after their defeat by the Israelis in 1967 was intolerably humiliating, and thus they saw some benefits in defeat which, if well fought, would at least raise their self-esteem and prestige: one Egyptian diplomat reportedly argued that it was important to "destroy Israel's image of military invincibility, irrespective of whether Egypt finally won or lost" (Shevchenko 1985, 254; see also Keegan 1990, 77–78). It is possible, in fact, that the Egyptians even preferred defeat to the unsatisfactory status quo, in which case war would have been entirely sensible from their perspective and could not have been deterred no matter how low their chances of winning. Or even if they preferred the status quo to defeat—but not by much—they might well have chosen war even if they stood only a small chance of winning it. Suppose, to put things in numerical form, the Egyptians could be said to have placed a value of 50 on the expected utility of the status quo, a glorious 500 on the value of victory, and −10 on the value of defeat. In that case they would have gone to war even if they believed they stood only a .2 chance of victory. In their estimation, the expected utility of the status quo (50) would have been far less than the expected utility of war: $500 \times .2 + (-10) \times .8 = 100 - 8 = 92$. The same sort of logic could be used with the Japanese decision to attack Pearl Harbor (see Mueller 1968).

Deterrence apparently did not fail in 1973 because the Israelis failed to convince the Egyptians that Egypt would probably lose a war. Rather, the Egyptians' value of defeat was insufficiently unpleasant in comparison to their rather low expected utility for the status quo while their visions of the value of a victory over Israel were blissfully high. If appeasement was not an option, the Israelis' best deterrent hope was probably to make the Egyptians' value of defeat far more penalizing, perhaps by promising devastating destruction of Egyptian values or society.

But the Israelis were unable to do this credibly because of their own obvious preference for quick, decisive, and inexpensive wars. For the Arabs, even defeat was not all that bad given their apparent misery with the status quo.

CRISIS STABILITY AND GENERAL STABILITY

This approach can be used to distinguish between two kinds of stability: crisis stability and general stability. Discussions of deterrence and of defense policy in general have been preoccupied with crisis stability, the notion that it is desirable for disputing countries to be so militarily secure that they can adequately deal with a surprise attack: even if successfully surprised, they can absorb the attack and rebound from it with an effective counteroffensive. If each side is militarily confident in this way, then neither side would see much advantage in launching a surprise attack, and thus neither side would be tempted to start a war out of fear that the other could get a jump on it. Crises, therefore, would be "stable"—both sides would be able to assess events in a luxuriously slow manner and not feel compelled to act hastily and with incomplete information. In expected utility terms, crisis stability means that a country's expected utility for a war it starts is not much different from the utility it expects from a war the other side starts: there is, then, no great advantage to initiating hostilities.

In the nuclear period, discussions of crisis stability centered around the technological and organizational problems of maintaining a secure "second strike" capability—that is, developing a retaliatory force so well-entrenched that a country can afford to wait out a surprise attack fully confident it will be able to respond with a devastating counterattack. Many argued that such crisis stability was "delicate": it could easily be upset by technological or economic shifts (Wohlstetter 1959; see also Snyder 1961, 97–109), and a great deal of thought went into assessing whether a given weapons system or military strategy was "stabilizing" or "destabilizing."

General stability is concerned with broader needs, desires, and concerns and is essentially what Kenneth Boulding (1978) calls "stable peace." It prevails when two countries, taking all the various costs, benefits, and risks into account, vastly prefer peace to war: their expected utility for peace, for the status quo, is much higher than their expected utility for war. It is the sort of thing that has prevailed for a century between the United States and Canada, and has broadened considerably in the developed world in the wake of the quiet cataclysm.

For peace one would ideally like both crisis stability and general stability to prevail in a relationship between two countries. But efforts to improve one form of stability may weaken the other. For example, in an effort to enhance crisis stability, a country may try to improve its second strike capability by building up its military forces; but its opponent may find this provocative, concluding that the buildup is actually a prelude to an attack. On the other hand, generous appeasement concessions, designed to raise a potential aggressor's satisfaction with the status quo by reducing provocation and thus enhancing general stability, may tempt that aggressor to attack by giving it reason to believe it could win cheaply in a quick strike: in a spectacularly futile effort to placate the Germans in the 1930s, Holland decided to remain quiet and neutral while, to decrease "provocation" to Hitler, Belgium broke off its alliance with France and Denmark disarmed.

However, when general stability is high, crisis instability is of little immediate concern. Technically, crisis stability between Russia and the United States has declined since the quiet cataclysm because of Russia's increased military disarray. But, since general stability has increased so much, no one even seems to notice.

In addition, this line of thinking suggests that many concerns about changes in arms balances, while valid in their own terms, miss the broader issue. A defense may increase or decrease crisis stability but this may not alter the broader picture significantly. When general stability is high, the question of who could fight the most ingenious and effective war becomes irrelevant. Deterrence, and therefore peace, prevails.

Chapter 5

THE ESSENTIAL IRRELEVANCE
OF NUCLEAR WEAPONS

The approach applied in Chapter 4 helps to bring deterrence considerations into closer conformity with the realities of decision making in war initiation (or avoidance) and it comfortably builds into the discussion not only military aspects, but also such important nonmilitary considerations as economics, morality, goodwill, prestige, inertia, international opinion, and national pride and self-image. It also broadens the concept of stability, suggesting that deterrence is most firm when general stability prevails—when two countries, taking all costs, benefits, and risks into account, vastly prefer peace to war, even, in most cases, to victorious war.

These considerations can be used as background to examine the long peace that prevailed between East and West after World War II and that mellowed even more after the quiet cataclysm. It is the central argument of this chapter that during the Cold War period (and since), general stability has prevailed in the contest between the major countries. Moreover, this stability has generally been in the cards: nuclear weapons have not been necessary to provide it.

It has been widely assumed that, for better or worse, the existence of nuclear weapons has profoundly shaped our lives and destinies. Some find the weapons supremely beneficial. Because the United States and the USSR had huge nuclear arsenals and because the proclaimed purpose of these arsenals was to deter an attack by the other side, some concluded that the weapons produced the long peace that prevailed between them. Thus, defense analyst Edward Luttwak said, "we have lived since 1945 without another world war precisely because rational minds . . . extracted a durable peace from the very terror of nuclear weapons" (1983b, 82). And Robert Art and Kenneth Waltz concluded, "The probability of war between America and Russia or between NATO and the Warsaw Pact is practically nil precisely because the military planning and deployments of each, together with the fear of escalation to general nuclear war, keep it that way" (1983, 28; see also Knorr 1985, 79; Mearsheimer 1984/85, 25–26; Gilpin 1981, 213–219; Benthem van dem Bergh 1992, ch. 6). Others argued that the continued existence of the weapons promised eventual calamity: the doomsday clock on the cover of the *Bulletin of the Atomic Scientists* pointedly hovered near midnight for over 40 years, and in his influential bestseller of the early 1980s, *The Fate of the Earth,* Jonathan Schell dramatically concluded that if we do not "rise up and cleanse the earth of nuclear weapons," we will "sink into the final coma and end it all" (1982, 231).

This chapter takes issue with both of these points of view and concludes that nuclear weapons neither crucially defined a fundamental stability nor did they threaten severely to disturb it. It seems likely that the long peace enjoyed firmer foundations and that the deterrence calculation has been affected by many other elements. Stability—general stability—has been overdetermined: even without nuclear weapons the United States and the USSR would have been deterred from a war with each other.[1] Or, to put it another way, while nuclear weapons may have been *sufficient* to prevent another major war, they have not been *necessary* to do so.[2]

It is possible to imagine hypothetical situations in which nuclear weapons could make a difference in the future. But it seems that, so far at least, things would have turned out much the same had nuclear weapons never been invented.

The argument uses, of course, a counterfactual approach (see Fearon 1991): if nuclear weapons had never been invented, I contend, the history of the postwar world would have come out much the same. But my counterfactual argument is in response to another, older counterfactual approach that is implicit in a great deal of literature about our "atomic age" and "nuclear era." It essentially holds that, because of the bomb, world affairs have looked a great deal different than they would otherwise. This venerable counterfactual thesis, it seems to me, suffers on close examination.

While I certainly concede that nuclear weapons substantially influenced political rhetoric, public discourse, and defense budgets and planning during the Cold War, it is not at all clear they have had a significant impact on the history of world affairs since World War II. Specifically, they do not seem to have been necessary (1) to deter world war, (2) to determine alliance patterns, or (3) to cause the United States and the Soviet Union to behave cautiously.

●

DETERRENCE OF WORLD WAR

It is true there has been no world war since 1945 and it is also true that nuclear weapons have been developed and deployed in part to deter such a conflict. It does not follow, however, that the weapons have prevented the war—that peace has been, in Winston Churchill's memorable construction, the "sturdy child" of nuclear "terror."

---

[1]See also Holmes 1989, 238–248; Bundy 1988; Mueller 1985; Vasquez 1991; Luard 1986, 396.
[2]This formulation derives from Kaysen, McNamara and Rathjens 1991, 99.

Kenneth Waltz suggests that "nuclear weapons have drastically reduced the probability of [a war] being fought by the states that have them" (1990, 745). John Mearsheimer notes that nuclear deterrence is "much more robust than conventional deterrence" (1990, 31). Robert Jervis stresses that nuclear weapons can cause destruction that is "unimaginably enormous" to *both* sides, and can do so extremely quickly (1988, 31–36). John Gaddis argues that "the vision of future war that Hiroshima burned into everyone's mind was vastly more frightening than any that had existed before (1992, 109). And Carl Kaysen concludes that "these new technologies of war have amplified the message of this century's war experiences by many decibels, and set it firmly in the minds of the wide public as well as those of political and military leaders" (1990, 61).

It is appropriate to compare probabilities and degrees of robustness, to note increased degrees of destructiveness, or to calibrate burning visions or decibel levels. But it is important as well to consider what those levels were before they were changed. A jump from a fiftieth story window is quite a bit more terrifying to think about than a jump from a fifth story one, and quite a bit more destructive as well; but anyone who finds life even minimally satisfying is readily deterred from either misadventure. Nuclear weapons may well have "reinforced an already declining propensity on the part of great powers to fight one another," as Gaddis puts it (1992, 108). But in my view, this was essentially similar to the way a $1000 gift reinforces a millionaire's wealth or a straitjacket reinforces a Quaker's propensity to shun violence.

To assert that the ominous presence of nuclear weapons prevented a war between the two power blocs, one must assume that there would have been a war had these weapons not existed. But there have often been lengthy militarized rivalries between states that nevertheless did not end in war between them (see Goertz and Diehl 1993). In the specific case of the nuclearized rivalry between the United States and the USSR, there were several important war-discouraging factors: the memory of World War II; the general postwar contentment of the victors; the cautious emphasis of Soviet ideology—the chief upsetting element in the postwar world—on lesser kinds of warfare; and the fear of escalation.

THE MEMORY OF WORLD WAR II

The people who have been in charge of world affairs since World War II have been the same people or the intellectual heirs of the people who tried assiduously, frantically, desperately, and, as it turned out, pathetically, to prevent World War II. And when, despite their best efforts, world war was forced upon them, they found the experience to be incredibly horrible, just as they had anticipated. On the face of it, to expect these countries somehow to allow themselves to tumble into anything resembling a repetition of that experience—whether embellished with nuclear weapons or not—seems almost bizarre. That is, although the people who have been running world politics since 1945 have had plenty of disagreements, they have not been so obtuse, depraved, flaky, or desperate as to need visions of mushroom clouds to conclude that major war, win or lose, could be distinctly unpleasant.

It is true they could be expected to be even *more* hostile to a nuclear war, but for the most part nuclear weapons simply compound and dramatize a military reality that by 1945 had already become appalling: few with the experience of World War II behind them would contemplate a repetition with anything other than horror. Even before the bomb had been perfected, world war had become spectacularly costly and destructive, killing some 50 million worldwide. As former Secretary of State Alexander Haig put it in 1982: "The catastrophic consequences of another world war—with or without nuclear weapons—make deterrence our highest objective and our only rational military strategy."[3] To demonstrate that nuclear weapons have made an important difference, Carl Kaysen argues if that nuclear weapons had been invented in the eighteenth century, the war-loving absolute monarchs of that era "would certainly change their assessment of the relative virtues of war and peace" (1990, 61–62). But the leading countries since 1945 *already* vastly preferred peace to major war, and thus needed no conversion.

POSTWAR CONTENTMENT

For many of the combatants World War I was as destructive as World War II, but its memory did not prevent another world war. Of course, as will be discussed more fully in Chapter 9, most nations *did* conclude from the horrors of World War I that such an event must never be repeated: if the only nations capable of starting World War II had been Britain, France, the USSR, and the United States, the war would probably never have occurred. Unfortunately other major nations sought direct territorial expansion, and conflicts over these desires finally led to war.

Unlike the situation after World War I, however, the only powers capable of creating another world war since 1945 have been the big victors, the United States and the Soviet Union, each of which emerged comfortably dominant in its respective sphere: as Waltz has observed, "The United States, and the Soviet Union as well, have more reason to be satisfied with the status quo than most earlier great powers had" (1979, 190; see also Nye 1987, 377). (Indeed, except for the dismemberment of Germany, even Hitler might have been content with the empire his archenemy Joseph Stalin controlled at the end of the war.) While there have been many disputes since the war, neither power had a grievance so essential as to make a world war—whether nuclear or not—an attractive means for removing it.

---

[3]*New York Times*, 7 April 1982. See also Michael Mandelbaum's comment in a book which in this respect has a curious title, *The Nuclear Revolution:* "The tanks and artillery of the Second World War, and especially the aircraft that reduced Dresden and Tokyo to rubble might have been terrifying enough by themselves to keep the peace between the United States and the Soviet Union" (1981, 21). And of course, given weapons advances, a full-scale *conventional* World War III could potentially be even more destructive than World War II.

SOVIET IDEOLOGY

Although the Soviet Union and international Communism had visions of changing the world in a direction they preferred, their ideology stressed revolutionary procedures over major war. The Soviet Union may have had hegemonic desires as many argued but, with a few exceptions (especially the Korean War) to be discussed below, its tactics, inspired by the cautiously pragmatic Lenin, stressed subversion, revolution, diplomatic and economic pressure, seduction, guerrilla warfare, local uprising, and civil war—activities for which nuclear weapons have little relevance. The Communist powers never—before and after the invention of nuclear weapons—subscribed to a Hitler-style theory of direct, Armageddon-risking conquest, and they have been extremely wary of provoking Western powers into large-scale war.

At a conference of the Nuclear History Program in Washington, D.C., in September 1990, Georgy Kornienko, a member of the Soviet foreign ministry since 1947, said he was "absolutely sure" the Soviets would never have initiated a major war even in a nonnuclear world. The weapons, he thought, were an "additional factor" or "supplementary," and "not a major reason." In his memoirs, Nikita Khrushchev is quite straightforward about the issue: "We've always considered war to be against our own interests"; he says he "never once heard Stalin say anything about preparing to commit aggression against another [presumably major] country"; and "we Communists must hasten" the "struggle" against capitalism "by any means at our disposal, *excluding war*" (1974, 511, 533, 531, emphasis in the original). The Soviets were concerned about wars launched *against* them by a decaying capitalist world, but at least since 1935 they held such wars to be potentially avoidable because of Soviet military strength and of international working class solidarity (Burin 1963, 339).[4]

[4]For the argument that the Soviets never contemplated, much less planned for, an offensive to the West, see Ambrose 1990. Arkady Shevchenko, while stressing that "the Kremlin is committed to the ultimate vision of a world under its control," insists that the Soviets "are patient and take the long view," believing "that eventually [they] will be supreme—not necessarily in this century but certainly in the next" (1985, 285–286). Similarly, Michael Voslensky asserts that Soviet leaders desired "external expansion," but their "aim is to win the struggle between the two systems without fighting"; he notes that Soviet military ventures before and after World War II have consistently been directed only against "weak countries" and only after the Soviets have been careful to cover themselves in advance—often withdrawing when "firm resistance" has been met (1984, 320–330). Richard Pipes concludes that "Soviet interests . . . are to avoid general war with the 'imperialist camp' while inciting and exacerbating every possible conflict within it" (1984, 65). William Taubman says that Stalin sought "to avert war by playing off one set of capitalist powers against another and to use the same tactic to expand Soviet power and influence without war" (1982, 12). MacGregor Knox argues that for Hitler and Mussolini "foreign conquest was the decisive prerequisite for a revolution at home," and in this respect those regimes differ importantly from those of Lenin, Stalin, and Mao (1984, 57). See also Jervis 1984, 156; McGwire 1985, 122. For a study stressing the Soviet Union's "cautious opportunism" in the Third World, see Hosmer and Wolfe 1983.

Moreover, if the memory of World War II deters anyone, it probably did so to an extreme degree for the Soviets. Officially and unofficially they seemed obsessed by the memory of the destruction they suffered. In 1953 Ambassador Averell Harriman, certainly no admirer of Stalin, observed to a *Newsweek* interviewer that the Soviet dictator "was determined, if he could avoid it, never again to go through the horrors of another protracted world war" (16 March 1953, 31). And the Soviets presumably picked up a few things from World War I as well; as Taubman notes, they learned the "crucial lesson . . . that world war . . . can destroy the Russian regime" (1982, 11).

THE FEAR OF ESCALATION

Those who started World Wars I and II did so not because they believed that costly wars of attrition were desirable, but because they felt that escalation to wars of attrition could be avoided. In World War I the offensive was considered to be dominant, and it was widely assumed that conflict would be short and decisive.[5] In World War II, both Germany and Japan experienced repeated success with bluster, short wars in peripheral areas, and blitzkrieg, augmented by the counterproductive effects of their opponents' appeasement and inaction.[6]

Insofar as military deterrence has been necessary, world war in the post-1945 era has been prevented not so much by visions of nuclear horror as by the generally accepted belief that conflict can easily escalate to a level, nuclear or not, that the essentially satisfied major powers would find intolerably costly.

To deal with the important issue of escalation, it is useful to assess two phenomena of the early postwar years: the Soviet preponderance in conventional arms and the Korean War.

THE SOVIET ADVANTAGE IN CONVENTIONAL ARMS.   Some have argued that the Soviets would have been tempted to take advantage of their conventional strength after World War II to snap up a prize like western Europe if its chief defender, the United States, had not possessed nuclear weapons. As Winston Churchill put it in 1950: "Nothing preserves Europe from an overwhelming military attack except the devastating resources of the United States in this awful weapon" (Evangelista 1982/83, 110).

---

[5]See Snyder 1984; Van Evera 1984, 80–117; and the essays in *International Security*, Summer 1984.

[6]Hitler, however, may have anticipated (or at any rate, was planning for) a total war once he had established his expanded empire—a part of his grand scheme he carefully kept from military and industrial leaders who he knew would find it unthinkable: see Overy 1982a. The Japanese did not want a major war, but they were willing to risk it when their anticipated short war in China became a lengthy, enervating one, and they were forced to choose between wider war and the abandonment of the empire to which they were ideologically committed: see Chapter 7 and Butow 1961, ch. 11.

This argument requires at least three questionable assumptions: (1) that the Soviets really thought of western Europe as a prize worth taking risks for[7]; (2) that, even without the atomic bomb to rely on, the United States would have disarmed after 1945 as substantially as it did; and (3) that the Soviets actually ever had the strength to be quickly and overwhelmingly successful in a conventional attack in western Europe.[8]

However, even if one accepts these assumptions, the Soviet Union would in all probability still have been deterred from attacking western Europe by the enormous potential of the American war machine. Even if the USSR had had the ability to blitz western Europe, it could not have stopped the United States from repeating what it did after 1941: mobilizing with deliberate speed, putting its economy onto a wartime footing, and wearing the enemy down in a protracted conventional major war of attrition massively supplied from its unapproachable rear base.

The economic achievement of the United States during the war was astounding. While holding off one major enemy, it concentrated with its allies in defeating another, then turned back to the first. Meanwhile, it supplied everybody. With eight million of its ablest men out of the labor market, it increased industrial production 15 percent per year and agricultural production 30 percent overall. Before the end of *1943* it was producing so much that some munitions plants were closed down, and even so it ended the war with a substantial surplus of wheat and over $90 billion in surplus war goods (national governmental expenditures in the first peacetime year, 1946, were only about $60 billion). As Denis Brogan observed at the time, "To the Americans war is a business, not an art."[9]

If anyone was in a position to appreciate this, it was the Soviets. By various circuitous routes the United States supplied the Soviet Union with, among other things, 409,526 trucks, 12,161 combat vehicles (more than the Germans had in 1939), 32,200 motorcycles, 1,966 locomotives, 16,000,000 pairs of boots (in two sizes), and over one-half pound of food for every Soviet soldier for every day of the

---

[7]This assumption was certainly not obvious to Bernard Brodie: "It is difficult to discover what meaningful incentives the Russians might have for attempting to conquer Western Europe" (1966, 71–72). Nor to George Kennan: "I have never believed that they have seen it as in their interests to overrun Western Europe militarily, or that they would have launched an attack on that region generally even if the so-called nuclear deterrent had not existed" (1987, 888-889). Hugh Thomas characterizes Stalin's postwar policy as "conflict which should not be carried into real war. . . . Thus, though expansion should be everywhere attempted, it should not come too close to fighting in zones where the United States, and probably Britain, would resort to arms" (1987, 102).

[8]This assumption is strongly questioned in Evangelista 1982/83, 110–138. See also Ulam 1968, 414; Mearsheimer 1983, ch. 6; and Posen 1984/85. Among Stalin's problems at the time was a major famine in the Ukraine in 1946 and 1947 (Khrushchev 1970, ch. 7).

[9]Quoted, Nevins 1946, 21. Despite shortages, rationing, and tax surcharges, Americans increased consumer spending by 12 percent between 1939 and 1944. See Lingeman 1970, 133, 357, and ch. 4; Milward 1977, 63–74, 271–275; Rosebery 1944, xii.

war (much of it Spam).[10] It is the kind of feat that concentrates the mind, and it is extremely difficult to imagine the Soviets willingly taking on this somewhat lethargic, but ultimately hugely effective, juggernaut. That Stalin was fully aware of the American achievement—and deeply impressed by it—is clear. Adam Ulam has observed that Stalin had "great respect for the United States' vast economic and hence military potential, quite apart from the bomb," and that his "whole career as dictator had been a testimony to his belief that production figures were a direct indicator of a given country's power" (1971, 95, 5).[11] As a member of the Joint Chiefs of Staff put it in 1949, "If there is any single factor today that would deter a nation seeking world domination, it would be the great industrial capacity of this country rather than its armed strength" (Huntington 1961, 46; see also Millis 1951, 350–351). Or as Hugh Thomas has concluded, "If the atomic bomb had not existed, Stalin would still have feared the success of the U.S. wartime economy" (1987, 548).

After a successful attack on western Europe the Soviets would have been in a position similar to that of Japan after Pearl Harbor: they might have gains aplenty, but they would have no way to stop the United States (and its major unapproachable allies, Canada and Japan) from eventually gearing up for, and then launching, a war of attrition.[12] All they could hope for, like the Japanese in 1941, would be that their victories would cause the Americans to lose their fighting spirit. But if Japan's Asian and Pacific gains in 1941 propelled the United States into war (perhaps unwisely, as argued in Chapter 7), it is to be expected that the United States would find a Soviet military takeover of an area of far greater importance to it—western Europe—to be alarming in the extreme. Not only would the United States be outraged at the American casualties in such an attack and at the loss of an important geographical area, but it would very likely conclude (as many Americans did conclude in the late 1940s even without a Soviet invasion of Europe) that an eventual attack on the United States itself was inevitable. Any Hitler-style protests by the Soviets that they had no desire for further territorial gains would not be very credible.

Thus, even assuming that the Soviets had the conventional capability for an easy takeover of western Europe, the credible American threat of a huge, conti-

---

[10]Deane 1947, 92–95; Jones 1969, app. A. Additional information from conversation with Harvey DeWeerd.

[11]In essence, Stalin seems to have understood that in Great Power wars, as Paul Kennedy has put it, "victory has always gone to the side with the greatest material resources" (1987, 439). Nor is it likely that this attitude changed later: "The men in the Kremlin are absorbed by questions of America's political, military, and economic power, and awed by its technological capacity" (Shevchenko 1985, 278). Edward Luttwak, while concerned that the Soviets might actually be tempted to start a war, notes the existence of "the great deterrent": the Soviet fear that "more aggressive expansion will precipitate an Alliance-wide mobilization response which could quickly erode the Kremlin's power position down to a 'natural' level—a level, that is, where the power of the Soviet Union begins to approximate its economic capacity" (1983a, 116). Or Khrushchev: "those 'rotten' capitalists keep coming up with things which make our jaws drop in surprise" (1974, 532).

[12]Interestingly, one of Hitler's "terrible anxieties" before Pearl Harbor was that the Americans and Japanese might work out a rapprochement, uniting against Germany (Rich 1973, 228, 231, 246).

nent-hopping war of attrition from south, west, and east could be a highly effective deterrent—all this even in the absence of nuclear weapons.[13]

LESSONS FROM THE KOREAN WAR. Despite the vast American superiority in atomic weapons in 1950, Stalin was willing to order, approve, or at least acquiesce in an outright attack by a Communist state on a non-Communist one, and it must be assumed that he would have done so at least as readily had nuclear weapons not existed. The American response was essentially the result of the lessons learned from the experiences of the 1930s: comparing this to similar incursions in Manchuria, Ethiopia, and Czechoslovakia (and partly also to previous Soviet incursions into neighboring states in eastern Europe and the Baltic area), Western leaders resolved that such provocations must be nipped in the bud. If they were allowed to succeed, they would only encourage more aggression in more important locales later. Consequently it seems likely that the Korean War would have occurred in much the same way had nuclear weapons not existed.

For the Soviets the lessons of the Korean War must have enhanced those of World War II: once again the United States was caught surprised and under-armed, once again it rushed hastily into action, once again it soon applied itself in a forceful way to combat—and in this case for an area that it had previously declared to be of only peripheral concern. If the Korean War was a limited probe of Western resolve, it seems the Soviets drew the lessons the Truman administration intended. Unlike Germany, Japan, and Italy in the 1930s, they were tempted to try no more such probes: there were no Koreas after Korea. It seems likely that this valuable result would have come about regardless of the existence of nuclear weapons, and it suggests that the Korean War vividly helped to delimit the methods the Soviet Union would be allowed to use to pursue its policy.[14]

That is, it is conceivable that the USSR, in carrying out its ideological commitment to revolution, might have been tempted to try step-by-step, Hitler-style military probes if it felt these would be reasonably cheap and free of risk. The policy of containment, of course, carrying with it the threat of escalation, was designed precisely to counter such probes. If the USSR ever had any thoughts about

---

[13]In fact, in some respects the memory of World War II was *more* horrible than the prospect of atomic war in the immediate postwar period. Western proponents of an atomic preventive war against the USSR were countered by General Omar Bradley and others who argued that this policy would be "folly" because the Soviets would still be able to respond with an offensive against Western Europe which would lead to something *really* bad: an "extended, bloody and horrible" struggle like World War II (1949; see also Baldwin 1950). The conventional threat might be more credible than atomic retaliation even in an era of U.S. nuclear monopoly because an American retaliatory threat to level Moscow with nuclear weapons could be countered with a threat to destroy a newly captured Western city like Paris. And of course once both sides had nuclear capabilities, the weapons could be mutually deterring as has often been noted in debates about deterrence in Europe. Moreover, the Soviets could use nuclear weapons to destroy a landing force, as concerned American officials noted in 1950; see Jervis 1980, 578.

[14]Soviet military intervention in Afghanistan in 1979 was an effort to prop up a faltering pro-Soviet regime. As such it was not like Korea, but more like American escalation in Vietnam in 1965 or like the Soviet interventions in Hungary in 1956 or Czechoslovakia in 1968. For discussions of the importance of the Korean War in shaping Western perspectives on the Cold War, see Gaddis 1974; Jervis 1980; and May 1984.

launching such military probes, the credible Western threat that these probes could escalate (demonstrated most clearly in Korea, but also during such episodes as the Berlin crisis of 1948–49) would be significantly deterring—whether or not nuclear weapons awaited at the end of the escalator ride.

The Korean experience may have posed a somewhat similar lesson for the United States. In 1950, amid talk of "rolling back" Communism and sometimes even of liberating China, American-led forces invaded North Korea. This venture led to a costly and demoralizing, if limited, war with China, and resulted in a considerable reduction in enthusiasm for such maneuvers. Had the United States been successful in taking over North Korea, there might well have been noisy calls for similar ventures elsewhere—although, of course, these calls might equally well have gone unheeded by the leadership.

It is not at all clear that the United States and the Soviet Union needed the Korean War to become viscerally convinced that escalation was dangerously easy. But the war probably reinforced that belief for both of them and, to the degree that it did, Korea was an important stabilizing event.

ALLIANCE PATTERNS

If nuclear weapons have been unnecessary to prevent world war, they do not seem to have crucially affected other important developments either, including the bipolar structure of the Cold War. As argued in Chapter 2, the Cold War was an outgrowth of various disagreements between the United States and the USSR over ideology and over the destinies of eastern, central and southern Europe. The American reaction to the perceived Soviet threat in this period mainly reflects prenuclear thinking, especially the lessons of Munich.

For example, the formation of the North Atlantic Treaty Organization (NATO) and the division of the world into two alliances centered on Washington and Moscow suggest that the participants were chiefly influenced by the experience of World War II. If the major determinant of these alliance patterns had been nuclear strategy, one might expect the United States and, to a lesser extent, the Soviet Union, to be only lukewarm members, for in general the alliances included nations that contribute little to nuclear defense but possessed the capability unilaterally of getting the core powers into trouble: as Michael May observes, "The existence of nuclear weapons, especially of nuclear weapons that can survive attack, helps make empires and client states questionable sources of security" (1985, 150). And one would expect the small countries in each alliance to tie themselves as tightly as possible to the core nuclear power in order to have maximum protection from its nuclear weapons. However, any weakening of the alliances which occurred during the Cold War came from the minor, not the major, partners.

The structure of the alliances therefore better reflects political and ideological bipolarity than sound nuclear strategy. As military economist (and, later, Defense Secretary) James Schlesinger once noted, the Western alliance "was based on some rather obsolescent notions regarding the strength and importance of the European nations and the direct contribution that they could make to the security of the United States. There was a striking failure to recognize the revolutionary impact that nuclear forces would make with respect to the earlier beliefs regarding European defense" (1967, 6). Or, as Warner Schilling has observed, American policies in Europe were "essentially pre-nuclear in their rationale. The advent of nuclear weapons had not influenced the American determination to restore the European balance of power. It was, in fact, an objective which the United States would have had an even greater incentive to undertake if the fission bomb had not been developed" (1961, 26). Or Kenneth Waltz: "Nuclear weapons did not cause the condition of bipolarity. . . . Had the atom never been split, [the United States and the USSR] would far surpass others in military strength, and each would remain the greatest threat and source of potential damage to the other" (1979, 180–181; see also Chapter 2; Gaddis 1992, 112).

CRISIS BEHAVIOR

Because of the harrowing image of nuclear war, it is sometimes argued, the United States and the Soviet Union were notably more restrained than they might otherwise have been, and thus crises that might have escalated to dangerous levels were resolved safely at low levels (Gaddis 1987, 229–232; Gilpin 1981, 218; Blacker 1987, 46; Gaddis 1992, 110–112; Holsti 1991, 305).

There is, of course, no definitive way to refute this notion since we are unable to run the events over again without nuclear weapons. And it is certainly true that decision makers are well aware of the horrors of nuclear war and cannot be expected to ignore the possibility that a crisis could lead to such devastation.

However, it should not be assumed that crises normally lead to war. Indeed, very often they do not (see Kennedy 1983, 170). Moreover, this idea—the notion that it is the fear of nuclear war that has kept behavior restrained—looks far less convincing when its underlying assumption is directly confronted: the assumption that the major countries would have allowed their various crises to escalate if all they had to fear at the end of the escalatory ladder was a sweet little exercise like World War II. Whatever the rhetoric in these crises, it is difficult to see why the unaugmented horror of repeating World War II, combined with a considerable comfort with the status quo, would not have been enough to inspire restraint.

Once again, escalation is the key: what deters is the belief that escalation to something intolerable will occur, not so much the details of the ultimate unbearable punishment. Where the belief that the conflict will escalate is absent, nuclear countries *have* been militarily challenged with war—as in Korea, Vietnam, Afghanistan, Algeria, and the Falklands.[15]

---

[15]On this point, see also Evan Luard: "There is little evidence in history that the existence of supremely destructive weapons alone is capable of deterring war. If the development of bacteriological weapons, poison gas, nerve gases and other chemical armaments did not deter war before 1939, it is not easy to see why nuclear weapons should do so now" (1986, 396).

None of this is meant to deny that the sheer horror of nuclear war is impressive or mind-concentratingly dramatic, particularly in the speed with which it could bring about massive destruction. Nor is it meant to deny that decision makers, both in times of crisis and otherwise, are fully conscious of how horribly destructive a nuclear war could be. It is simply to stress that the sheer horror of repeating World War II is not all that much less impressive or dramatic, and that powers essentially satisfied with the status quo will strive to avoid anything that they feel could lead to *either* calamity. World War II did not cause total destruction in the world, but it did utterly annihilate the three national regimes that brought it about. People remember things like that.

Did the existence of nuclear weapons keep the Korean conflict restrained? As noted, the Communist venture there seems to have been a limited probe—although somewhat more adventurous than usual and one that got out of hand with the massive American and Chinese involvement. As such there was no particular reason—or meaningful military opportunity—for the Soviets to escalate the war further. In justifying *their* restraint, the Americans continually stressed the danger of escalating to a war with the Soviet Union—something of major concern whether or not the Soviets possessed nuclear weapons.

Nor is it clear that the existence of nuclear weapons has vitally influenced other events. For example President Harry Truman was of the opinion that his nuclear threat drove the Soviets out of Iran in 1946, and President Dwight Eisenhower, that his nuclear threat drove the Chinese into productive discussions at the end of the Korean War in 1953. McGeorge Bundy's reassessment of these events suggests that neither threat was very well communicated and that, in any event, other occurrences—the maneuverings of the Iranian government in the one case and the death of Stalin in the other—were more important in determining the outcome.[16] But even if we assume the threats *were* important, it is not clear why the threat had to be peculiarly *nuclear*—a threat to commit destruction on the order of World War II would also have been notably unpleasant and dramatic.

Much the same could be said about other instances in which there was a real or implied threat that nuclear weapons might be brought into play: the Taiwan Straits crises of 1954 and 1958, the Berlin Blockade of 1948–49, the Soviet-Chinese confrontation of 1969, the Israeli Six-Day War in 1967, the Yom Kippur War of 1973, Cold War disagreements over Lebanon in 1958, Berlin in 1958 and 1961, offensive weapons in Cuba in 1962. Morton Halperin argues that "the primary military factors in resolving the crisis" in the Taiwan Straits in 1954 were "American air and naval superiority in the area," not nuclear threats (1987, 30). Alexander George and Richard Smoke note that crises in Berlin in 1948–49 and in the Taiwan Straits in 1958 were broken by the ability of the Americans to find a

---

[16]Bundy 1984, 44–47; Bundy 1988, 232–233, 238–243. For the argument that Truman never made a threat, see Thorpe 1978, 188–195. See also Gaddis 1987, 124–129; and Betts 1987, 42–47.

technological solution to them (1974, 383). Betts suggests that even if the American alert was influential with the Soviets in 1973 (which is quite questionable), it is "hard to argue against the proposition that the conventional force elements in it were sufficient, the nuclear component superfluous" (1987, 129). He also finds "scant reason to assume . . . that the nuclear balance would be a prime consideration in a decision about whether to resort to nuclear coercion" (1987, 218–219). As for the Soviet-Chinese confrontation, Roy Medvedev notes Soviet fears of "war with a poorly armed but extremely populous and fanatical China" (1986, 50; see also Shevchenko 1985, 165–166; on many of these issues, see Bundy 1988). All were resolved, or allowed to dissipate, at rather low rungs on the escalatory ladder.

Interestingly, it seems that even in the great "nuclear" crisis over Cuba in 1962 the central figures would have been about equally anxious if all they had to worry about was escalation to a war of the kind they had already experienced. "I have participated in two world wars," Khrushchev wrote Kennedy at the height of the crisis, "and know that war ends only when it has carved its way across cities and villages, bringing death and destruction in its wake" (Medvedev 1986, 190; Allison 1971, 221). In a speech to Soviet textile workers a year after the crisis, Khrushchev recalled the loss of his son in World War II and the millions of other deaths suffered by the Russians, and then laid into the Chinese: "Some comrades abroad claim that Khrushchev is making a mess of things, and is afraid of war. Let me say once again that I should like to see the kind of bloody fool who is genuinely not afraid of war." The Soviet press reported that it was this statement that was cheered more loudly and wholeheartedly than any other by his audience (Werth 1964, xii).[17] And Kennedy was haunted by the experience with the conventional conflagration that began in 1914. He had been greatly impressed by Barbara Tuchman's *The Guns of August* and concluded that in 1914 the Europeans "somehow seemed to tumble into war . . . through stupidity, individual idiosyncracies, misunderstandings, and personal complexes of inferiority and grandeur." He had no intention of becoming a central character in a "comparable book about this time, *The Missiles of October*" (Kennedy 1971, 40, 105; see also Sorensen 1965, 513).

While the horror of a possible nuclear war was doubtless clear to the participants in these various crises and confrontations, it is certainly not apparent that they would have been much more casual about escalation if the worst they had to fear was a repetition of World War II.

---

[17]For an able refutation of the popular notion that it was American nuclear superiority that determined the Soviet backdown in the Cuban missile crisis, see Lambeth 1972, 230–234. Marc Trachtenberg has presented an interesting, if "somewhat speculative," case that Soviet behavior was influenced by their strategic inferiority. His argument is largely based on the observation that the Soviets never went on an official alert, and he suggests this arose from fear of provoking an American preemptive strike. But the essential hopelessness of the tactical situation and the general fear of escalation to what Lambeth (quoting Thomas Schelling) calls "just plain war" would also seem to explain this behavior (Trachtenberg 1985, 156–163). Relatedly, Hannes Adomeit sees "no congruence between increased Soviet military capabilities and enhanced Soviet propensities to take risks" (1986, 42–43).

CONCLUSION: THE ROLE OF NUCLEAR WEAPONS

The argument suggests, then, that stability has been overdetermined—that the postwar situation contained and continues to contain redundant sources of stability. The United States and the Soviet Union were essentially satisfied with their lot and, fearing escalation to another costly war, were quite willing to keep their conflicts limited. As suggested earlier, nuclear weapons may well have enhanced, or in Gaddis' expression, reinforced, this stability (1992, 108). And they are certainly dramatic reminders of how horrible a big war could be. But it seems highly unlikely that, in their absence, the leaders of the major powers would be so unimaginative as to need such reminding. Wars are not begun out of casual caprice or idle fancy, but because one country or another decides that it can profit from (not simply win) the war—the combination of risk, gain, and cost appears preferable to peace.[18] Even allowing considerably for stupidity, ineptness, miscalculation, and self-deception in these considerations, it does not appear that a large war, nuclear or otherwise, has been remotely in the interest of the essentially contented, risk-averse, escalation-anticipating powers that have dominated world affairs since 1945.

Central throughout has been the issue of escalation. Both sides were fully aware that any severe conflict between them could easily escalate to an all-out fight, and each adopted deterrence policies designed to make that threat credible to the other. Insofar as military considerations are relevant, then, it was escalation—the conviction on both sides that a war between them would become massively costly—that determined the issue, not the peculiar qualities of the horrors that waited at the end of the escalatory ladder. As long as the two sides anticipated that they would be worse off with war than with the rather pleasant status quo, deterrence held. Nuclear weapons have not been required to bring these two cautious contestants to this elemental conclusion.

Thus, if a would-be aggressor thinks a move might very well escalate to something terrible like a world war (with or without nuclear weapons), caution is likely to ensue. However, where that fear is lacking—as with the Argentines when they launched military action against the interests of the (nuclear-armed) United Kingdom in 1982—war can come about.[19] The belief in escalation may be some-

---

[18]Thus, as discussed in Chapter 4, the notion that there is a special danger if one side or the other has a "war-winning" capability is misguided; there would be danger only if a war-*profiting* capability exists. The second does not necessarily follow from the first. As Lebow argues: "History indicates that wars rarely start because one side believes it has a military advantage. Rather they occur when leaders become convinced that force is necessary to achieve important goals" (1984, 149).

[19] Waltz argues that "contemplating war when the use of nuclear weapons is possible focuses one's attention not on the probability of victory but on the possibility of annihilation. . . . The problem of the credibility of deterrence, a big worry in a conventional world, disappears in a nuclear one" (1990, 734). British nuclear retaliation was certainly possible, yet the Argentines apparently did not find it credible. On this issue, see also Luard 1986, 396; Gaddis 1992, 110. Jervis suggests that the fear of escalation is more vivid and dramatic in the nuclear case (1988, 35–36). This may be true, but, again, it is necessary in addition to demonstrate that those running world affairs have needed such vivid reminders.

thing of a myth—certainly the major countries during the Cold War were remarkably good at carrying out their various tangles and disagreements far below the level of major war (Mueller 1989a, 236–240). Thus, although the trends with respect to major war seem to be quite favorable, peace could nevertheless be shattered by an appropriately fanatical, hyperskilled, and anachronistic leader who is willing and able to probe those parameters of restraint. Accordingly, it would be sensible to maintain vigilance.

Thus, although I hold that nuclear weapons have not been very important in shaping the course of international history and although I contend that nuclear weapons have not been necessary to keep leaders cautious about major war, I do believe there are imaginable circumstances under which it might be useful to have nuclear weapons around—such as the rise of another lucky, clever, risk-acceptant, aggressive fanatic like Hitler. Therefore, even if one concludes that nuclear weapons have not been necessary to preserve peace, it might still make sense to have some for added insurance against severe anachronism. Insofar as a military deterrent was necessary, the fear of another World War II has been quite sufficient (indeed, far more than sufficient, I expect) for the *particular countries* which have actually existed since 1945. But it does not follow that that fear alone could prevent all imaginable wars.

However, in the world we have actually experienced, major war does not seem ever to have really been in the cards,[20] and accordingly any enhancement of stability that nuclear weapons may engender has been purely theoretical—extra insurance against unlikely calamity. Nuclear weapons do add a new element to international politics: new pieces for the players to move around the board (missiles in and out of Cuba, for example), new terrors to contemplate. But in counter to Albert Einstein's famous remark that "the atom has changed everything save our way of thinking" (1960, 426), it seems rather that nuclear weapons have changed little except our way of talking, gesturing, and spending money.

---

[20]Thus, George Kennan: "The atom has simply served to make unavoidably clear what has been true all along since the day of the introduction of the machine gun and the internal combustion engine into the techniques of warfare—what should have been clear to people during World War I and was not: namely, that modern warfare in the grand manner, pursued by all available means and aimed at the total destruction of the enemy's capacity to resist, is, unless it proceeds very rapidly and successfully, of such general destructiveness that it ceases to be useful as an instrument for the achievement of any coherent political purpose" (1961, 391).

Chapter 6

ENOUGH ROPE: OVEREXTENSION
VERSUS CONTAINMENT

As promulgated in 1947 by one of its chief architects, George Kennan, the policy of containment fashioned a strategy to deal with the "implacable challenge" posed by Soviet Communism. Because of their ideology and history, he held, the Soviets were dangerous. They were highly disciplined—albeit cautious and flexible—and fundamentally expansionary, feeling it their "duty eventually to overthrow the political forces beyond their borders" (1947, 582, 569).

Fortunately for the West, there existed, Kennan argued, a strong possibility that "Soviet power, like the capitalist world of its own conception, bears within it the seeds of its own decay, and that the sprouting of these seeds is well advanced" (1947, 580). Kennan stressed three such "seeds." First, the population of Russia, he believed, was "physically and spiritually tired" as well as "disillusioned, skeptical and no longer as accessible as they once were to the magical attraction which Soviet power still radiates to its followers abroad." Second, "Soviet economic development, while it can list certain formidable achievements, has been precariously spotty and uneven" (1947, 577–578).

And the third involved the "great uncertainty" that hung over the "political life of the Soviet Union." This was "the uncertainty involved in the transfer of power from one individual or group of individuals to others." By his calculation, the Soviets had taken twelve years to consolidate the transfer of power after the death of Vladimir Lenin, and Kennan anticipated problems at least as great when Stalin met his eternal reward. This derived not only from "the personal position of Stalin," but from "the dangerous congealment of political life in the higher circles of Soviet power" (1947, 578–579).

To deal with the Soviet threat, Kennan called for "a long-term, patient but firm and vigilant containment of Russian expansive tendencies." More specifically, the United States should enter upon "a policy of firm containment, designed to confront the Russians with unalterable counter-force at every point where they show signs of encroaching upon the interests of a peaceful and stable world." He felt it clear "that the Soviet pressure against the free institutions of the western world is something that can be contained by the adroit and vigilant application of counter-force at a series of constantly shifting geographical and political points, corresponding with the shifts and manoeuvers of Soviet policy" (1947, 575, 581, 576).

Harry Truman reflected a similar perspective in his farewell address in January 1953. "As the free world grows stronger, more united, more attractive to men on both sides of the Iron Curtain—and as the Soviet hopes for easy expansion are blocked—then there will have to come a time of change in the Soviet world" (1966, 378). Similarly, as another President, George Bush, put it in 1989, "The grand strategy of the West during the postwar period has been based on the concept of containment—checking the Soviet Union's expansionist aims in the hope that the Soviet system itself would one day be forced to confront its internal contradictions."

Truman was unwilling to predict when or how this change would happen: "Nobody can say for sure when that is going to be, or exactly how it will come about, whether by revolution, or trouble in the satellite states, or by a change inside the Kremlin." Kennan, however, seems to have put greatest stress on his last "seed"—the succession problem—because he suggests a time frame. Although at one point he calls the contest a "duel of infinite duration," he suggests that great dilemmas—and ultimately, he hoped, doom—would be created for Soviets if "the western world finds the strength and resourcefulness to contain Soviet power over a period of ten to fifteen years" (1947, 576).[1] That time projection, it seems likely, is based on a estimate of how long it might take before the tyrannical Soviet leader, Joseph Stalin, then sixty-eight years old, was summoned to meet his presumably distinctly unamused maker.

THE QUESTIONABLE SUCCESS OF CONTAINMENT

If this is a fair analysis of Kennan's thinking, he was clearly woefully wrong about the depth of the succession dilemma. Stalin died in 1953, and after a few years of jockeying around (and very little bloodshed), the mantle of leadership was passed on to new Communists. However, while the process took much longer than Kennan probably anticipated, and while succession hardly proved to be the central dilemma he postulated, he was essentially right about the disillusionment

---

[1]In 1950 Kennan argued that even if it took an extremely long time—like thirty years—for the "defeat of the Kremlin" to occur, the "tortuous and exasperatingly slow devices of diplomacy" were surely preferable to a "test of arms" which was unlikely to bring about "any happy or clear settlement" of international differences (Gaddis 1982, 49).

and skepticism of the Russian population, about the fundamental precariousness of Soviet economic development, and about "the dangerous congealment of political life in the higher circles of Soviet power."

Eventually, in the 1980s under the leadership of Mikhail Gorbachev, the Soviets did mellow their foreign policy decisively, and shortly after that the whole country imploded. It is natural to conclude from this experience, as most people have, that the wisdom of the containment strategy has been affirmed. But while the policy *intended* a certain desirable effect, it does not follow that the policy *caused* it.

In fact, the policy of containment is logically flawed. If the Soviet system really was as rotten as Kennan and Truman more or less accurately surmised, then the best policy would not have been to contain it, but to give it enough rope—to let it expand until it reached the point of terminal overstretch. Indeed, one of Kennan's favorite quotes comes from Gibbon: "there is nothing more contrary to nature than the attempt to hold in obedience distant provinces" (Gaddis 1982, 47; Gellman 1984, 53). If that is true, an expansive country will discover this lesson faster if it is allowed to gather in new distant provinces than if it is contained. That is, if the goal was to speed the Soviet Union's inevitable rendezvous with its decadent destiny, it might have been wiser to let it expand to the rotting point. Containment may actually have done it a favor by postponing the climax.

Thus it may not be sound to wallow in self-congratulation in the wake of the Cold War, and to conclude that "We won." Rather, it would be much more sensible to conclude that the Soviet Union lost: almost all the calamities that brought it to its desperate condition and compelled it to abandon its expansionary ideology were self-induced.

DOMESTIC DILEMMAS

As Kennan suggested, it is clear that the major problem for the Soviet Union was the staggering failure of its bureaucratic and economic system. Based on some utopian notions that sought to repeal human greed (or self-interest) and to replace the price system with managed arrangements, the Soviets eventually invented an economic and social system that stifled initiative and enshrined inefficiency. But Westerners can take little credit for creating this dilemma. They tried to exacerbate it with various trade policies, but the basic problem was fabricated by the Soviets themselves. Indeed, if the Soviets had taken Western advice, they would never have adopted their system in the first place.

ARMS EXPENDITURES

Much the same holds for arms policy. It is true that the Soviets' vast, economy-straining arms buildup was in part a reaction to Western defense spending. But much of this buildup would have happened anyway. As Kennan pointed out in 1947, central to the classic Soviet Communist view of the world was an intense suspiciousness of, and hostility toward, the surrounding capitalist world, a view that often verges on, and sometimes transcends, paranoia. Massive arms expenditures are a necessary concomitant of this worldview, and they were likely no matter how the West chose to array its arsenal.

Indeed, the West tried to level or reduce arms expenditures several times—in the mid-1940s, the 1960s, and the 1970s. Each time the Soviets responded by continuing to build. Their policy seems to have been "too much is not enough." As Jimmy Carter's Secretary of Defense, Harold Brown, concluded with exasperation, "When we build, they build; when we cut back, they build," and as it happened, it was under Carter that the "Reagan defense buildup" began. The value of that expensive policy is not at all clear. It probably helped the Soviets (particularly Gorbachev) to appreciate the depth of the country's economic dilemma, but the effect may have been fairly marginal since the Soviets were *already* vastly overspending for defense. Moreover, the buildup came at a severe cost (or waste) to the American economy which was then forced to devote much of the 1990s trying to dig out.

IMPERIAL OVERSTRETCH

As discussed in Chapter 2, Soviet ideology also had at its center an almost messianic drive to undermine the capitalist enemy. As Kennan put it in 1947, the Communists believed that for capitalism to perish, "a final push was needed from a proletariat movement in order to tip over the tottering structure" (1947, 567).

As noted, it is on this drive that containment focused most directly, and the assumption was that if the Soviets' expansionary impetus were systematically frustrated, their foreign policy would eventually mellow because of changes from within. Accordingly the United States sought to apply "unalterable counter-force at every point where they show signs of encroaching upon the interests of a peaceful and stable world," which included not only areas of highest concern, like western Europe, but also such peripheral places as Korea, Laos, and the Congo.

Kennan does not mention it in his 1947 article, but at its core the policy of containment applied the lesson of Munich: when a country bent on expansion gains more territory, the experience only whets its appetite for more. Thus when Communist expansion was thwarted—as in Greece in the 1940s, in Korea in the 1950s, or in central Africa in the 1960s—the policy was held to have been successful. When areas fell into the Communist camp—as in eastern Europe in the late 1940s, China in 1949, North Vietnam in 1954, Cuba in 1959, and portions of Laos in 1961—containment was held to have suffered a setback.

But what ultimately helped to bring about the mellowing of Soviet expansionism was not containment's success, but its failure.

Wherever they expanded, the Soviets sought, often brutally, to suppress ancient nationalisms and freedoms. Kennan anticipated that the Soviets would find maintaining control over eastern Europe to be difficult. In 1947, he proclaimed it "unlikely" that the 100 million Soviets could permanently hold down not only their own minorities, but "some 90 millions of Europeans with a higher cultural level and with long experience in resistance to foreign rule" (Gaddis 1982, 43; Taubman 1982, 170). By the 1980s, the Soviets' empire in eastern Europe had indeed became a severe economic drain and a psychic problem—although this, of course, cannot be credited to Western policy which strenuously opposed the occupation from the beginning.

Then in 1975 three countries—Cambodia, South Vietnam, and Laos—toppled into the Communist camp. Partly out of fear of repeating the Vietnam experience, the United States went into a sort of containment funk and watched from the sidelines as the Soviet Union, in what seems in retrospect to have been remarkably like a fit of absent-mindedness, opportunistically gathered a set of Third World countries into its imperial embrace: Angola in 1976, Mozambique and Ethiopia in 1977, South Yemen and Afghanistan in 1978, Grenada and Nicaragua in 1979. The Soviets at first were quite gleeful about these acquisitions—the "correlation of forces," they concluded, had magically and decisively shifted in their direction.

However, far from whetting their appetite for more, these gains ultimately not only satiated their appetite for expansion but, given the special properties of the morsels they happened to consume, the process served to give the ravenous expanders a troubling case of indigestion. For almost all the new acquisitions soon became economic and political basket cases, fraught with dissension, financial mismanagement, and civil warfare. In 1979 the situation in neighboring Afghanistan had so deteriorated that the Soviets found it necessary to send in troops, and descended into a long period of enervating warfare there.

As each member of their newly expanded empire turned toward the Soviet Union for maternal warmth and sustenance, many Soviets began to wonder about the wisdom of the venture. Perhaps, it began to seem, they would have been better off contained. Charles Wolf and his colleagues at the RAND Corporation (1983) estimated that the cost of the Soviet empire (excluding the costs of maintaining troops in eastern Europe, but including the costs of the war in Afghanistan) rose enormously between 1971 and 1980 from about 1 percent of its Gross National Product to nearly 3 percent when measured in dollars, or from under 2 percent to about 7 percent when measured in rubles. (By comparison, insofar as the United States could be said to have a comparable empire, the costs were less than one-half of 1 percent of its GNP.)

Anti-Soviet wars in the Third World also presented a new opportunity for the United States. In the 1980s it started backing some of them, particularly ones in Nicaragua (controversially) and Afghanistan (noncontroversially). This might be seen as an application of containment policy (although in principle containment eschews such "rollback" policies), and the war in Afghanistan, in particular, certainly helped raise Soviet imperial costs. But that war was started and perpetuated by Afghan resentment at Soviet occupation, not by the containment strategy. The arms sent there by the United States may have enhanced the damage anti-Soviet forces could inflict, but the central dilemma for the Soviets—the reality that made the war a "running sore," as Mikhail Gorbachev was soon putting it—was the willingness of the rebels to fight for decades if necessary to free their country.

SOVIET CONTRADICTIONS

The "internal contradictions" the Soviets came to confront, then, were a direct result of misguided domestic and foreign policies, and these contradictions would have come about—as Kennan seems to suggest—no matter what policy the West chose to pursue. Soviet domestic problems derived from decades of mismanagement, mindless brutality, and fundamental misconceptions about basic economic and social realities. Their defense dilemmas came from a conspiratorial ideology that creates external enemies and then exaggerated the degree to which the enemies would use war to destroy them.

And their foreign policy failures stemmed from a fundamentally flawed, and often highly romantic, conception of the imperatives of history and of the degree to which foreign peoples will find appeal in the Communist worldview. It took forty years but, plagued by economic and social disasters and changes, the Soviets finally were able, as Kennan and Truman had hoped, to rise above ideology, embrace grim reality, and adopt serious reform.[2]

THE BENEFITS OF CONTAINMENT

Although the Western policy of containment probably deserves little special credit for bringing about this belated rendezvous with reality, the policy does seem to have had some beneficial effects.

In particular it deserves credit for keeping some countries outside the Soviet orbit. Without a containment war in the 1950s, South Koreans would probably now be living as miserably as their fellows in the North. Thailand, Malaysia, and Singapore need only look to the Indochina states to see what might have happened if Communist rebels had been successful in their countries. And it is possible, although far from certain, that some western European countries would have succumbed to Communism in the late 1940s had the containment policy not been in effect.[3]

It could also be argued—very speculatively—that containment helped reduce the danger of a major war. The principal containment wars in Korea and Vietnam and the Cuban missile crisis may have had this effect.

If the North Koreans had been successful in 1950 in overrunning the South, hawks in the international Communist movement would surely have been encouraged to consider employing the technique elsewhere. Instead, as noted in Chapter 5, the sour experience in Korea seems permanently to have discredited such mili-

---

[2]As suggested in Chapter 2, however, it does not follow that economic and social travail *necessarily* lead to a mellowing of ideology. Leaders, in this case Gorbachev, had to *choose* that policy route. Faced with the same dilemmas, a conservative leader might have stuck to the faith while suffering gradual decline (like the Ottoman empire) or one might have adopted more modest reforms to maintain the essential quality of the system—and the privileges of its well-entrenched elite. For a discussion of the possible value of applying a policy of containment (rather than war) to vulnerable and vastly overextended Japan after Pearl Harbor, see Chapter 7.

[3]Takeovers in western Europe would likely not have been much of a boon for the Soviets because they presumably would have mismanaged them just as assiduously as they did those in their part of Europe. They did, after all, take over several Western-type European countries—East Germany, Czechoslovakia, and Hungary—and were unable to make them very productive.

tary probes—there have been no Koreas since Korea. Most historians now agree, however, that the main impetus toward that war came from the North Koreans, not from Stalin's Kremlin which greatly feared a wider war. Thus precipitous military action was not very likely even in the wake of a quick Korean success.

Had South Vietnam been allowed to collapse to Communism in 1965 the event would have been profoundly encouraging to Communist theorists—particularly those in China—who were almost hysterically committed to the view that the United States and other Western states were "paper tigers" and in the process of terminal decline. The event would certainly have served to encourage movements toward similar wars elsewhere (although there were plenty of these at the time anyway). And it is at least possible that a more direct confrontation between a humiliated United States and a euphoric China was prevented (see Mueller 1989a, ch. 8).

As the Korean War discredited direct, if limited, military probes as a method for advancing the Communist cause, the Cuban missile crisis of 1962 discredited the methodology of crisis. Basic to Leninist theory is the notion that capitalist countries will inevitably fight among themselves, and Nikita Khrushchev and other Soviet leaders often saw the manipulation of these imperialistic "contradictions" to be a potentially fruitful method for advancing their cause. After the trauma of 1962, this dangerous notion was abandoned—the Soviets fomented no crises after that, and most analysts have trouble seeing how a major war could come about unless an episode of crisis or at least of severely heightened tension were to precede it. However it seems clear in retrospect that, as Kennan believed from the outset, the Soviets never saw major war (whether nuclear or not) to be remotely in their interest (see Chapter 5). While crisis was a dangerous game, the Soviets were unlikely ever to let it get out of hand and, since the United States had a similar aversion, it is questionable whether major war has ever really been in the cards.

CONCLUSION

The Western policy of containment, then, has helped to keep some countries free from Communism, and it may have further reduced the already low danger of major war. But insofar as it was devised to force the Soviets to confront their inherent contradictions, the history of the Cold War suggests a curious paradox. Kennan and the other early containment theorists were correct to conclude that Soviet Communism is a singularly undesirable and fundamentally flawed form of government, and they were right to anticipate that it would inevitably have to mellow when it could no longer avoid confronting its inherent contradictions. But Soviet Communism would probably have reached this point somewhat earlier if its natural propensity to expand had been tolerated rather than contained.

Chapter 7

REASSESSING PEARL HARBOR

In some important ways, the experience of the demise of the Cold War and of the collapse of Communism during the quiet cataclysm can alter the way we look at the past. In this chapter, I attempt to reassess Pearl Harbor and its consequences with the benefit of such hindsight.

The first part of the chapter evaluates the damage inflicted by the Japanese attack on Pearl Harbor on December 7, 1941. Postmortems generally describe the attack in dramatic, almost apocalyptic, terms. The Joint Congressional Committee that investigated the event after the war labeled the attack "the greatest military and naval disaster in our Nation's history" (U.S. Congress 1946b, 65), and leading students of the attack use similar language. John Toland has characterized Pearl Harbor as a "catastrophe" (1961, 38) and as "the worst military disaster in [American] history" (1970, 237), while Samuel Eliot Morison calls the attack "devastating" and an "overwhelming disaster" for the United States (1963, 68, 70). Gordon Prange dubs the attack a "debacle" (1986, 534) and "one of the worst defeats the United States suffered in its 200 years" (1988, xiii; similarly, see Puleston 1947, 111). Ronald Spector, Roberta Wohlstetter, and Louis Morton call it a "disaster" as well, and Spector and Wohlstetter also agree on "catastrophe" (Spector 1985, 93; Morton 1962, 144; Wohlstetter 1962, 3, 398). Melvin Small finds it a "crushing blow" and "our worst military disaster" (1980, 234, 253; see also Melosi 1977, x).

In a direct military sense these dramatic characterizations are excessive: militarily, the attack on Pearl Harbor was more of an inconvenience than a catastrophe or disaster for the United States. The destruction inflicted by the Japanese was not terribly extensive, and much of it was visited upon military equipment that was old and in many cases obsolete or nearly so. In addition, much of the damage was readily and quickly repaired, and its extent was soon made all but trivial by the capacity of America's remarkable wartime industry to supply superior replacements in enormous numbers. Moreover, the attack did not significantly delay the American military response to Japanese aggression, nor did it importantly change the pace of the war: the United States was unprepared to take the offensive at that time in any case, and the damage at Pearl Harbor increased this unpreparedness only marginally. I also conclude that the persistent exaggerations of damage stem more from the tendency of writers to apply dramatic terms to notable events than from the efforts of the U.S. government to use the incident to generate support for the war effort.

In the second part of the chapter, however, I apply the experience of the postwar Cold War and conclude that in broader political and strategic ways, Pearl Harbor may well have been truly a disaster. It clearly was one for the attackers, of course, because it triggered a conflict that eventually destroyed Imperial Japan, exacting in the process a huge price in blood and treasure. But it was also a disaster for the United States in an important sense because it utterly closed off careful thought there, propelling the country heedlessly into a long, ghastly war in Asia when the experience of the Cold War suggests that the country might have rolled back the Japanese empire at lower cost to all involved if it had continued its pre–Pearl Harbor policies of containment and harassment. And in broadest focus, the war triggered by Pearl Harbor may have been a disaster in that the vicious international overlordship it demolished in Asia at great cost was replaced with a set of local tyrannies that in many cases, especially China, were even worse.

PEARL HARBOR AS A MILITARY INCONVENIENCE

The Japanese attacked in two waves in the early morning of December 7, 1941. Some 183 fighters, bombers, and torpedo planes participated in the first wave and 168 in the second; 28 submarines and 5 two-man, two-torpedo midget subs also contributed (Prange 1981, 491–492; Willmott 1982, 134). The American targets were sitting ducks—the ships were arrayed in rows in the harbor, and the planes were bunched and lined up neatly on airfields to protect them against sabotage.

The Japanese planned carefully and achieved nearly complete surprise on the first wave. The second wave, which began an hour later, was hampered by intense anti-aircraft fire, and although many important targets remained, it accomplished little: about 90 percent of the damage was achieved by the first wave (Morison 1963, 59, 66–67). This difference suggests how risky the Japanese venture was, even in the short term. If their luck had gone a bit sour, giving the Americans hours or even minutes of warning, the Japanese would have done far less damage, and the local U.S. commanders, who were cashiered from authority after the attack and pilloried for decades for incompetence or worse, would instead have been celebrated as heroes and saviors.

The Japanese, operating under virtually ideal attack circumstances and with enormous luck, are commonly said to have "destroyed or severely damaged" as many as 21 American ships and 339 aircraft.[1] In addition they killed 2,403 people.[2]

NAVAL LOSSES

Most of the major ships in the Pacific Fleet, including all three aircraft carriers, were elsewhere at the time of the attack (see Table 7.1). The Japanese managed to strike 20 percent of the 101 ships at Pearl Harbor.

They principally targeted the 8 battleships (the United States had another in Puget Sound and 6 more in the Atlantic), and they hit all of them. As it happened, the youngest of these had been launched twenty years earlier, and all were in substantial need of modernization. As Thomas C. Hone observes, "None of the battleships at Pearl Harbor was a first-line warship"; in fact, four were due to be officially declared over-age in 1942 (1977, 58, 59n27).

Moreover, the battleship itself was rapidly declining in military significance. Admiral C. C. Bloch, the commandant of the Pearl Harbor district, points out that "the Japanese only destroyed a lot of old hardware." In a sense, he argues, "they did us a favor" by helping the United States to enter the modern naval age in which carriers are at the heart of the fleet (Prange 1981, 737). H. P. Willmott observes that the attack "removed from the scene some ships of rather questionable value and forced the Americans to recast the whole of their tactical doctrine." Doctrine had already been changing, but the attack caused strategic thinkers "to jettison any lingering ideas of the battleship remaining the arbiter of sea power"

---

[1]Sometimes commentators drop the "damaged" category entirely. Thus: "The Japanese were able to destroy 18 ships" (Small 1980, 253). Most analysts number the naval losses at 18 because they do not consider the floating drydock to be a ship and because they do not include in their count the small tugboat, *Sotoyomo*, and *Helm*, a destroyer lightly damaged by a near miss. Others also leave out the ancient ex-battleship, *Utah*. In the attack, Japan lost 29 planes while another 72 were damaged, some beyond repair. In all, about 129 Japanese died in the attack. See Slackman 1990, 235. The submarine portion of the attack was a fiasco: the subs did little or no damage and all 5 of the midget subs were quickly sunk or captured. In addition 1 large submarine (accounting for half of the Japanese dead) was sunk. Willmott argues that a result was a serious loss of face for Japanese submariners and a loss in confidence in submarines by the Japanese naval command that persisted throughout the war (1982, 134–135).

[2]This loss represents, of course, a substantial human tragedy. In assessing Pearl Harbor, perhaps rather callously, from a strictly military standpoint, however, the loss was readily manageable: within six months, the Navy alone had grown by over 250,000. Nonetheless, as David MacGregor has pointed out to me, the casualties at Pearl Harbor were notable even by later standards: the battle at Tarawa, often considered a bloodbath, claimed some 1,000 American lives, Guadalcanal claimed 1,600, Iwo Jima claimed 6,000, and Okinawa, the most costly battle of the Pacific War for the United States, claimed 12,000. When commentators refer to Pearl Harbor as the greatest military disaster in American history, however, they cannot be focusing on casualties: vastly greater losses were sustained in battles in World War I and in the Civil War, as well as in the Korean War. In all, the United States suffered some 300,000 battle deaths in World War II. Worldwide, some 30 to 50 million people perished in the conflict.

TABLE 7.1

The United States fleet

	The fleet on December 7, 1941			Ships added to fleet after 12/7/41
	Fleet totals	Pacific Fleet totals	At Pearl Harbor	
Aircraft carriers	7	3	0	18
Battleships	15	9	8	8
Heavy cruisers	na	12	2	13
Light cruisers	na	9	6	33
Destroyers	na	54	30	352
Submarines	na	22	4	203
	297	109	50	
Gunboats	na	1	1	
Minelayers	na	9	9	
Minesweepers	na	26	14	
Auxiliary ships	na	60	27	
	429	205	101	

na, Not available.

Sources: Wallin 1968, 52–56; U.S. Congress 1946a, Part 12, 345–346, 348–349; King 1946, 252–286.

and obligated them "to develop the war-winning concept of the fast carrier task force" (1982, 139).[3]

Furthermore, the damage inflicted on Pearl Harbor's old boats was actually quite limited. The Japanese achieved surprise in considerable part because American intelligence had mistakenly concluded that torpedoes dropped from planes could not function in Pearl Harbor's shallow water, which was dredged to about 40 feet in the channels and was less than 30 feet elsewhere (Wohlstetter 1962, 369–370; see also U.S. Congress 1946a, Part 39, 311–312). As it happens, it is a basic physical law that ships sunk in shallow water do not go down very far. Consequently when the attackers left, even the ships they had sunk or capsized were readily available for repair, resting accessibly, if uncomfortably, on the bottom. Moreover, alert crews were able to beach two damaged ships (the battleship *Nevada* and the repair ship *Vestal*) before they could sink.

That the United States was surprised at Pearl Harbor, in fact, was something of an advantage. In a 1964 interview, Admiral Chester W. Nimitz, who became commander in chief of the Pacific Fleet three weeks after the attack, concluded that "it was God's mercy that our fleet was in Pearl Harbor on December 7." If Admiral Husband Kimmel, the commander in Hawaii, had "had advance notice

---

[3]In Admiral Frederick Sherman's words, "The portion of our sea power which was put out of action was the part that was already obsolete in the new era of fighting" (1950, 41–42). For a discussion of changing naval doctrine, including the observation that the U.S. Navy had been giving carrier production priority over battleship production well before Pearl Harbor, see Rosen 1988, 151–158. For a somewhat different perspective, see Weigley 1973, 253, 271.

that the Japanese were coming, he most probably would have tried to intercept them. With the difference in speed between Kimmel's battleships and the faster Japanese carriers, the former could not have come within rifle range of the enemy's flattops. As a result, we would have lost many ships in deep water and also thousands more in lives" (Prange 1982, 9; see also Wallin 1968, 290).

When repair and restoration are considered, the United States suffered a dead loss of only 2 out of the harbor fleet of over 100 (see Table 7.2). The two ships that were total losses were both battleships and, as it happened, they were two of the oldest in the fleet and among the four scheduled to be declared overage in 1942. One was the *Arizona*, which had been launched in 1913, a year after its namesake state entered the Union. It was scavenged for machinery, scrap metal, and fuel oil, and the sunken remnants rest there still, a memorial to the day. The other was the *Oklahoma*, a year newer than the *Arizona*, which was stripped and scavenged, raised, and sold for scrap. It accidentally sank again (this time in deep water) when being towed to the mainland after the war.

Another battleship, *West Virginia* (launched in 1921), was repaired, but did not rejoin the fleet until the middle of 1944. Two others, *California* (1919) and *Nevada* (1914), rejoined the fleet within two years. The other three damaged battleships were repaired and ready for action within three weeks. A Japanese torpedo also destroyed the *Utah*. This craft is sometimes listed as a battleship, which indeed it was when it was launched in 1909. But in 1941 it was serving as a target ship for American aircraft: by sinking it, the Japanese merely accomplished what the U.S. Navy had not yet managed to do itself.

Beyond this the Japanese badly damaged 3 of the 30 destroyers at Pearl Harbor (there were 54 in the Pacific Fleet). These, however, were safely afloat again in 2 months or so, were disassembled and reoutfitted on new hulls, and rejoined the Fleet within 10 to 18 months.[4] The other ships hit by the Japanese were soon back in action, most of them by early in 1942.

The effective naval losses at Pearl Harbor should therefore not casually be reckoned as some 21 ships "destroyed or severely damaged." Rather, 2 very old battleships (and 1 target ship) were lost except for their salvage value, 3 slightly younger battleships were put out of action for between 1 and 2 1/2 years, and 3 destroyers required very extensive repairs. With only minor exceptions, the 12 other damaged ships were repaired rather quickly and soon rejoined the fleet. (The impact of this destruction on the American ability to respond immediately to Japanese advances is discussed below.) As a result, except for 2 battleships (and the target ship), all the ships struck at Pearl Harbor participated in the naval battles that brought defeat to Japan in 1945. Of the 6 U.S. battleships that helped to administer the important Japanese naval defeat at Leyte Gulf in 1944, 5 had been damaged at Pearl Harbor (Wallin 1946, 1521). If the "real objective of the Japanese was to cripple the American Fleet" (Wallin 1946, 1523), the mission was a spectacular failure.

---

[4]Of the two worst-damaged destroyers, "The remarkable truth was that practically all of the electrical equipment, machinery, and armament in *Cassin* was found to be salvable, while even in *Downes* 90 per cent of her machinery and one-third of her electrical motors could be retrieved" (Alden 1961, 36).

TABLE 7.2

Naval damage at Pearl Harbor

Battleships

Arizona (1913). Substantially destroyed and sunk. Scavenged for machinery, ordnance material, scrap metal, and fuel oil. Became part of a memorial structure.

Oklahoma (1914). Capsized. Floated on November 3, 1943, and scavenged. Sold for scrap in 1946, and sank in a storm when being towed back to the mainland in 1947.

West Virginia (1921). Sunk. Floated on May 17, 1942, and placed in drydock on June 9; sailed to Seattle for modernization and ready for action again on July 4, 1944; won five battle stars.

California (1919). Sunk. Floated and moved to drydock on April 9, 1942; sailed to Puget Sound Navy Yard for modernization on October 10, 1942; rejoined the fleet less than a year later, and won seven battle stars.

Nevada (1914). Severely damaged and beached by crew. Floated on February 12, 1942; sailed to Seattle under own power on April 22 for modernization; back in service by the end of 1942, and won seven battle stars.

Pennsylvania (1915). Considerably damaged. Repaired and back in action on December 20; sailed to mainland for overhaul.

Maryland (1920). Considerably damaged. Fully repaired by December 20.

Tennessee (1919). Some serious damage. Repaired and back in action on December 20.

Light cruisers

Raleigh (1922). Substantial destruction of machinery, serious flooding. Repaired by February 14, 1942; sailed to California for new engine parts and electrical repairs.

Helena (1939). Substantial destruction of machinery, some flooding. Repaired by December 21. Left for California on January 5, 1942, for further work.

Honolulu (1936). Considerable damage and flooding. Repaired by January 12, 1942.

Destroyers

Downes (1936). Heavily damaged. Floated on February 6, 1942. Fifty percent salvaged and installed on new hull in California; launched on May 20, 1943; won four battle stars.

Cassin (1935). Heavily damaged. Floated on February 18, 1942. Fifty percent salvaged and installed on new hull in California; launched on June 21, 1943; won seven battle stars.

Shaw (1935). Great damage. Bow replaced, able to sail to repair facility in California on February 9, 1942; returned to full duty in the fall of 1942; won eleven battle stars.

Helm (1937). Light damage. Repaired quickly after January 15, 1942.

Repair ship

Vestal (1908). Some damage, serious flooding, beached by crew. Floated in ten days; completely repaired in drydock by February 18, 1942.

TABLE 7.2 (CONTINUED)

Minelayer

> *Oglala* (1907). Capsized. Given low priority due to age; back in service in February 1944 after repairs in California; still in service in 1968.

Seaplane tender

> *Curtiss* (1940). Serious damage. Repaired by its own crew by May 28, 1942, after replacement parts arrived.

Auxiliary

> *Floating drydock Number 2.* Sunk. Floated on January 9, 1942; repaired and in limited use by January 26, 1942; fully repaired by May 15.

> *Sotoyomo,* small tugboat. Burned and sunk. After long wait for parts, repaired by late summer, 1942.

> *Utah,* former battleship (1909), had been in use as a target ship. Capsized. Scavenged for ordnance material and fuel oil.

Note: Dates in parentheses are the years the ships were launched.

Sources: Wallin 1968, 1946; U.S. Congress 1946a, Part 12, 348–349, 354–357; Morison 1963, 63–64; Morison 1948, 143–146; Prange 1986, 538–539; Slackman 1990, 263–271; Alden 1961, 32–41.

The destruction of two battleships and the temporary removal from duty of several others, in fact, may have been something of a short-term advantage to the United States. At the time, suggests Willmott, "trained manpower in the U.S. Navy was in critically short supply." After Pearl Harbor, naval personnel without ships were redeployed, which meant that "escort forces could be properly manned, and the carrier task forces could be properly constituted and balanced" (1982, 139).[5]

Moreover, in evaluating the impact of the attack, one must consider what American industry could do to replace the losses. To compensate for the 2 old battleships that were sunk and for the 3 that were badly damaged at Pearl Harbor, 8 new ones, far larger and far better, joined the Fleet over the next four years. Of these, 3 were commissioned by May 1942 while another came along in August. To compensate for the 3 severely damaged destroyers, no less than 352 new ones were added during the course of the war, 7 of them by the end of February 1942 and 3 more in March. In addition, during the war the Fleet grew by 18 aircraft carriers, 9 light aircraft carriers, 77 escort carriers, 2 large cruisers, 13 heavy cruisers, 33 light cruisers, 412 destroyer escorts, and 203 submarines, not to mention 55 high-speed transports and 83,219 landing craft (King 1946, 252–286). Clearly, the Pearl Harbor losses were overwhelmingly and, particularly in the case of the destroyers, quite quickly, made up.

---

[5]I would like to thank Chaim Kaufmann for bringing this issue to my attention.

An illuminating comparison is provided by H. P. Willmott: "Such was the scale of American industrial power that if during the Pearl Harbor attack the Imperial Navy had been able to sink every major unit of the entire U.S. Navy and then complete its own construction programs without losing a single unit, by mid-1944 it would still not have been able to put to sea a fleet equal to the one the Americans could have assembled in the intervening thirty months" (1983, 522).[6]

AIRCRAFT LOSSES

A somewhat similar picture emerges when one looks at aircraft losses. Some 151 American aircraft were damaged in the attack, and 188 were destroyed or soon cannibalized out of existence.[7] However, many of the attacked planes, including over one-third of the destroyed Army planes, were obsolescent types, and many of the others were small scouting and patrol craft (see Tables 7.3 and 7.4).

Furthermore, nearly 40 percent of the Army planes were in various states of disrepair and were out of commission on December 7. After the attack, massive efforts were made not only to repair damaged planes, but also to put those that were undamaged, but out of commission, into operation. It was found that of the 120 damaged Army planes, fully 80 percent could be salvaged. In addition, 29 shiny new B-17s were rushed over from the mainland, more than replacing the 4 destroyed in the attack. As a result, in less than two weeks the Army had almost as many planes in operation in Hawaii as it had had before the attack (U.S. Congress 1946a, Part 22, 60–61; Part 7, 3068, 3070; Part 24, 1784).

In evaluating the aircraft destruction it is most important to consider, as with the ships, what the United States was able to do to replace the losses. On January 6, 1942, President Franklin Roosevelt dramatically called upon American industry to produce 60,000 aircraft in 1942 and another 125,000 in 1943. His speech helped boost morale, but his targets had to be scaled back somewhat, in part because there were not yet enough landing fields, hangars, and maintenance facilities to handle that many planes. As it happened, however, the country did manage to turn out some 47,836 military aircraft in 1942 (to Japan's 8,861), another 86,000 or so in 1943 (to Japan's 16,693), and a total of 299,300 over the course of the war.[8] The United States lost 4 B-17s at Pearl Harbor, but between 1940 and 1945 American industry produced 12,692 new ones; it lost 32 P-40s in the attack, but

---

[6]I would like to thank Bruce Russett for leading me to this quotation.

[7]Army aircraft damaged, 120 (80 pursuit planes, 6 reconnaissance planes, and 34 bombers): U.S. Congress 1946a, Part 7, 3069–3070. Navy aircraft damaged, 31: Morton 1962, 133. Army aircraft destroyed or cannibalized, 96: U.S. Congress 1946a, Part 12, 323; Morton 1962, 133. Navy aircraft destroyed, 92: U.S. Congress 1946a, Part 12, 357–358.

[8]Smith 1959, 141–142; Civilian Production Administration 1947, 540. Smith observes (p. 142n) that Roosevelt's ambitious 1942 and 1943 targets for merchant shipping and antiaircraft guns were actually overfulfilled. Japanese figures from United States Strategic Bombing Survey (1946, vol. 7, 155). See also Milward 1977, 74. Milward notes (p. 67) that American man-hour (actually, in this case, substantially woman-hour) output was twice that of the Germans, five times that of the Japanese.

TABLE 7.3

Destruction and delivery of Army combat aircraft

	Aircraft in Hawaii		Destroyed in attack	Aircraft delivered from 1/40 to 12/45
	Before attack	After attack		
B-17			4	12,692
In commission	6	4		
Out of commission	6	4		
B-18°			12	
In commission	21	11		
Out of commission	12	10		
B-12°			0	
In commission	1	1		
Out of commission	2	2		
A-20			2	7,385
In commission	5	5		
Out of commission	7	5		
A-12°			0	
In commission	2	1		
Out of commission	0	1		
P-40			32	13,738
In commission	64	33		
Out of commission	35	34		
P-36°			4	
In commission	20	16		
Out of commission	19	19		
P-26°			6	
In commission	10	4		
Out of commission	4	4		
O-47			0	
In commission	5	5		
Out of commission	2	2		
O-49			1	
In commission	2	1		
Out of commission	0	0		
OA-8			0	
In commission	1	1		
Out of commission	0	0		
OA-9			2	
In commission	3	1		
Out of commission	0	0		
TOTALS				
In commission	140	83		
Out of commission	87	81		
Total destroyed	227	164	63	

°Characterized by the Army as "Obsolescent types."

Sources: U.S. Congress 1946a, Part 12, 323; Smith 1959, 27.

TABLE 7.4

Naval and Marine Corps aircraft on Hawaii

Total aircraft present before attack	169
Destroyed aircraft	
Fighters	13
Scout bombers	26
Patrol bombers	46
Observation/Scouts	1
Utility	3
Training	1
Transports	2
Total destroyed	92
Damaged	31

Sources: U.S. Congress 1946a, Part 12, 357–358; Morton 1962, 133; U.S. Congress 1946b, 69.

built 13,738 (see Table 7.3). At 1942 rates of production, all the planes lost at Pearl Harbor could be replaced with aircraft that were brand new, and generally far superior, in less than three days.

AMERICAN NONLOSSES

In determining whether the Pearl Harbor attack was a "disaster" for the United States, one might also consider the many targets that were left untouched by the huge Japanese offensive. The Japanese failed even to hit half of the light cruisers, 86 percent of the destroyers, or any of the heavy cruisers or submarines in the harbor, and they missed several other major targets as well. As Homer Wallin points out, the extensive shore facilities suffered little damage, and "the tremendous oil stowage adjacent to Pearl Harbor" which was filled to capacity "was not attacked at all" (1946, 1524).[9]

Moreover, it happened that none of the 3 aircraft carriers in the Pacific Fleet was at Pearl Harbor on the day of the attack—2 were at sea and 1 was in San Diego—and the Japanese had no idea where they were. It was the carrier, not the battleship, that was to prove to be the major naval weapon in the Pacific War, and so this absence was important.[10]

---

[9]In addition, he observes, "The Japanese failed to drop at least a few bombs which might have started a conflagration that would have proved disastrous, especially to the mobility of the undamaged vessels of the Fleet in the days to follow December 7." See also Morton 1962, 133; Willmott 1982, 140–141; Goldstein et al. 1991, 176.

[10]If the two Honolulu-based carriers had been at their berths, they would have been the primary targets for the Japanese (Slackman 1990, 12; Willmott 1982, 131–133). Admiral Sherman argues that "there is little doubt" that the carriers "would have been totally destroyed" (1950, 41). Carriers are more fragile than battleships, but even if the carriers had been sunk in the shallow harbor, they might well eventually have been recoverable. And, of course, fewer bombs would have been targeted at other ships. During the war, incidentally, it took some thirty-two months to build a battleship, but an aircraft carrier could be built twice as fast (King 1946, 13).

In addition to the carrier, the submarine proved to be an especially effective naval weapon in the war. Few of the Pacific Fleet's submarines were at Pearl Harbor, and none of these was damaged. And, as noted, American industry was soon turning out better ones by the scores anyway.

DID PEARL HARBOR DELAY THE AMERICAN
MILITARY RESPONSE?

If Morison is correct that the Japanese set out with "the double purpose of wiping out the major part of the Pacific Fleet at Pearl Harbor, and destroying all military aircraft on Oahu," then the attackers failed miserably (1963, 46). Admiral Frederick Sherman suggests, however, that Japan's mission was more modest: "The purpose of the raid was to immobilize our Pacific Fleet in order to gain time and ensure freedom of action for the Japanese invasions of the Philippines and the Netherlands East Indies" (1950, 33).

The attack did delay America's ability to respond quickly to early Japanese aggressions in the Pacific. As Prange notes, "Any hope of reinforcing the Philippines or Singapore vanished in the smoke of the Hawaiian debacle" (Prange 1986, 534). But the Japanese carried out these attacks at such lightning speed and with such total success that in all probability the ships based at Pearl Harbor, insufficient in number and slow of speed, would not have been able to get there in time, would scarcely have made much difference to the outcome even if they had been able to, and might well have been sunk—this time in deep water—if they had tried.[11] Indeed, a dash to the South Seas would have played into the hands of the Japanese whose war plans specifically proposed that they should "endeavor by various means to lure the main fleet of the United States [to the Far East] and destroy it" (Ike 1967, 248.)[12]

Morison makes American unpreparedness quite clear: "The Pacific Fleet was too weak in many types, especially destroyers and auxiliaries, too deficient in anti-aircraft protection, to go tearing into waters covered by enemy land-based air power." There was a plan for the relief of the Philippines if they were attacked, but it would have taken six to nine months to accomplish this even assuming the Pearl Harbor fleet remained intact. Thus, "even at the most optimistic the Japanese could have conquered everything they wanted in the Philippines and Malaya by leaving Pearl Harbor alone and relying on submarines and aircraft in the Mandates to deal with our Pacific Fleet."[13]

----

[11]The three badly damaged destroyers, *Shaw*, *Downes*, and *Cassin*, were in drydock on December 7 undergoing major repairs and alterations (Alden 1961, 33). Thus they would not have been immediately available for such a venture in any case.

[12]As Scott Sagan points out, the traditional strategy for the Japanese navy involved "forcing the American fleet to cross the Pacific, attriting the fleet through submarine attacks during its voyages, and attempting to win what was expected to be the decisive battle near Japan" (1988, 913).

[13]Thus," Morison concludes, "the surprise attack on Pearl Harbor, far from being a 'strategic necessity,' as the Japanese claimed even after the war, was a strategic imbecility" (1948, 132).

Actually, things were even worse than that for the United States. The U.S. plan depended upon a military buildup in the Philippines that would have allowed the forces there to hold out for at least six months. That buildup was underway, but at the time of Pearl Harbor it was still at least two months from completion (Sherman 1950, 44).[14] Thus, the military premise upon which the plan was based was not fulfilled when the war began, and the operation could not have been put into action, at least according to the plan, whether Pearl Harbor had been attacked or not.

In fact, one of the reasons the Americans were surprised at Pearl Harbor was that they realized the fleet there would never have been able to cramp Japan's style in a southward thrust. As one war plans officer recalled, "I did not think they would attack at Pearl Harbor because I did not think it was necessary for them to do so." Because of many deficiencies, "we could not have materially affected their control of the waters they wanted to control whether or not the battleships were sunk at Pearl Harbor" (U.S. Congress 1946a, Part 26, 207).

The officer's anticipation seems to have been correct. In early January 1942, Army planners advised that in order to relieve the Philippines they would need at least 1,500 aircraft, 7 to 9 battleships, 5 to 7 carriers, 50 destroyers, 60 submarines, and a full complement of auxiliary ships (Spector 1985, 114). Regardless of the destruction at Pearl Harbor, the United States probably would not have been able to gather such a huge armada in time.

Moreover, even this force might not have been enough. Admiral Sherman argues that "the Pearl Harbor attack knocked [our] plans into a cocked hat" and forced a defensive war in the Pacific. This, he says, is because the United States had a total of only 7 aircraft carriers (3 in the Pacific, 4 in the Atlantic) to Japan's 10: "We had short-sightedly allowed the Japanese to . . . achieve superiority in this paramount class of warships" (1950, 45). But by this account it was the carrier imbalance that knocked things into that cocked hat—an imbalance that was in no way affected by Pearl Harbor. As Spector notes, "The loss of so many aging battleships did not delay the start of an American offensive nearly so much as did the shortage of aircraft carriers (of which never more than four were available in the Pacific at any time before late 1943), amphibious shipping, and destroyers" (1985, 83–84).

An additional consideration is that Germany declared war on the United States four days after war began in the Pacific. Even if there had been no losses at Pearl Harbor, the United States could not have launched a viable offensive to the South Seas without unacceptably diverting forces from what was now clearly the primary theater of war: the Atlantic.[15]

---

[14]Notes Sherman, "This was one reason why the military and naval leaders had urged the President and State Department to delay a showdown with Japan until we were more nearly ready" (1950, 44).

[15]See also Spector 1985, 114. Malcolm Muir argues, "Pearl Harbor immediately ended any possibility of a cross-Pacific offensive by the battle line. This setback, coupled with the entry of Germany and Italy into the conflict, confronted American naval planners with an unprecedented challenge: to fight major wars in two oceans at once—and with a fleet crippled on the opening day" (1990, 4). It seems rather that, given the size of the American Navy, it was the challenge attendant on fighting a two-ocean war that would have "ended any possibility of a cross-Pacific offensive," quite apart from any losses at Pearl Harbor.

The central issue here is that the Americans were substantially unprepared at the end of 1941 for the massive, two-theater (or multi-theater) war into which they plunged; the destruction at Pearl Harbor reduced this preparedness only marginally.[16] In the summer of 1940, the commander-in-chief of the Pacific Fleet, Admiral James O. Richardson, observed that the Navy simply was not ready for war because it lacked advanced bases, was too small, and had substantial shortages of ammunition, fuel, spare parts, and essential supplies. Because of this, he concluded that a war would take four years: two years of buildup and two years of hard fighting (Carney 1981, 49).[17] This was the broad, grim reality, and it was not significantly altered by Pearl Harbor: militarily, the damage inflicted was more of an inconvenience than a disaster.

The Origins and the Persistence of the Disaster Image

It is not entirely clear why the attack on Pearl Harbor has been so persistently labeled a military catastrophe, an overwhelming disaster, a crushing blow. Since the attack propelled the United States into a long and costly war, there may have been some psychological need at the time to maximize the justification for the war by exaggerating the damage suffered in the triggering event. Perhaps those exaggerations simply became embedded in later discussions and descriptions.

If this is the case, however, it was not due to propaganda efforts by the U.S. government which, in fact, went out of its way to downplay the damage, not to exaggerate it. Startled and enraged by the attack, many Americans initially assumed the worst, and rumors quickly spread that the entire Pacific Fleet had been sunk, that more than 1000 planes had been destroyed on the ground, that more than 10,000 men had been killed, and that shiploads of corpses were quietly being transported to New York to be dumped into a common grave. Fearing that such rumors might hurt morale, Franklin Roosevelt went on the radio in February 1942 to denounce "the rumor-mongers and the poison peddlers in our midst," and to announce that only 2,340 had been killed, that only three combatant ships had been put permanently out of commission, that most damaged ships were under repair or had already rejoined the fleet, and that the repairs would make them "more efficient fighting machines." Moreover, he stressed that Japanese gains in the Philippines had been made possible not by success at Pearl Harbor, but because "even if the attack had not been made, your map will show that it would have been a hopeless operation for us to send the fleet to the Philippines through

---

[16]"In no material respect were they ready for war," as Willmott has put it (1982, 115).

[17]Richardson strongly opposed basing so much of the fleet at Pearl Harbor because it could not be quickly sent off to war from that base. As he put it in a September 1940 memo, "In case of war [it would be] necessary for the Fleet to return to mobilization ports on the West Coast or accept partial and unorganized mobilization measures resulting in confusion and a net loss of time" (Richardson 1973, 325–326; see also U.S. Congress 1946a, Part 1, 264; Part 14, 956).

thousands of miles of ocean, while all those island bases were under the sole control of the Japanese."[18]

Similarly, in late 1942, the Navy Department issued an evaluation of the attack that is a model of descriptive restraint: "On the morning of December 7, 1941, Japanese aircraft temporarily disabled every battleship and most of the aircraft in the Hawaiian area. Other naval vessels, both combat and auxiliary, were put out of action and certain shore facilities . . . were damaged. Most of these ships are now back with the fleet. The aircraft were all replaced within a few days and interference with the facilities was generally limited to a matter of hours" (Thursfield 1943, 128). But despite such early, authoritative, and basically accurate debunking, words like "catastrophe" and "disaster" continued, and continue, to be applied.

In 1941, as Willmott notes, the world "was still accustomed to measuring sea power in terms of battleships" (1982, 137). The war proved that to be a faulty measure, but from that perspective it was easy to exaggerate the importance of the attack.

In addition, the attack itself was dramatic and spectacular, and perhaps such events tend to inspire equally highly charged rhetoric in some military writers. That is, writers, impressed or mesmerized by the sheer drama of the event and by its historic importance, simply found their fingers tapping out the words, "Disaster at Pearl Harbor." The more nearly accurate "Inconvenience at Pearl Harbor" simply does not get the juices flowing. It is difficult, otherwise, to explain why thoughtful writers like Morison, Prange, Spector, Toland, and the Congressional investigators of the attack use words like "disaster" and "catastrophe" when their own works provide extensive information detailing how limited the damage was, how quickly it was repaired, and how irrelevant it was to the later war effort. In a generally valuable book on the event published in 1990, Michael Slackman furnishes an extensive discussion of the success of the naval salvage and repair operation. Yet he says at one point, "The *destruction* of the battle line at Pearl Harbor *eradicated* the mainstay of U.S. surface forces in the Pacific" (1990, 263, emphasis added).[19] It is difficult to see from the evidence in his own book how such extreme verbiage is justified.

Photographs did not play a role in the initial reaction since none were published for a month or two after the attack (suggesting that pictures are hardly necessary to convey a dramatic event's impact), but conceivably they helped influenced the longer-term reaction. At any rate, the most dramatic, and therefore most-often shown, pictures of the attack depict damaged ships spewing out huge volumes of smoke, and the general impression is one of total devastation. Pictures of facilities being reconstructed and of ships being floated, repaired, and re-

---

[18]*New York Times,* 24 February 1942, 4. At the time, the President was pushing things a bit. His estimates of ship damage proved accurate, but that is not the way it seemed to the people engaged in the repair work in Hawaii: "When the president gave . . . the list of ships which were lost, it seemed highly improbable that the list would work out to be that short. . . . Within four or five months the salvage work had proceeded so favorably that it was clear that the president's list of losses could not only be met but considerably shortened" (Wallin 1946, 1526).

[19]Similarly, John Dower casually refers in passing to "the destruction of the U.S. fleet at Pearl Harbor" (1986, 101).

PHOTO 7.1

Typical Pearl Harbor photograph: smoke and fire.
Source: Stillwell 1981, 137; U.S. Naval Institute Collection.

launched simply do not have the same dramatic appeal and thus were not as widely circulated (see Photos 7.1 and 7.2).[20]

Whatever the reason, the misguided use of such words as "disaster" and "catastrophe" to describe the Pearl Harbor attack has helped to exaggerate the perceived (or anticipated) effectiveness of conventional bombing—an exaggeration, however, that antedates the war (see, for example, Bialer 1980). People still use words like "destroyed," "annihilated," "knocked out," "devastated," "eradicated," "demolished"—words that strongly imply permanent disablement—to describe the results of an air attack on a target when "put out of commission for a few weeks, days, or hours" would be far more accurate.[21] For example, a report in the *New York Times* from the Vietnam era noted that American bombers had "crippled anew" a North Vietnamese power plant that was "extensively damaged in a raid two months ago and subsequently rebuilt" (17 August, 1972, 3). "Crippled," a word that implies a permanent, not a temporary, condition, hardly seems the right term to describe damage that puts a target out of operation for at most two months. "Temporarily disabled," a phrase used in the 1942 Navy report on Pearl

---

[20]A book of photographs from Pearl Harbor, purporting to show "the way it was" does not include a single picture of the reconstruction (Goldstein et al. 1991). Similarly, everyone has seen the pictures of the devastation at Hiroshima, but there seem to be no pictures showing that electrical service was restored within one day, railroad and trolley service within two, and telephone service within seven (U.S. Army, Manhattan Engineer District 1946, 13). See also Mueller 1989a, 89–90).

[21]However, if the war is short (as the Japanese hoped in 1941), temporary disablement could be militarily sufficient. I am indebted to Sean Lynn-Jones for suggesting this caveat.

PHOTO 7.2

Atypical Pearl Harbor photograph: substantial reconstruction
four days after the attack.

*Source: Office of the Chief of Military History 1952, 17. U.S. Army files Dept. of
Defense. The caption reads: "CONSTRUCTION WORK AT WHEELER FIELD, 11
December 1941. After the Japanese raid many destroyed or damaged buildings were
rebuilt."*

Harbor, seems more apt. Or there is the picture in *Aviation Week* showing four
craters in a North Vietnamese airstrip, "effectively blocking its use," according to
the caption (3 July 1972, 13). Since the North Vietnamese, often using battalions
of little old ladies (Arnett 1972), were routinely able to fill such holes very quickly,
the phrase, "for a few hours," might appropriately have been appended to the description.

More generally, as will be discussed in Chapter 9, there has been a strong
tendency in the writing of military history over the ages to exaggerate—presumably for dramatic effect—the extent of damage in wars. Writers characteristically
find death and destruction more vivid and notable than their absence.

For example, for centuries a legend prevailed that Germany had suffered a 75
percent decline in population during the Thirty Years War when the correct figure was probably more like 20 percent.[22] More recently, reporters from the
Washington Post began their description of the "highway of death" in the 1991

---

[22]Compare the legend reported in Wedgwood (1938, 516), with the estimate of 20 percent in Parker
(1984, 211).

Gulf War with these vivid words: "As far as the eye can see along this road to Iraq lies a tangled sea of scorched, twisted metal littered with bodies of Iraqi soldiers." Later in the report, however, the reporters estimate how far it is that the eye can, in fact, see—they note that the "tangled sea" of metal and bodies occupies only 1 mile of this "road to Iraq." And they incidentally record that, so far, only forty-six bodies had been found "littered" among the "scorched, twisted metal" (Claiborne and Murphy 1991). It would have been possible to place the story in a wider frame: despite the appearance of massive destruction, the story might stress, the array of vehicles occupies only a 1-mile stretch of road and the attack appears to have caused remarkably few Iraqi casualties. Similarly, a *Los Angeles Times* report discusses another road on which "Iraqi military units sit in gruesome repose, scorched skeletons of vehicles and men alike, black and awful under the sun." The report goes on to note, essentially, that there were only one or two vehicles per mile along this particular road and that the number of "scorched skeletons" numbered in the "scores" (Drogin 1991). Again, vividness is stressed over proportion or context, and, not surprisingly, analysts were soon casually referring to the destruction on the "highway of death" as a "classic slaughter" (Tsouras and Wright 1991, 115).[23]

PEARL HARBOR
AS A STRATEGIC AND POLITICAL DISASTER

Although the Pearl Harbor attack was far from a disaster in strict military terms for the United States, the term *disaster* may still apply in a broader sense, certainly for Japan, and perhaps for the United States and Asia as well.

DISASTER FOR JAPAN

The Japanese were at least as interested in inflicting psychological shock on the United States as material damage. Their war plans emphasized that they must "endeavor to destroy the will of the United States to fight" and to use "strategic propaganda" to point out "the uselessness of a Japanese-American war" while directing American public opinion "toward opposition to war" (Ike 1967, 248, see also 153). As Roberta Wohlstetter puts it, they assumed "that the United States, with ten times the military potential . . . would after a short struggle simply accept

---

[23]At the same time, the media were far less interested in the real slaughter of the Gulf War. Hasty early estimates—probably greatly exaggerated—that the Iraqis suffered tens or even hundreds of thousands of deaths in battle received front page treatment. By contrast, careful studies concluding that tens of thousands of Iraqi children died—individually and less picturesquely—in the aftermath of the war received only secondary treatment. On these issues, see Mueller 1994b.

the annihilation of a considerable part of its air and naval forces and the whole of its power in the Far East" (1962, 355). Or as Prange suggests, Japan presumed "that in the face of this type of attack the American people might think the Japanese such a unique and fearless race that it would be useless to fight them" (1981, 21).[24]

This proved, of course, to be one of the greatest miscalculations in military history, but a thoughtful caveat by Scott Sagan ought to be kept in mind: "Anyone who has lived through the war in Vietnam cannot easily dismiss the possibility that the United States public and elite opinion might have decided that the costs of continuing a war in Asia were greater than any possible gains to be made" (1988, 916). Indeed, in the next section I will argue that such a calculation might have led to the wisest policy in World War II for the United States and for Asia. Be that as it may, the attack on Pearl Harbor was phenomenally successful in its shock effect, but the shock was exactly the opposite of the one the Japanese hoped for. As Prange observes, "The American people reeled with a mind-staggering mixture of surprise, awe, mystification, grief, humiliation, and, above all, cataclysmic fury" (Prange 1981, 582; see also Lord 1957, 216). Ten years after the war a Japanese admiral who participated in the Pearl Harbor attack was asked if he had received any medals from the Emperor. "On the contrary," the admiral responded, "I should have received medals from the American side rather than from the Emperor" since "but for the Pearl Harbor attack, the United States would not have been united as one people for war" (Prange 1986, 540).[25] As it turned out, then, Pearl Harbor was indeed a "disaster"—for the attackers.

Pearl Harbor was a disaster for the Japanese in another way as well. Together with their other amazing successes in the opening weeks of the war, Pearl Harbor contributed substantially to a dangerous overconfidence or "victory disease," as the Japanese dubbed it after the war (Stephan 1984, 124; Slackman 1990, 248; Morison 1963, 140; Prange 1982, 370; Dower 1986, 114). Flushed to euphoria with their remarkable military triumphs and increasingly of the belief that the Americans "lack the will to fight" (Spector 1985, 166), the Japanese launched themselves carelessly into a vast and overly ambitious adventure in which they sought to "annihilate" the Pacific Fleet of their new American enemy, and to establish dominance over the Solomons, the Coral Sea, Midway Island, Samoa, New Caledonia, the Fijis, and the Western Aleutians (Morison 1963, 140). Many

---

[24]The Japanese "gave virtually no serious thought to how the conflict might be terminated. Somehow, before too long, they hoped, the Allies would tire of the struggle and agree to a compromise settlement" (Dower 1986, 293). See also Russett 1972, 55.

[25]Until Pearl Harbor, the United States had, as Willmott puts it, "no clear idea what Japanese action, if any, could constitute sufficient aggression to involve the United States in war" (1982, 120). The Japanese attack instantly resolved that conundrum. One should not, however, assume there was absolutely no puzzlement in the American population: six months after Pearl Harbor only 53 percent of the population said it had a clear idea of what the war was about (comparable to responses found during the Vietnam War), although this percentage grew later (Mueller 1973, 63).

Japanese, in fact, anticipated that they could even conquer the Hawaiian Islands (Stephan 1984).

At a time when the Japanese should have been changing their tactics to confront enemies who were getting stronger and becoming better prepared, they continued to follow their old modes of operation and committed themselves to a widespread and fragmented effort not only against the Americans in the central Pacific, but into the southwest Pacific and the Indian Ocean as well.[26] Unlike the Pearl Harbor attack, the Japanese, now ventured forward, in Prange's words, with "overconfidence, careless planning, slipshod training, and contempt for the enemy" (1982, xii), and soon propelled themselves into the battle of Midway, in which they sustained massive losses from which they were never able to recover an experience that can justifiably be categorized as a disaster.[27]

DISASTER FOR THE UNITED STATES AND ASIA:

HOT WAR, RATHER THAN COLD

If Pearl Harbor was a disaster for Japan, perhaps there is a sense in which it was one for the rest of Asia and for the United States as well. Morison contends that "the Japanese high command, by their idiotic act, had made a strategic present of the first order to the United States: they had united the country in grim determination to win victory in the Pacific" (1963, 69). It may be useful to consider how valuable this "present of the first order" actually was.

Before Pearl Harbor, American policy toward Japanese expansion was essentially one of containment—although, as Paul Schroeder observes, after the summer of 1941 American policy became more dynamic, demanding that Japan not merely stop its expansion, but that it withdraw from China (1958, ch. 8). American tactics stressed economic pressure, a military buildup designed to threaten and deter, and assistance to anti-Japanese combatants, especially to China where the Japanese had become painfully bogged down (although Japan's problems there were due far more to Chinese resistance than to U.S. aid, which was actually quite modest) (Utley 1985, 135–136).[28] Should Japan abandon its expansionary imperial policy, the United States stood ready, as the American ambassador put it at the time, to help Japan peacefully to gain "all of the desiderata for which she allegedly started fighting—strategic, economic, financial, and social security" (Butow, 1961, 341). (After the war the United States had a chance to carry out this promise and did so in full measure.)

---

[26]Willmott 1983, 34, 78–79. In fact, Willmott concludes, Japan "managed to pick what was arguably the wrong course of action every time it was confronted with a choice."

[27]At Midway, notes Willmott, "For reasons that will always defy rational analysis [Japanese commander] Yamamoto insisted upon a tactical deployment that incorporated every possible risk and weakness and left his forces inferior to the enemy at the point of contact, despite their having what should have been an irresistible numerical and qualitative superiority" (1983, 515). For a catalogue of Japan's many mistakes in the crucial battle of Midway, see Prange 1982, ch. 40. As for the Japanese army, Willmott observes, "One cannot ignore the simple fact that not a single operation planned after the start of the war met with success" (1982, 91).

[28]Utley notes that U.S. aid authorizations in July 1941 were 821,000 tons for Britain, 16,000 for China. See also Russett 1972, 46.

This American concern with Asia has had its critics. Melvin Small observes that "the defense of China was an unquestioned axiom of American policy taken in along with mother's milk and the Monroe Doctrine. . . . One looks in vain through the official papers of the 1930s for some prominent leader to say, 'Wait a second, just why is China so essential to our security?'" (1980, 238–239). Jonathan Utley has a different perspective, but he comes to a similar conclusion: "It was not through a careful review of national policy or the stakes involved in Asia that the United States would place itself in the path of Japanese expansion, but incrementally, without long-range planning, and as often as not as a stopgap measure necessitated, or so the planners thought, by the events in Europe" (1985, 58). And Warner Schilling observes crisply, "At the summit of foreign policy one always finds simplicity and spook," and he suggests that "the American opposition to Japan rested on the dubious proposition that the loss of Southeast Asia could prove disastrous for Britain's war effort and for the commitment to maintain the territorial integrity of China—a commitment as mysterious in its logic as anything the Japanese ever conceived" (1965, 389).[29]

But until Pearl Harbor this policy, however spooky, was comparatively inexpensive. After the attack, however, it no longer became possible even to consider the question, as Schilling phrases it, of "just how much American blood and treasure the defense of China and Southeast Asia was worth." Americans were enraged, threatened, humiliated, and challenged by what Roosevelt called the "unprovoked and dastardly" blow that had come without warning or a declaration of war, at a time when Japanese officials were in Washington, deceptively seeming to be working for a peaceful settlement. With the attack, virtually all remaining reservations vanished as everyone united behind a concerted effort to lash back at the treacherous Japanese, to exact revenge, and to kick butt.[30] After suffering the loss of some 2,500 people at Pearl Harbor, the Americans, without thinking about it any further, launched themselves furiously and impetuously into a war in which they lost hundreds of thousands more.

CONTAINING JAPAN.   The war killed millions of people in Asia, and it finally forced the Japanese out of their imperial possessions. But the United States could have pursued a continued policy of cold war rather than hot—that is, of harassment and containment, economic pressure, arming to deter and to threaten, assistance to anti-Japanese combatants, and perhaps limited warfare on the peripheries. The goal of a continued containment policy would have been limited. It would have sought only to compel Japan to retreat from its empire, not, like the

---

[29]By contrast, at the time of major escalation in the Vietnam War, American decision makers carefully assessed, reassessed, and debated the policy premises of the American commitment there. see Mueller 1989a, 168–176; Barrett 1993.

[30]As Morison observes, "Isolationism and pacifism now ceased to be valid forces in American politics" (1963, 69). Or, in Toland's words, "With almost no exceptions 130,000,000 Americans instantly accepted total war" (1961, 37). As Morison points out, it was Pearl Harbor, not the subsequent, more costly and more important attack on the Philippines that moved American opinion (1963, 77–78). Wohlstetter agrees: "For some reason the damage done to these other American outposts in the Pacific is not considered in the same category of crime" (1962, 340).

war, to force the country to submit to occupation. Such a policy might well eventually have impelled Japan to withdraw from its empire at far lower cost to the United States, to Japan, and to the imperialized peoples.

Although the strategy of containment is associated with postwar U.S. policy toward the Soviet Union, it was also basically the initial policy of the British and French in response to the German invasion of Poland in 1939. The Allies did not launch direct war, but instead harassed the Germans in places like Norway, put on economic pressure, built up their forces behind defensive barriers, looked for opportunities to aid resistance movements and to exploit fissures in the German empire, and sat back patiently. It was cold war, though it was called "phoney war" (for a discussion, see Quester 1977, 135-138). The crucial defect in the containment policy directed at Germany was that Germany was (obviously) capable of invading and defeating France. By contrast, Japan could not invade and defeat the United States. Furthermore, Germany did not at the time present a ripe opportunity for punishing harassment because it was not entangled in a continental war the way Japan was in China, nor could it as readily be economically strained. Thus a policy that failed against Germany had a far greater chance of success against Japan, had it been tried.

That containment can be effective under the right conditions has of course now been demonstrated. After the war the United States and its allies were confronted with another expanding and threatening empire, this one based in Moscow and directed by Josef Stalin, one of history's greatest monsters. A major war against that empire at the time—perhaps with the Germans and Japanese now as allies and with American industry again cranked up for maximum military effort—might very well have been successful, and the costs might have been no higher than those incurred in defeating the Japanese empire. With victory in this war, the gains of 1989–91, including the toppling of Soviet Communism, might have been achieved forty years earlier. However, although the Soviets may have been expansionary and even more murderous than the Japanese, and although they may ultimately have presented a more visceral and wide-ranging threat to American values than the comparatively localized Japanese, the Soviets, unlike the Japanese, were not so foolhardy in the course of expansion as to attack American property directly.[31] Accordingly, as discussed in Chapter 6, the United States adopted and maintained a patient policy of containment, economic pressure, arms buildup, peripheral war, and harassment against its new enemy.[32] It took a long time—some forty-five years—for the Soviet empire to disintegrate (and as argued in the previous chapter, the containment policy might not have been necessary to bring this about), but it is difficult to find people who think that fighting a war like

---

[31]Curiously, when American troops were being sent to Saudi Arabia in 1990 to deter a possible Iraqi attack on that country, American leaders were greatly concerned that their as yet outnumbered forces might be attacked at any moment (Woodward 1991, 274, 304). No one, it appears, considered that a would-be aggressor might find the example of the American reaction to the Pearl Harbor attack to be sobering. On this issue, see Mueller 1994a, 123.

[32]Unlike the Soviets, the Japanese may not have been planning a permanent empire. They said they were willing to promise in 1941 that after peace was established in China, they would remove their troops in 25 years (Ike 1967, 210).

World War II (even one without nuclear weapons) to speed that process up would have been worthwhile.

A similar firm, patient policy of cold war rather than hot might well have worked with the Japanese after Pearl Harbor—and probably much more quickly. They were already vastly overextended by their intervention in China, begun in 1937. Their army there of a million and a half had made many initial gains but, as Willmott notes, it "was bogged down in a war it could not win. It did not have the strength to advance, and in any case there were no worthwhile objectives it could hope to secure. It could not force the 'final battle' that would end the war. It could not properly pacify the areas it held. It was tied to the railways and major lines of communication, and was draining the industrial and financial resources of Japan without adequate compensation. The army had impaled itself in an impossible position, and had produced a disastrous situation for Japan herself" (Willmott 1982, 55; see also Fujiwara 1990, 155; Butow 1961, 129).

The economic drain on Japan of this venture was considerable. Military expenditures skyrocketed from 9 percent of gross national expenditures to 38 percent (Nakamura 1983, 39) and the difference was made up by the Japanese consumer: by 1941 real consumption per capita had dropped almost 20 percent from 1937 levels (Gleason 1965, 436). As early as 1938 Japan's export industries had become paralyzed, and its ability to import needed materials had plummeted. Production of almost all commodities, including steel, either fell or else rose much more slowly than the military required, and shortages of labor, especially skilled labor, developed (Barnhart 1987, 91, 96, 200–201).

Unable to bring themselves to retreat from China, and under severe economic pressure from the United States and from their own misguided economic policies, the Japanese leaders accused members of the Planning Board (which had been spewing out dire analyses and predictions) of Communist activity and arrested them. Then in late 1941, although already stretched thin militarily, Japan lashed out, going to war, as Michael Barnhart notes, "on a shoestring—and a ragged one at that" (1987, 200, 238, 269). Besides attacking Pearl Harbor, Japan conquered huge areas in Southeast Asia, including some vital oil fields in the Dutch East Indies, which they hoped would provide them with adequate resources to maintain their far-flung ventures.

Although these advances began with some impressive and famous victories, they hardly resolved Japan's problems. The Chinese continued to fight, and the Japanese now found themselves in charge of an empire that was even larger and even more unwieldy than before. Among the difficulties was their inability to become effective colonists, and the brutal conquerors mainly inspired an intense hatred among the imperialized peoples which in many cases still persists and which at the time guaranteed resistance and hostility and exacted enormous occupation costs.[33]

---

[33]As Willmott observes, "The very morale that sustained the Japanese in the advance gave rise to a casual and blind cruelty at almost every turn, and these actions ensured a lasting enmity on the part of subject peoples who might have been won over with decent treatment" (1982, 91).

Moreover, the advance by no means solved Japan's oil problem. In principle, there was enough oil in the newly conquered areas to supply Japan's needs, but the country did not have a tanker fleet big enough to transport all the oil it required. In addition it took time and effort to get the new oil fields into production, and in the meantime it was necessary to draw on the dwindling reserves. As a result, two prewar Japanese studies calculated that even assuming there were no major naval engagements for three full years, the Japanese would be faced with a major oil crisis, or worse, by 1944 (Willmott 1982, 68–70).

Somewhat related was the problem of merchant shipping upon which the island empire depended. Before the war 40 percent of Japan's imports were delivered on foreign ships. In its attacks Japan was able to capture some merchant ships, but it was still confronted with a 25 percent drop in shipping. It could build new ships and refit old ones, but this was a slow and agonizing process at best because its shipyards were small and inefficient and because of the huge demands the military was making on the industrial sector. In its conquests Japan gained the resources of Southeast Asia, but because of these shipping reductions, its own resources actually declined (Willmott 1982, 88–89, 451).

Thus Imperial Japan was in deep trouble, and it was accordingly an auspicious target for a policy of containment. It was far more so, it would seem, than the postwar Soviet Union. The Soviets expanded their empire only marginally and in contiguous areas, and they did not have to rely on lengthy and vulnerable sea-lanes for survival. Moreover, the people they conquered had little fight left in them and in many cases initially welcomed the conquerors. As suggested in Chapter 6, the strains in their empire really began to show only after they had unwisely expanded their commitments in the late 1970s. Even without direct American military efforts, Japan's huge empire in Asia was already costly and unwieldy, and in time it might have become as debilitating, as obsolete, and as pointless as the British, French, or Dutch ones there.[34] And eventually Japan might have come to realize this.

It is true that at the time of Pearl Harbor, Japan was in the control of a fanatical, militaristic group, and it is true that there was a considerable war fever among many elements in the population (though no one was anxious to have a war with the United States if it could be avoided) (Fujiwara 1990, 157–159; Butow 1961, 167, 251–252, 332–333). But the grip of the romantic, imperial militarists in Japan

---

[34]On this issue, see also Russett 1972, 44–62. For another critique of American entry into the war, see Small 1980, 215–267. See also Mueller 1968, 30; and Morison 1963, 45. It may not be completely whimsical in this regard to suggest that Japan over the last century and a half has always been some 15 to 25 years out of date. In 1853 it set out to catch up with the West in military technology. After doing so, it decided to become a late entrant into the Great Power club by the accepted means of defeating an established Great Power—Russia—in a war in 1904–05. It then sought to add the accoutrements of power by collecting an empire in the 1930s, even as the other Great Powers were tiring of theirs. In World War II it learned, as almost all Europeans had learned in World War I, that getting into big wars is a really terrible idea. Noticing in the postwar period that Greatness was now being associated with economic prosperity, it set about to achieve that. Now, having prospered, it is seeking to become a political leader, an international good citizen, and a paternalistic guide to less fortunate peoples—rather in the manner of the United States in the 1940s and 1950s.

was neither complete nor necessarily permanent. Substantial misgivings about the enervating, even disastrous, expansionary policy and about the "holy war" in China were being felt not only by some top Japanese civilians, but also by some important military leaders and by the Emperor. It seems entirely conceivable that these critics would have been able to moderate, and in time quietly to dismember, the frustratingly costly imperial policy.

It is also true that the war thoroughly and (we hope) permanently destroyed the militaristic group in Japan and its values. The postwar experience with the Soviet Union suggests (although of course it does not guarantee) that favorable results could have been achieved eventually through a policy of containment rather than war. The Soviet Union at the outset of the Cold War was similarly controlled by a set of dangerous, expansionary ideologues, but, as discussed in Chapter 6, minds eventually changed as Soviet policies proved hopelessly unproductive. This experience suggests, then, that the United States might well have been able productively to exacerbate Japan's dilemma of overexpansion helping to impel it to retreat from its empire, and that this might have been accomplished with far less misery and bloodshed by using containment rather than war.[35]

THE QUESTIONABLE "GAINS" OF THE PACIFIC WAR. What, after all, was gained by using hot rather than cold war to cause the Japanese to abandon their empire? Ronald Spector notes that the United States managed to acquire "a strong democratic ally in the new Japan" (1985, 561). This can, I suppose, be accounted a gain, but it cannot be entirely irrelevant to point out that in order to achieve the liberalization of Japan it was necessary to depopulate the country by some two million souls. Moreover, there had long been a substantial impetus toward liberalism in Japan, and in calmer times this might well have revived, as eventually it revived (after a long period of dedicated suppression) in Russia.

In defending the Pacific War, Spector also argues that because of it the region became "more safe and stable than the older system in which Japan, the Soviet Union, and the European powers struggled for supremacy in a weak and divided China." Things are generally looking up in much of Asia today, but for the first few decades of the postwar era most of the area did not experience much in the way of safety and stability. Rather it was the scene of bloody civil and international war, economic and social mismanagement often of spectacular proportions, and occasionally outright genocide. And he would not want to trade, he says, "the vibrant, rapidly growing new nations of Asia—like Singapore, Taiwan, India, and Malaysia—for the stagnant, impoverished, and exploited colonies of the 1930s"

---

[35]Although the Japanese expansion in Asia cut the United States off from the sources of some important raw materials, these supplies were not crucial, as Roosevelt had publicly pointed out in 1940 (and as was to be demonstrated during the war) because the United States could produce synthetic rubber, acquire tin from Bolivia, and produce more manganese at home. See Utley 1985, 85.

(1985, 561). But would those colonies have remained stagnant without the war? And would Spector or anyone else similarly prefer present-day North Korea, Vietnam, Burma, or Cambodia?

Above all, there is the issue of China where most of the population of the former Japanese empire lived. A major reason the United States fought the Pacific War was to keep the heroic, persecuted, war-racked Chinese from being dominated by a vicious regime. As Schroeder puts it, "There is no longer any real doubt that the war came about over China" (1958, 209); and Morison observes, "The fundamental reason for America's going to war with Japan was our insistence on the integrity of China" (1963, 45). In discussing the drive toward war, Bruce Russett also stresses the importance of China in the perceptions of Roosevelt and his advisers who had become convinced that "Japanese ambitions in China posed a long-term threat to American interests," were affected by the "sentimental American attitude toward China as a 'ward'," and may have seen China as a significant economic partner—although "by embargoing Japan in 1941 the United States was giving up an export trade at least four times that with China" (1972, 58–60).[36]

In the war the United States devastated Japan and saved China—for Mao Zedong and the Chinese Communists. The imperial Japanese occupiers were often cruel and murderous, but Mao seems to have surpassed them substantially in callousness, incompetence, and sheer viciousness (as well as in hostility toward the United States). In the war from 1937 to 1945, the Chinese may have lost three million people or more.[37] But in its first three years alone, the Communist regime probably executed two million (Meisner 1986, 81).[38] Then, in the four years after the start of the Great Leap Forward of 1958, the regime inflicted on the Chinese people the greatest famine in history, one that is now estimated to have taken thirty million lives (Ashton et al. 1984). It seems difficult to escape the conclusion that China could hardly have been worse off in Japanese hands. Or, to put it an-

---

[36]Utley sees the China issue as less central, but he agrees it triggered the war: "It was the issue of China that in the final hours stood as an insurmountable obstacle between Japan and the United States" (1985, 177). "The final point of disagreement between the two countries was on the withdrawal of Japanese forces from China. If war was to be prevented, Japan had to yield on this point" (Fujiwara 1990, 154). "The chief issue between Japan and the United States was the future of China" (Small 1980, 238).

[37]An estimate of three million military and civilian deaths is given by Sivard (1987, 30); while Messenger estimates 2,500,000 (1989, 243). Battle deaths for the Nationalist Chinese are estimated at 1,310,224 Encyclopedia Britannica, 1991 ed., vol. 29, 1023. Some put total Chinese battle deaths as high as 2,200,000: Snyder 1982, 126. Encyclopedia Americana accepts this higher estimate and then observes that "Chinese civilian losses are unknown but probably numbered several million" (1988 ed., vol. 29, 530).

[38]Demographer John S. Aird notes that, while estimates generally range from 1 to 3 million, some are much higher: one Hong Kong source puts the death toll at 10 million and quotes a 1981 Chinese journal that claims 20 million people were executed or died of unnatural causes during what it calls the "anti-rightist" and "people's communication" periods (1990, 2, 111n3).

other way, even if the containment policy retrospectively proposed here had not been successful eventually in forcing Japan out of China, it is not at all clear that China would have been less fortunate under that fate than it was under the one supplied by the liberating war.

And it should also be pointed out that, having saved Asia from Japanese imperialism at great cost, the United States was soon back in the area centrally participating in the two bloodiest wars of the postwar era. In Korea—where it now found itself killing, rather than aiding, the Chinese—around three million civilian and military lives were lost. In Vietnam, some two million perished.[39] And insofar as the United States entered the war to preserve China as a trading partner or opportunity, the war proved to be an utter waste.

CONCLUSION

The argument here deals with the Pacific War, not the European one, and it obviously relies heavily on hindsight. After Pearl Harbor, American decision makers probably had no viable political option but to go to war in the Pacific (although they made no effort to search for an alternative, either), nor could they possibly have been able to anticipate the postwar horrors. Moreover, I am not arguing that American participation in the Pacific War was necessary for the various horrors in Asia to have taken place—they might well have happened in any case.

But, given what we now know, was it wise to pursue war after Pearl Harbor? Was the vicious and gruesome Pacific War worth it? If the point of the war was to force Japan to retreat from its empire and to encourage it to return to more liberal ways, a policy of cold war might well eventually have had the same result at a far lower overall cost. If the point of the war was to prevent further horrors and somehow to bring peace, justice, freedom, and stability to the rest of Asia, the war was a substantial failure. From that perspective it certainly seems that Pearl Harbor, which propelled the United States into that terrible war, was a disaster after all.

---

[39]These estimates of military and civilian deaths are from Sivard 1987, 31. Battle deaths alone have been estimated at 2 million for Korea and 1.2 million for Vietnam: see Singer 1991, 60–61.

Chapter 8

WAR: NATURAL,
BUT NOT NECESSARY

The brief Gulf War of 1991 was the first standard international war to take place in the aftermath of the quiet cataclysm. Although the war soon faded into notable obscurity, it seemed all-consumingly important to many at the time (see Mueller 1994a), and when U.S. president George Bush proclaimed on launching it that the war would "chart the future of the world for the next hundred years," he was taken seriously (1991, 314).

Many who watched the war and the five-month crisis that led to it were impressed by the passion and even exhilaration ("bloodlust," some called it) that many people in such supposedly war-averse countries as Britain and the United States took to the enterprise. It is easy to conclude from such an experience that, since the fascination with war continues, the institution itself is likely to persist. This conclusion does not follow. Formal dueling retains its fascination and its romance, but it still has became obsolete. Chainsaw massacres apparently continue to intrigue, but that does not mean people will necessarily rush out to engage in the practice.[1]

At base, war is a hopeless problem, but it does not seem to be a serious one. The problem is hopeless because it is clearly impossible to make war impossible. It may be true that on some perfectly reasonable level war is a ludicrous, even childish, enterprise. The experience of millennia, however, has shown that people, if effectively organized and inspired, will dutifully embrace the absurdity and

---

[1]Thus the following exchange, which takes place between two characters in Bernard Shaw's play, *Major Barbara*, is a non sequitur: "Well, the more destructive war becomes, the sooner it will be abolished, eh?" "Not at all, the more destructive war becomes the more fascinating we find it."

march off to slaughter each other in large numbers, that they will accept the experience as appropriate and sensible, and that they may often find it exhilarating and fascinating.[2] The knowledge about how to make war and the capacity to do so, in other words, will always be with us—they can never be fully expunged.

The problem would be a serious one if war were also somehow necessary—if it were a requirement of the human condition or if it fulfilled a crucial social function. I will argue in this chapter that, although war exploits natural instincts and proclivities, it is neither necessary nor inevitable. Accordingly, it can go into decline without a notable change or improvement in human nature and without being replaced by anything else. The chapter concludes by suggesting that this process is already well underway, at least in substantial portions of the developed world—an argument that is further extended in Chapter 9. In important areas where war was once endemic, it has been considerably discredited as a method for expressing aggression and for resolving conflict. People, it seems, can live quite well without it.

WAR AS AN EXPRESSION OF HUMAN NATURE

In an article published in 1868, Leo Tolstoy, a strong opponent of war, glumly concluded that people kill each other in war because by doing so they fulfill "an elemental zoological law which bees fulfill when they kill each other in autumn, and which causes male animals to destroy one another." This was, he observed, "an inevitable necessity" (1966, 1372).

Another legendary pacifist, the psychologist William James, similarly traces war's existence and persistence to "the rooted bellicosity of human nature" and to man's "innate pugnacity" (1911, 269, 300–301). Somewhat more hopeful than Tolstoy, he proposed in a famous essay in 1910 that these unfortunate qualities could be purged if one established a "moral equivalent of war." This would involve the "military conscription of the whole youthful population" for "a certain number of years" during which time the draftees would be forced to dig mines, wash dishes, build roads, construct tunnels, create skyscrapers. This cathartic experience, James felt, would knock the "childishness" out of them while embedding the "martial virtues" in them, and they would "come back into society with healthier sympathies and soberer ideas; . . . they would tread the earth more proudly, the women would value them more highly, they would be better fathers and teachers of the following generation" (1911, 290–291).

Imbued with a similar perspective, Sigmund Freud concluded in a 1915 paper that war is a "natural thing" with a "good biological basis." At that time he was as fatalistic as Tolstoy about the issue, arguing that "war cannot be abolished" (1957, vol. 14, 229). By 1932, however, he had come closer to James' position: al-

---

[2]The paradox is neatly suggested by a statement made by U.S. General H. Norman Schwarzkopf in October 1990, a few months before he ordered hundreds of thousands of troops into war: "War is a profanity because, let's face it, you've got two opposing sides trying to settle their differences by killing as many of each other as they can" (Woodward 1991, 313).

though he still found war "in practice to be scarcely avoidable," he now felt it might be ameliorated if "civilization" could somehow "divert" or "displace" "human aggressive impulses" and the "instinct for hatred and destruction" so that "they need not find expression in war" (1957, vol. 22, 209, 212–214; see also Roazen 1968, ch. 4).

Another version of this perspective was embodied in the widely discussed book, *On Aggression*, by Konrad Lorenz, published in the 1960s. Lorenz finds war to be "unreasoning and unreasonable" as well as "abjectly stupid and undesirable." He concludes that it can only be explained if one assumes that such behavior "far from being determined by reason and cultural tradition alone, is still subject to all the laws prevailing in all phylogenetically adapted instinctive behavior" (1966, 228–229). That is, man has bred into him an "aggression drive for which in the social order of today he finds no adequate outlet" (1966, 235). Lorenz particularly focuses on "militant enthusiasm" which is "a specialized form of communal aggression" (1966, 259). This is "a true autonomous instinct" and when it is released, "like the sexual urge or any other strong instinct, it engenders a specific feeling of intense satisfaction" (1966, 262).

Like Freud and James, Lorenz proposes to handle the war impetus by engineering devices for "discharging aggression in an innocuous manner" (1966, 269). He finds sport to be such a "healthy safety valve" (1966, 272).[3] He also advocates "personal acquaintance between people" because "personal acquaintance, indeed every kind of brotherly feeling for the people to be attacked, constitutes a strong obstacle to aggression" (1966, 273)—blithely ignoring the fact that many of the most murderous wars have been civil ones, conducted between groups who knew each other only too well. Beyond this, Lorenz also holds out hope for the anti-aggressive effects of education, science, medicine, art ("the universal appreciation of Negro music is perhaps an important step toward the solution of the burning racial problem in America"), humor, love, friendship, and even reason (1966, 277–290).

A related approach is presented by Sue Mansfield. She applies formulations from gestalt psychology to suggest that aggression is less a drive or urge than a "physiological and psychological capacity . . . that is available for satisfying externally or internally defined needs of the organism" (1982, 10). For her, war uses aggression in an attempt to satisfy "deep-seated psychic needs" (such as "the infantile desire for revenge on powerful parents, the anxiety-based insatiability for goods and power, a paranoid sense of powerlessness") and in an effort to "force nature and the divine (the environment) to conform to human will" (1982, 19). Unfortunately war is incapable of fully satisfying these needs, she concludes, and thus it becomes an unconscious and unfulfilled gestalt figure which people strive

---

[3]Writing in 1623, the French peace advocate, Eméric Crucé, unlike Lorenz, recognized multiple reasons for war: [wars] were undertaken, he believed, "for honor, for profit, for righting some wrong, and for exercise." But he came to a Lorenzian conclusion about expatiating the last of these causes, which he felt was the most "difficult to remedy." He too set great stock in sport—tournaments and mock battles—as well as in hunting which he found "a noble and fitting exercise for warriors." He added that not only would wild beasts "serve as suitable opponents for working off this desire for violence," but also "savages that do not use reason" and "pirates and thieves who do nothing but steal" (1972 ed., 8, 18, 22–23).

to complete by repetitive aggression (1982, 13–17). The process fails to produce the necessary "intergenerational reconciliation, security, or a centered sense of power," and therefore "human societies have seemingly been condemned to an unending and ultimately boring compulsiveness" (1982, 19). At the end, she does hold out the rather lame hope that "our current neurotic dependency on war" can be cured if we somehow increase "our sense of individual empowerment and re-sponse-ability as well as our contact with, and our tolerance for, a diverse and con-flictful environment" (1982, 242).

THE PROBLEM OF EXTRAPOLATION

From the perspective of the political scientist and from that of the diplomatic and military historian, there are at least two central problems with the notion that war is an expression of a natural aggressive impulse or drive or that it is necessary to satisfy deep psychic needs. First, even if we grant that there is a natural aggres-sive impulse, it is remarkably heroic to extrapolate from that impulse to a huge, complicated societal phenomenon like war.

Indeed, many students of war would argue that, while emotion, passion, psy-chic needs, and instinct are not irrelevant to decisions to go to war, for the most part war is, as Clausewitz put it long ago, "merely the continuation of politics by other means" (1976, 87–88). In counter to the rather casual assertions of Lorenz and others, military historian Michael Howard concludes after a lifelong study of war that "the conflicts between states which have usually led to war have normally arisen, not from any irrational and emotive drives, but from almost a superabun-dance of analytic rationality. . . . Men have fought during the past two hundred years neither because they are aggressive nor because they are acquisitive ani-mals, but because they are reasoning ones." He adds, "Wars begin by conscious and reasoned decisions based on the calculation, made by both parties, that they can achieve more by going to war than by remaining at peace" (1984, 14–15, 22). Evan Luard, in his masterful study of war since 1400, concurs: "Throughout the whole of the period . . . it is impossible to identify a single case . . . in which it was not, at the time the war broke out, the deliberate intention of at least one party that war should take place. . . . [W]ar is regarded by states as an instrument which it may be in their interests to use, in certain circumstances, to promote or defend their interests. But it remains an instrument that is used deliberately and inten-tionally" (1986, 232; see also Blainey 1973, ch. 9; Bueno de Mesquita 1981, ch. 2; Mueller 1989a, 227–232; Hinsley 1963, 348).

This issue might be illustrated best by a consideration of the process by which Europe went to war in 1914—surely one of the most thoroughly examined events in history. Some historians suggest that aggression and a spirit of bellicosity were relevant to the initiation of that war, but all would stress that the decisions were far more complicated. That is, an aggressive impulse or capacity may have helped to facilitate the decisions to go to war, but much more was required to bring it off: impulse alone would never have been sufficient.

Consider in this regard the conclusions of Hartmut Pogge von Strandmann about the process by which Germany began the war: "The concept of expansion based on a military victory found enough support to command a consensus among the military, political, and business leaders of Wilhelmine Germany. The drive to the east and to the west was underpinned by an imperialist culture which spread the virtues of Social Darwinism, the conquest of markets, the penetration of spheres of influence, competition between capitalist partners, the winning of living-space, and the rising power of the state. Buoyed up by an assumed military superiority, general economic strength and particular industrial vigor, widespread optimism and a mood of belligerence, the military and political leaders found, when they made the decision to push for war, that this was an acceptable option to many Germans, possibly even to the majority. . . . Confidence, determination, and the belief in victory were the ingredients of a willingness to fight an expansionist war, disguised as a defensive or preventive action, which was widely shared by political and military leaders, political groupings, as well as large sectors of the population." He does include "a mood of belligerence" in his catalogue, but clearly Germany did not go to war merely because of that. In fact, argues Pogge von Strandmann, reason is needed: "no power slides into war" and "decisions which lead to war are made deliberately" (1988, 97).

THE PROBLEM OF CONTROLLED AGGRESSION

Second, students of battle would argue that the major problem in warfare is not so much to channel man's natural instinct for aggression, hatred, and destruction, but rather to keep soldiers from giving in to a natural instinct to run and hide (a phenomenon that is surely vastly more common in animal behavior than aggression). To deal with natural fear in combat, as John Keegan has pointed out, military discipline and morale have been maintained by the careful application of bribery, liquor, drugs, religious appeals, patriotism, male bonding, and sheer, murderous compulsion (1987, 196–197; see also Keegan 1976).[4] In a similar analysis, William Hauser stresses four factors: submission to military authority; loyalty to buddies, leaders, unit, country, and cause; pride in one's unit and oneself; and the fear of the dangers of rearward flight, of punishment, and of disgrace (1980, 188–195; see also Smith 1949; Rapoport 1992, 196).

---

[4]As military observers have often noted, it is frequently—perhaps usually—true that the outcome of a battle or war is determined more by an army's fighting spirit than by anything else: few would disagree with Napoleon's dictum that "in war, moral considerations account for three-quarters, the balance of actual forces only for the other quarter" (for a discussion of this in relation to the Gulf War, see Mueller 1994b). Accordingly anything that buoys this fighting spirit facilitates the prosecution of war. Religion—in particular the notion that an instrumental and guiding god is one's ally—has very often served that purpose (see also Kaeuper 1988). In 1466, a soldier put it this way: "I believe that God favors those who risk their lives by their readiness to make war to bring the wicked, the oppressors, the conquerors, the proud and all who deny true equity, to justice" (Vale 1981, 30). Or, as Gerald Linderman observes of the American Civil War, "A conviction of wide currency was that God would ensure the victory of the army whose collective faith was the sturdiest" (1987, 10). In 1911 a British writer, Harold F. Wyatt, argued that war is the "Court of God": "Whichever people shall have in it the greater soul of righteousness will be the victor" (1911, 602). Religion and the belief in god can also aid the conduct of warfare by helping soldiers overcome their natural terror of battle—there are, as they say, no atheists in foxholes (see Smith 1949, 172–188). For this reason, commanders have often used religious ritual and appeals to buck up their forces as they gird for battle. Religion is not the only mechanism for accomplishing this, of course, but there can be little doubt that the belief in the existence of a guiding and instrumental god has helped to facilitate the sacrificial, uncertain, masochistic, improbable, and fundamentally absurd activity known as warfare.

Beyond this, there is another reason battle (and therefore war) is possible. This reason, however, more closely reflects the perspective of Freud and Lorenz. At least for some soldiers, battle turns out to be a high—war, as James observed, is "supremely thrilling excitement" and "the supreme theater of human strenuousness" (1911, 282, 288). For example, the attitudes of a fifteenth-century soldier were put this way: "What a joyous thing is war. . . . When you see that your quarrel is just and your blood is fighting well, tears rise to your eyes. A great sweet feeling of loyalty and pity fills your heart on seeing your friend so valiantly exposing his body to execute and accomplish the command of our Creator. And then you prepare to go and live or die with him, and for love not to abandon him. And out of that there arises such a delectation, that he who has not tasted it is not fit to say what a delight it is. Do you think that a man who does that fears death? Not at all; for he feels so strengthened, he is so elated, that he does not know where he is. Truly he is afraid of nothing" (Vale 1981, 30). And the young Winston Churchill wrote, "There are men who derive as stern an exaltation from the proximity of danger and ruin, as others from success," and "Nothing in life is so exhilarating as to be shot at without result" (Manchester 1989, 28).

Comments about the delectation of battle became much rarer after World War I—a phenomenon assessed in Chapter 9—but that does not mean combat has ceased to be an elating experience for some. Glenn Gray, an American soldier in World War II, discusses what he calls "the enduring appeals of battle" and stresses three. One of these is "the delight in seeing." He exults in the "fascination that manifestations of power and magnitude hold for the human spirit," and argues that "the chief aesthetic appeal of war surely lies in this feeling of the sublime" which is distinctive for "its ecstatic character in the original meaning of the term, namely, a state of being outside the self." The second is "the delight in comradeship," and he suggests that "there must be a similarity between this willingness of soldier-comrades for self-sacrifice and the willingness of saints to die for their religious faith." And the third is "the delight in destruction" or "the satisfaction that men experience when they are possessed by the lust to destroy and kill their kind" (1959, 33, 47, 52).[5]

Vietnam veteran William Broyles (1984) has come to a similar conclusion: "War is ugly, horrible, evil, and it is reasonable for men to hate all that. But I believe that most men who have been to war would have to admit, if they are honest, that somewhere inside themselves they loved it too, loved it as much as anything that has happened to them before or since." It is "an experience of great intensity;" it "replaces the difficult gray areas of daily life with an eerie, serene clarity"; "if you come back whole [a notable qualification] you bring with you the knowledge that you have explored regions of your soul that in most men will always remain uncharted"; the most "enduring emotion of war" is "comradeship", and "brotherly love," a "utopian experience" in which "individual possessions and advantage count for nothing, the group is everything." "War may be the only way in which most men touch the mythic domain of our soul. It is, for men, at some terri-

---

[5]Similarly, the Icelandic sagas refer to the "lust for battle" (Snorri 1966, 83).

blc level the closest thing to what childbirth is for women: the initiation into the power of life and death." "Most men who have been to war . . . remember that never in their lives did they have so heightened a sexuality. War is, in short, a turn-on."

· And there is more: war can impel soldiers into the exhilaration of superhuman achievement. In a classic study, physiologist Walter B. Cannon has observed that "in times of strong excitement there is not infrequent testimony to a sense of overwhelming power that sweeps in like a sudden tide and lifts the person to a new high level of ability." This often occurs "in the tremendous adventure of war where risks and excitement and the sense of power surge up together, setting free unsuspected energies, and bringing vividly to consciousness memorable fresh revelation of the possibilities of achievement" (1929, 238–239).

Vivid examples of such superhuman achievements can be found in many descriptions of battle. In his history of the Normandy invasion of World War II, Keegan tells the story of the American Staff Sergeant Harrison Summers who was leading a unit against a series of farm buildings held by the Germans. Looking back, he realized that no one was following him and concluded, rather irrationally, "I've got to finish it." Thereupon he almost single-handedly charged each building, spraying the defenders with his sub-machine-gun. When the battle was over five hours later he collapsed in exhaustion and was asked, "How do you feel?" He replied, "Not very good. It was all kind of crazy." Or there was Lieutenant Louis Levy who, in what Keegan calls "the strange euphoria of combat," attacked German tanks with grenades and rifle fire while "helmetless, bleeding from the shoulder and 'laughing like a maniac'" (Keegan 1982, 104, 108–110).

The Vikings had a word for such behavior, one that has made it into the English language: they called it "going berserk." Viking raiding parties would have a select group of berserkers who did not have to row, but were expected to go into a superhuman combat high when the time was appropriate. When they worked themselves into what the medieval Latin sources called *furor berserkicus* they would howl savagely, bite their shields, and fight with a wild increase of strength. After the battle they would fall into a stupor of exhaustion (Foote and Wilson 1970, 285; Williams 1920, 253–254; Lid 1956).

In some respects these observations enforce the notion that war can be visualized as a natural, if terrible, outlet for instincts of aggression, destruction, and perhaps hatred. William H. McNeill has argued that "human beings live with inherited propensities for organized violence that run far deeper than our consciousness" (1990, 192). But while the existence of those natural instincts may help in an important way to make war *possible,* they do not make it inevitable or necessary. This is because there seems to be no natural requirement that these qualities be expressed. Gray suggests as much when he observes that "thousands of youth who never suspected the presence of such an impulse in themselves have learned in military life the mad excitement of destroying" (1959, 52). War may have brought out this "impulse," but it was not something that would necessarily have come out by itself.

Moreover, once these qualities have been expressed in war, soldiers seem to be able to live out the rest of their lives without again releasing them. Broyles (who has since gone on to a substantial literary career and is the creator of the

American television series set in Vietnam, "China Beach") makes this clear: "I never want to fight again," and "I would do everything in my power to keep my son from fighting." And Gray, who became a professor of philosophy at Colorado College, concludes his book by speculating about what will be required "if war is to be extirpated from our race" (1959, 226).

Indeed, the argument can be made even stronger. If men were unable to control the expression of these aggressive qualities in a more or less rational manner, war would be impossible.

For wars to be fought men must be able to let their instincts go only on command, and they must be able to rein them in when ordered even when severely provoked (holding their fire when being fired upon, for example). The berserkers did not go into their euphoric state randomly, but when ordered to do so.[6] Furthermore, after experiencing the combat high, soldiers must be able, like Gray and Broyles, to slump comfortably back into drab peacetime endeavors without seeking to recreate the combat experience on their own (those few unable to make the transition are locked up in prisons or mental institutions).[7]

Thus, in order to prosecute war, commanders may call upon instincts and proclivities that seem base and terrible to many. But while these instincts and proclivities can be activated if necessary, it is not necessary that they be activated.

Contrary to aggression theory, then, the natural instincts which permit war to happen should be seen as tools that can be exploited rather than as dynamic forces of nature which must be unleashed, diverted, or bottled up (see also Berkowitz 1989).[8] Tools that no longer seem useful or have become out of date can—like a rusty old rake—simply be neglected with neither anxiety nor remorse.

---

[6]One source suggests that the berserker was "mentally instable" and "a kind of psychopath." But it also points out that the "ability to go berserk" was a rational one: "to a large extent the berserk seems to have been able to control his animal excitement" (Lid 1956). It is interesting in this regard that players in the National Hockey League, allowed from an early age to give in to their instincts for violent aggression as part of the game, were able to restrain these proclivities when they came up against smooth-skating Soviet players who did not fight back and, accordingly, gained an advantage by avoiding the penalty box.

[7]That such control is entirely possible is suggested, somewhat surprisingly, by Lorenz. "I have found," he observes, "that even highly irascible people who, in a rage seem to lose all control of their actions, still refrain from smashing really valuable objects, preferring cheaper crockery." He quickly adds, however, that "it would be a complete error to suspect that they could, if they only tried hard enough, keep from smashing things altogether!" (1966, 270). The error may not be quite so "complete." It would not be at all surprising to learn that Summers and Levy, after their remarkable adventures in the battle of Normandy, lived out the rest of their lives without ever again exhibiting such violently aggressive behavior.

[8]Something similar could be said about another instinct that many people would consider to be base: our fascination with the grotesque. This instinct was regularly pandered to when there were freak shows, visitation periods for the public at insane asylums, and public executions, institutions which moralists over the last century or two have effectively managed to abolish. People generally seem to be able to function quite well without them, even though it is extremely unlikely that the basic instinct has been bred or repressed out of existence. After all, the phenomenon of "rubbernecking" remains viable: an automobile accident causes traffic problems even if it occurs on the other side of a divided roadway because people, however guiltily, slow down to see if they can spot any gore. The servicing of this instinct through fiction, on the other hand, seems to continue unabated—movies and television may today be performing the function once served by live theater (like Punch and Judy shows) and lurid folk tales.

WAR AS A USEFUL SOCIAL INSTITUTION

A different perspective on the problem of war has been supplied by Margaret Mead. Writing in 1940, she notes that anthropologists had found peoples, like the Eskimo, who, while "turbulent and troublesome," never go to war. She argues therefore that war is not a natural instinct, but rather merely a social "invention" like "writing, marriage, cooking our food instead of eating it raw, trial by jury or burial of the dead." Peoples will "go to war if they have the invention, just as peoples who have the custom of dueling will have dueling and peoples who have the patterns of vendetta will indulge in vendetta," while "people who do not know of dueling will not fight duels" (1964, 270, 272).

For Mead the problem is that "once an invention is made which proves congruent with human needs or social forms, it tends to persist" (1964, 273). Since warfare is now "part of our thought" and is "firmly entrenched," it can be eliminated only if it is replaced by a new invention: "a form of behavior becomes out of date only when something else takes its place" (1964, 273–274). To support her point, Mead argues that the inventions of ordeal and trial by combat disappeared only when they were replaced by another invention, trial by jury. A somewhat similar conclusion has been reached by many diplomatic analysts. William Rappard, for example, argued in 1940 that war "is a method of settling conflicts of interests and ambitions between sovereign States," and therefore if "war is to be eliminated from international relations, a pacific method of settlement must be substituted for it" (1940, 103–104).

In this Mead and Rappard are in at least partial harmony with James, Freud, Lorenz, and Mansfield. Mead specifically denies that war is either a "biological necessity" or a "sociological inevitability" (1964, 269), but she does conclude that, once invented by a society, war serves, or at least is held to serve, a valued social function (on this issue, see also Park 1964). Where James, Freud, Lorenz, and Mansfield argue that war cannot be eliminated until some method is found to channel, divert, or displace instinctual aggressiveness or bellicosity, or to fulfill psychic needs, Mead and Rappard argue that war cannot be abolished until a new device is invented to service the valued social function the institution performs.

As noted, Mead illustrates the process by pointing to the way trial by jury replaced trial by combat. But she also cites dueling as an example of a custom which has died out. That institution, however, was never really replaced by anything. Formal dueling seems to have evaporated mainly because it came to be taken as a ridiculous mode of behavior, not because it was superseded by some other method to resolve disputes (see Stevens 1940, 280–283; Cochran 1963, 287; Baldick 1965, 199; Mueller 1989a, 9–11). It may be true that there were improvements in the responsiveness and effectiveness of the legal system as dueling was dying out. But duels were only rarely fought over issues that the legal system can handle, either then or now: typically they were inspired by conflicts over matters of honor and personal dignity, not over who stole whose cow. Moreover, particularly in the United States, duelists were hardly alienated from the judicial system or disenfranchised from it. In fact, many were lawyers—some 90 percent in Tennessee, for example (Seitz 1929, 30).

Thus, it is entirely possible for an institution that serves, or seems to serve, a useful and valued social function to become obsolete and to fade away without being replaced by any sort of newly-invented functional substitute. It was once held that "dueling, like war, is the necessary consequence of offense," as a dueling manual put it in 1847 (Stowe 1987, 15). Young men of the social set that once engaged in formal dueling do not seem to have noticeably changed their basic nature: they have not become any less contentious or self-centered; they still seem to be deeply concerned about matters of honor and self-image; and they still are quick to take offense. But dueling is no longer a consequence, necessary or not, of such offense. In fact, it does not even occur to them that dueling might be an option. A fabled institution that had been used for centuries to settle differences simply died out and has not been replaced.

Slavery is another institution—one as important in history as war—that has been all but eradicated from the human experience without replacement (see Mueller 1989a, 11–12; Ray 1989; Winter 1989, 200–201). Something similar could be said for other institutions that have died out or have been severely reduced in occurrence over the ages: vendetta or family feuding, for example, or capital punishment, flogging, eunuchism, self-flagellation, piracy, colonialism, infanticide, human sacrifice. None required the invention of substitutes. People simply found that they could get along quite well without them.

—

THE DECLINE OF WAR IN EUROPE

No matter how much fascination it retains, war could be on its way to joining these obsolete or obsolescent institutions. Like dueling, war is a costly, but often effective, method for resolving quarrels. Like slavery, it has been an important historical institution. But, like both of these obsolete institutions, war is necessary neither to satisfy human impulses nor to make society function. Unlike breathing, eating, or sex, war is not something that is somehow required by the human psyche, by the human condition, or by the forces of history.

As discussed more fully in Chapter 9, the experience in Europe helps to support this conclusion. The various peoples of that continent used to get into wars all the time—it was probably the most warlike place in the world. In medieval times, as Georg Schwarzenberger points out, a premise of international law was "In the absence of an agreed state of truce or peace, war was the basic state of international relations" (cited in Nadelmann 1990, 486). In the early Middle Ages, as Philippe Contamine notes, "years without military expeditions were always sufficiently exceptional for them to be mentioned in the Annals" (1984, 23).[9] Between

---

[9]Later, during the reign of Henry III (1216–1272), England lapsed into a period of what Contamine considers to be peace: in 56 years, the country only fought four wars on the continent, five in Wales, and two on the Scottish border, while sustaining four civil wars (1984, 65). After that "respite," England descended into the Hundred Years War with France.

1815 and 1854, however, there was an era of near-total peace within Europe, something that was utterly unprecedented in its history. There were several short wars on the continent between 1854 and 1871, and then, from 1871 until 1914, another period of near-total peace within Europe that was even longer than the first. As Luard observes, although there were some civil wars, the two long stretches in the nineteenth century in which all major European countries "were at peace with each other, both in Europe and outside, despite many disputes and much competition for territory," represent "a dramatic change from the pattern of war in the preceding age, when major powers were in recurrent warfare against each other" (1986, 58–59).

This pattern of substantial peace was, of course, shattered by the two World Wars of the twentieth century, but since 1945 Europe has experienced the longest continuous period of peace—particularly international peace—since the days of the Roman Empire (Mueller 1989a, 3; Schroeder 1985, 88). As Luard observes, "Given the scale and frequency of war during the preceding centuries in Europe, this is a change of spectacular proportions: perhaps the single most striking discontinuity that the history of warfare has anywhere provided" (1986, 77). Thus, while war persists elsewhere and while civil war inflicts some areas of Europe, there has been a very remarkable decline in international war in what was once the world's most warlike continent.

Some European countries, of course, continued to engage in wars on other continents, and it could be argued that they were satisfying their natural aggressive urges there. But this is not true for all the states of Europe. Some, including many that were once among the most warlike, appear to have abandoned war entirely.

For example, 500 years ago the Swiss were fierce fighters and were widely sought after as mercenaries. As Lynn Montross has observed, "After their triumph over Burgundy (1477) the Swiss could have challenged any army on the continent." Yet they soon began to betray what Montross calls "a curious indifference to political or territorial aggrandizement" (Levy 1983, 45). Switzerland has now stayed out of all international war for almost two centuries, and it sustained its last civil war in 1847. Anyone who holds that war is required by human nature or that the institution can only vanish when an appropriate substitute is invented needs to supply an explanation for the curious warless condition of the once-warlike Swiss: are they peculiar? have they discovered a moral equivalent (downhill skiing perhaps)? are they a mass of suppressed neuroses?

Other countries have followed a similar path. Scandinavia, home to the warloving Vikings, has been trying to be war-free for over a century and a half: the Swedes fought their last war in 1815. As a great power, Holland once got into its quota of wars, but it has been working to avoid them since 1713. Spain and Portugal have effectively remained out of all European wars since 1815 (see Mueller 1989a, 19–21; Luard 1986, 62–63).

Or consider England. Two people musing early in the seventeenth century about the English character (perhaps after a performance of any part of Shakespeare's *Henry VI*), might well conclude that civil war, if not endemic to human nature, is surely endemic to English nature. England was enjoying a hiatus of civil peace at the time, but the two raconteurs might well conclude that sooner or later the English would again show their true nature by lapsing into a period of civil warfare. And they would have been right. But astoundingly, after the civil war period in the middle of that century, England (if not Britain) abandoned civil war entirely. Once experts at civil war—addicts perhaps—the English have now lived without it for over three centuries and show little sign either of strain or relapse. They have successfully kicked the habit.

Over the last century, then, the ancient institution of war, without losing its inherent fascination, has become substantially discredited, at least within the developed world, as a mechanism for carrying out international affairs and for resolving conflicts among nations (and, for the most part, within them).[10] This has required neither an improvement in human nature nor the invention of new devices or institutions to channel instincts or to settle issues.

PEACE, WAR, CONFLICT, AND COOPERATION

This certainly does not mean that conflict has been eliminated. Conflict, like war, is natural. But unlike war, conflict is necessary and inevitable because it is impossible for everyone to have exactly the same interests.[11] Samuel Huntington contends that one should not ignore "the weakness and irrationality of human nature," and he stresses that although human beings are capable of generosity and wisdom, they are "also often stupid, selfish, cruel, and sinful." As long "as human beings exist," he insists, "there is no exit from the traumas of history" (1989, 10). But it does not follow that the human race is fatalistically condemned to express these qualities, and to expatiate its traumas, in war. I know of no evidence that young men of the Alexander Hamilton–Aaron Burr class are as a group any less stupid, selfish, cruel, sinful, or contentious today than they were 200 years ago. They simply no longer use the device of formal dueling to express, or resolve, their conflicts (although, of course, street fighting and gang warfare do persist in other social groups).

As members of the set that once engaged in formal dueling now manage to resolve (or simply live with) their inevitable conflicts without dueling, the nations in a warless world would similarly have to cope. France and Germany today do not by any means agree about everything but, shattering the pattern of the century previous to 1945, they no longer even conceive of using war or the threat of it to resolve their disagreements.

Some of the conceptual problem in this area has come from peace advocates over the centuries who have very often argued that peace cannot be secured un-

---

[10]The experience of World War I seems to have been crucial to this process of discrediting: see Chapter 9. Nuclear weapons, on the other hand, do not seem to have been necessary for the change: see Chapter 5.

[11]It is also undesirable: if the potential buyer and seller of food value the product exactly the same, no purchase would take place and starvation would ensue.

less the world first achieves harmony, inner tranquility, cooperation, goodwill, love, brotherhood, equality, and/or justice. It is a reasonable counter to that position to argue that, given human nature and the depth of the difficulties, none of these rather vaporous qualities is ever likely to overwhelm the human race, and therefore that peace is impossible.

But peace does not require that there first be a state of universal love or perpetual harmony or broad justice. Peace is not opposed in principle to any of these qualities, and in some cases it may very well facilitate their wider establishment. But peace is quite compatible as well with conflict, contentiousness, hostility, racism, inequality, hatred, avarice, calumny, injustice, petulance, greed, vice, slander, squalor, lechery, xenophobia, malice, and oppression. To achieve peace, people do not necessarily have to become admirable, nor do they need to stifle all their unpleasant instincts and proclivities; they merely need to abandon the rather absurd institution of war as a method for dealing with one another. The abolition of slavery may have made the world better, but it certainly did not make it perfect. Similarly, peace is not a utopian condition; it is merely better than the alternative. If we stop envisioning it as heaven on earth, it will be easier to achieve and to maintain.

Chapter 9

THE HISTORICAL MOVEMENT OF IDEAS: THE RISE OF WAR AVERSION AND THE RETREAT FROM DOOMSDAY

As observed in Chapter 2, ideas are often, in Robert Dahl's construction, "a major independent variable" (1971, 188). And, as suggested there, to ignore changes in ideas, beliefs, ideologies, and attitudes is to leave something important out of consideration.

This chapter assesses the idea of war aversion and, focusing particularly on attitude changes at the time of the First World War, it seeks to demonstrate that the remarkable growth in the acceptance of this idea over the last century or so is not the necessary consequence of changes in broader social or economic phenomena, but rather that it is the result of the success of idea entrepreneurs. And, more generally, the chapter attempts to develop an explanation for what Dahl calls "the historical movement of ideas."

CHANGING IDEAS: THE OBSOLESCENCE OF MAJOR WAR

In *Retreat from Doomsday* I concluded that "major war" (war among developed countries) may well be obsolescent. Since I was writing the book while a bloody international war was raging between Iran and Iraq, and while civil wars were going on in El Salvador, Ethiopia, Guatemala, Cambodia, Lebanon, Angola, Iraq, Nicaragua, Peru, Sudan, Burma, Sri Lanka, Afghanistan and several other places, it was fairly obvious that war had not exactly been extinguished on the

globe. Nonetheless, it seemed to me that an important and consequential historical change has taken place with respect to ideas about, and attitudes toward, the
institution of war—one rather akin to, though certainly not identical with, the
processes by which the once-venerated and widely accepted institutions of slavery
and formal dueling became extinct.

The book treats war as an idea, almost as a fad, and it focuses on changing attitudes toward war. It concludes that these have changed in highly significant ways
at least in the developed world. At one time Europeans widely viewed warfare as
something that was natural and normal: as Michael Howard has observed, "War
was almost universally considered an acceptable, perhaps an inevitable and for
many people a desirable way of settling international differences" (1984, 9). In
partial consequence of this point of view, Europe was, as discussed in Chapter 8, a
cauldron of both international and civil conflict—the continent was, in fact, the
most warlike in the world. Thomas Jefferson, with a mixture of amazement and
disgust, called it an "arena of gladiators" where "war seems to be the natural state
of man" (1939 ed., 262–263).[1]

Attitudes toward war have changed profoundly in the twentieth century in
Europe. There is no way to quantify this change except perhaps through a rough
sort of content analysis: a hundred years ago it was very easy to find serious writers, analysts, and politicians in Europe and the United States who hailed war "not
merely as an unpleasant necessity," as Roland Stromberg has observed, "but as
spiritual salvation and hope of regeneration" (1982, 1–2). For example, Oliver
Wendell Holmes told the Harvard graduating class in 1895 that war's message was
"divine," John Ruskin found war to be the "foundation of all the higher virtues and
faculties of men," Alexis de Tocqueville concluded that "war almost always en-
larges the mind of a people and raises their character," Émile Zola considered war
to be "life itself," Igor Stravinsky believed that war was "necessary for human
progress" (Mueller 1989a, ch. 2). By now, however, such views have become extremely rare. This may not quite be the "systematic evidence demonstrating that
Europeans believe war is obsolete" that John Mearsheimer has called for (1990,
41), but it does suggest that the appeal of war, both as a desirable exercise in itself
and as a sensible method for resolving international disagreements, has diminished markedly on that once war-racked continent. War has hardly become obsolete, but international war in the classic European sense has, I think, started to become so—it has begun to go out of style there (see also Keegan 1993, 59).

As will be discussed more fully later in this chapter, much of this change took
place at the time of World War I. Because of the change, it became the central
policy of almost all countries in the developed world after World War I to avoid
war—at least war with each other. The experience of World War II embellished
this process (and it was probably crucial for the distant Japanese), but I think that
war came to Europe in 1939 not because it was in the cards in any important

---

[1]Or, as Daniel Webster put it in 1826: "Wars for particular dynasties, wars to support or prevent particular successions, wars to enlarge or curtail the dominions of particular crowns, wars to support or to
dissolve family alliances, wars to enforce or to resist religious intolerance—what long and bloody chapters do not these fill in the history of European politics!" (Tucker and Hendrickson 1992, 168).

sense, but because it was brought about by the maniacally dedicated machinations of Adolf Hitler, an exceptionally lucky and spectacularly skilled entrepreneur.[2] Mearsheimer argues that "if any war could have convinced Europeans to forswear conventional war, it should have been World War I, with its vast casualties" (1990, 30; see also Van Evera 1990/91, 33). Although, as discussed below, I do not think the casualty count alone caused the change, a consequence of World War I was that the vast majority of Europeans *did* forswear war—at least war of that sort. Indeed, one of the reasons Hitler was so successful for so long was that his opponents assumed that, since it was so obvious that no one could want another war, he must be serious when he continuously professed his yearning for peace (see note 6 below).

To opt out of the war system there were two central paths war-averse countries could take. One was the pacifist (or Chamberlain) approach: be reasonable and unprovocative, stress accommodation and appeasement, and assume the best about one's opponent. The other was the deterrence (or Churchill) approach: arm yourself and bargain with troublemakers from a position of military strength. The chief lesson garnered by the end of the 1930s was that, while the pacifist approach might work well with some countries, an approach stressing deterrence and even confrontation was the only way to deal with others. To that degree, war remained part of the political atmospherics even for the war averse.[3]

After World War II, there was an important contest between East and West. It stemmed, I think, from the essential belief by many important Communists that international capitalism, or imperialism, was a profoundly evil system that must be eradicated from the face of the globe and by violence if necessary (see Chapters 2 and 6). Moreover, they felt they were duty-bound to assist in this inevitable historical process. I do not think the Soviets ever envisioned major war as a sensible method for carrying out this scheme (see Chapter 5), but they did consider valid such tactics as violent revolution, bluster and crisis, and revolutionary wars in what came to be called the Third World.

Western policymakers became alarmed at the dangers presented by international Communism, and the lesson learned, perhaps overlearned, from the interwar experience was that one is safest if one assumes the worst. It does not follow, therefore, that because countries maintain strong military defenses and the will and ability to use them, that they are necessarily in favor of war. Rather, it seems that, as Michael Howard has put, "today everyone in developed societies belongs to the 'peace movement', even those who, in the name of stability, are most zealously building up their national armaments" (1991, 175).

An important consequence of this change is that, as observed in the previous chapter, Europe (and the developed world in general) has experienced an almost complete absence of international warfare since 1945. Jack Levy calculates that "the probability of no war occurring between the handful of leading states in the system" for such a long time is about .005 (1991, 147).

---

[2]For a development of this argument, see Mueller 1989a, 64–71; and especially Mueller 1991d.

[3]For a discussion that does not seem to consider these distinctions, see Trachtenberg 1991. On these issues, see also Chapter 4.

By the time the book was completed in 1988 (see also Mueller 1986), it seemed to me that Communist ideology was in the process of very substantially mellowing on its central confrontational issue, and therefore that we might soon come to the end of the world as we knew it, that the arms race might reverse itself, and that East and West might soon find themselves linked in previously inconceivable alliance relationships.

In the period since the book came out, much of that has transpired, although with a speed and thoroughness I still find breathtaking. And, while armed conflict has hardly vanished from the globe, the likelihood of a major conflagration among developed nations—the kind of war most feared during the Cold War—has, as discussed in Chapter 1, very substantially diminished. With the quiet cataclysm, we have retreated even farther from doomsday.

The argument does not hold that everything is getting better in every way, nor does it claim that everything people generally consider bad will vanish from the earth. But things do change. As noted in the previous chapter, slavery used to be an institution as venerable and apparently as natural and inevitable as war. Formal dueling used to be widely accepted as an effective method for resolving certain kinds of disputes. Both became thoroughly discredited and then obsolete. There is reason to believe the institution of war could eventually join their ranks.[4]

●

IDEAS AS INDEPENDENT VARIABLES:
THE RISE OF WAR AVERSION

Randolph Siverson has suggested that analyses which rely "heavily on the claim that people's tastes have changed" are "lacking a theory" (1990, 1063). The implication, it seems, is that analyses that treat the historical movement of ideas as an independent variable cannot be considered a contribution to theory. My belief, by contrast, is that it is important to deal with what Francis Fukuyama has called the "autonomous power of ideas" (1989; see also Huntington 1989), and that theories that ignore the historical movement of ideas cannot come to grips with reality because they are misspecified: they leave out a key explanatory variable. And the rise over the last century of war aversion—the rising acceptance of the notion that

---

[4]Huntington notes that "murder has been unacceptable in civilized societies for millennia, and yet it seems unlikely that the murder rate in twentieth-century New York is less than it was in fifth-century Athens" (1989, 7). And, obviously, the list could be expanded to include things like rape, incest, robbery, and impure thinking. But slavery and formal dueling (and war) are institutions that require support and acceptance from society as a whole, or at least from significant relevant sections of it, and they cannot be effective if they go out of fashion with the relevant portions of society. Certain forms of social murder—crucifixion, human sacrifice, and capital punishment, as well as dueling—have, in fact, largely gone out of existence in the developed world. On the other hand, abortion, once considered a barbarity and still held to be a form of murder by many, has increased as social acceptance has grown.

war is a bad idea and ought to be eliminated from human affairs—seems an excellent case in point.

THE RISE OF WAR AVERSION AS A DEPENDENT VARIABLE

If the historical movement of ideas is an important explanatory variable, it becomes equally important to try to account for changes in ideas.

Some people argue that attitude changes arise from other causes. For example, Michael Howard, in general agreement with the conclusion of *Retreat from Doomsday,* has suggested that, although war will persist among "undeveloped" societies and although civil war might still occur within both undeveloped and developed ones, it is "quite possible that war in the sense of major, organized armed conflict between highly developed societies may not recur, and that a stable framework for international order will become firmly established" (1991, 176). And he chiefly derives this conclusion from a set of observations about ideas— about the way people in the developed world have changed their attitudes toward war.

In seeking to explain this important change in attitude, however, Howard treats ideas as a dependent variable. At one time, he notes, the developed world was organized into "warrior societies" in which warfare was seen to be "the noblest destiny of mankind." This was changed, he suggests, by industrialization which "ultimately produces very unwarlike societies dedicated to material welfare rather than heroic achievement" (1991, 176).

The main problem for this generalization, as Howard is quite aware, is that industrialization spoke with a forked tongue. Over the last two centuries the developed world has experienced the Industrial Revolution, enormous economic growth, the rise of a middle class, a vast improvement in transportation and communication, surging literacy rates, and massive increases in international trade. But it is not at all clear that the rise in war aversion was necessarily caused by these important social and economic developments. For if they encouraged some people to abandon the war spirit, they apparently propelled others to fall, if anything, more fully in love with the institution. Howard himself traces the persistence, even the rise, of a militaristic spirit that became wedded to a fierce and expansionist nationalist impetus as industrialization came to Europe in the nineteenth century. And, of course, in the next century industrialized nations fought two of the greatest wars in history. Thus industrialization can inspire bellicism as much as pacifism. Howard never really provides much of an explanation for how or why industrialization must inevitably lead to an antimilitary spirit, and he rather vaguely attributes the horrors and holocausts that accompanied industrialization to "the growing pains of industrial societies" (1991, 1).

Carl Kaysen has also concluded that major war is becoming obsolete, and he has advanced an argument similar to Howard's, but with far more detail about the process, particularly its economic aspects. He argues that "for most of human history, societies were so organized that war could be profitable for the victors, in both economic and political terms." However, "profound changes . . . following the Industrial Revolution, have changed the terms of the calculation" causing the potential gains of war to diminish and the potential costs to rise (1990, 49; see also Fukuyama 1992, 262).

Kaysen tends to minimize the economic costs of war before the modern era, but many studies suggest they could be extremely high. Richard Kaeuper's analysis of the economic effects of decades of war in the late Middle Ages catalogues the destruction of property, the collapse of banks, the severing of trade and normal commerce, the depopulation of entire areas, the loss of cultivated land, the decline of production, the reduction of incomes, the disruption of coinage and credit, the hoarding of gold, and the assessment (with attendant corruption) of confiscatory war taxes (1988, 77–117). By contrast, within a few years after a terrible modern war, World War I, most of the combating nations had substantially recovered economically: by 1929 the German economy was fully back to prewar levels, while the French economy had surpassed prewar levels by 38 percent (Overy 1982b, 16). The "most meaningful question," observes Alan Milward, "is whether the cost of war has absorbed an increasing proportion of the increasing Gross National Product of the combatants. As an economic choice war, measured this way, has not shown any discernible long-term trend towards greater costliness" (1977, 3).

Not only were there many hideously destructive, even annihilative, wars before the modern era, but there was a substantial belief that many of the wars had been even more horrible than they actually were. Often—in fact, *typically*—war stories would substantially exaggerate the extent of the destruction and bloodshed (see Chapter 7 and Mueller 1994b). Yet beliefs and experiences like this had never brought about a widespread revulsion to war as an institution nor did they inspire effective, organized demands that it be banished. Instead war continued to be accepted as a normal way of doing things.

Moreover, as with Howard's argument, the problem is that industrialization was accompanied not only by a rising peace movement, but also with a renewed romantic yearning for the cleansing process of war. In fact, industrialization made possible the "splendid little war": as Luard observes, "very short wars (two months or less) have been virtually confined to the last century or so, since it is only in this period that mobility has been sufficient to allow the type of lightning military campaign required" (1986, 79). For nineteenth-century war advocates like Heinrich von Treitschke, this condition was literally a godsend: one could still have wars with all their nobility, heroism, and sublimity, while, thanks to industrialization, the downside of war—the distasteful bloodshed—would be kept to a bearable minimum.[5]

---

[5]It is often argued that as economic interdependence increases, people will turn against war. For von Treitschke, however, the opposite was the case: because of the burgeoning, interdependent economic system, he argued, "civilized nations suffer far more than savages from the economic ravages of war, especially through the disturbance of the artificially existing credit system, which may have frightful consequences in a modern war. . . . Therefore wars must become rarer and shorter, . . . for it is impossible to see how the burdens of a great war could long be borne under the present conditions. But it would be false to conclude that wars can ever cease. They neither can nor should" (1916, 69–70).

THE RISE OF WAR AVERSION AS AN INDEPENDENT VARIABLE

It seems to me that people in the developed world have become disillusioned with war not because of the logical or atmospheric implications of industrialization, but for the same reasons they had become disillusioned with an equally old and venerable institution, slavery. Substantial efforts have been made by scholars and analysts to use material factors, particularly economic ones, to explain the origin and the amazing success of the idea that slavery ought to be abolished. But, as Stanley Engerman has observed, slavery never was in economic decline—indeed, at the same time that the abolition movement was taking flight the Atlantic slave trade was entering an extremely profitable phase. Consequently the success of the movement has to be explained by "political, cultural, and ideological factors" (1986, 339; see also Drescher 1987, Eltis 1987, Ray 1989, Nadelmann 1990).

Ideas, then, are very often forces themselves, not flotsam on the tide of broader social or economic patterns. War aversion has grown over the last century not because it was somehow required by social and economic change, but because the idea, skillfully promoted at the right time in the world's history, managed to catch on.

WAR AVERSION AND THE "LEVEL OF ANALYSIS." The consequences of treating war merely as an idea are substantial. In discussing the causes of international war, commentators have often found it useful to group theories into what they term levels of analysis. In a classic work Kenneth Waltz (1959) organizes the theories according to whether the cause of war is found in the nature of man, in the nature of the state, or in the nature of the international state system. More recently Jack Levy (1989a), partly setting the issue of human nature to one side, organizes the theories according to whether they stress the systemic level, the nature of state and society, or the decision making process. In various ways, I think, these level-of-analysis approaches may direct attention away from war itself and toward concerns which may influence the incidence of war.

I suggest rather that war should be visualized not as a sort of recurring outcome that is determined by other conditions, but rather as a phenomenon that has its own qualities and appeals. And over time these appeals can change. As argued in Chapter 8, war is merely an idea, an institution, like dueling or slavery, that has been grafted onto human existence. Unlike breathing, eating, or sex, war is not something that is somehow required by human nature, by the human condition, by the structure of international affairs, or by the forces of history. Accordingly war can shrivel up and disappear, and this can come about without requiring any notable change or improvement on any of the standard level-of-analysis categories. Specifically, war can die out without changing human nature, without modifying the nature of the state or the nation-state, without changing the international system, without creating an effective world government or system of international law, and without improving the competence or moral capacity of political leaders.

It can also go away without expanding international trade, interdependence, or communication; without fabricating an effective moral or practical equivalent;

without enveloping the earth in democracy or prosperity; without devising inge-nious agreements to restrict arms or the arms industry; without reducing the world's considerable store of hate, selfishness, nationalism, and racism; without increasing the amount of love, justice, harmony, cooperation, goodwill, or inner peace in the world; without establishing security communities; and without doing anything whatever about nuclear weapons.

EXPLAINING THE HISTORICAL MOVEMENT OF IDEAS. Ideas may be important, even crucial, but accounting for changes in them is a difficult undertaking. As Dahl puts it: "One can hardly exaggerate how badly off we are as we move into this terrain. If it is difficult to account satisfactorily for the acquisition of individual beliefs, it is even more difficult to account for historical shifts in beliefs" (1971, 182). That is, there may be something of an inherent and rather unpleasant mushiness in the study of the "historical movement of ideas," and analysis will tend to be inductive and after the fact, rather than predictive. (Actually, the problem may be even worse for those who value scientific progress: anyone who came up with a good method for predicting changes in ideas would be likely to keep it secret because the method, applied to stock markets and commodity production, would quickly make the theorist the richest person in the world.) But it does not seem wise in this area to ignore phenomena that cannot easily be measured, treated with crisp precision, or probed with deductive panache.

To begin to confront this issue, some people have used the concept, or metaphor, of "learning." While the metaphor has some valuable resonances, it is misleading and misdirecting for several reasons.

First, it suggests that an idea, once ingested, cannot be undone. When one learns how to swim or to ride a bicycle or to speak another language, that knowl-edge or aptitude can never be fully unlearned—one can never return to a state of complete ignorance.

Second, and relatedly, the learning analogy implies progress, betterment. Too much learning can be a bad or dangerous thing, and we sometimes speak of "learning bad habits." But for the most part we tend to believe that any learning, any increase of knowledge, is an improvement—or at any rate does no harm. But obviously, plenty of ideas that by most accepted standards prove to be bad ones—like state Communism, totalitarianism, trial by combat, genocide, the Spanish Inquisition, airplane hijacking—also get "learned." Few would find these develop-ments progressive.

Third, the learning metaphor tends to imply that new ideas can only be ac-quired slowly. We sometimes do talk about learning fast, but the concept gener-ally suggests gradual progress. However, while some ideas become accepted slowly, others (for example, that it is time for the countries of eastern Europe to be democratic) can catch on almost overnight.

Finally, learning implies success. That is, if one tries hard enough and has a good enough teacher, one will likely eventually learn the lesson.

Another metaphor stresses the "diffusion" of ideas. This also implies gradualism and irreversibility, and it suggests a certain inevitability. Moreover, it implies that individual people do little to influence the process—that the process is a rather passive one.

It seems to me that it is more promising to stress promotion and persuasion when trying to account for the historical movement of ideas. People do not learn ideas like war aversion, nor do they ingest them by a process of diffusion; they become persuaded to accept—or buy—them.

At any given time there are always a huge array of ideas around, and only a few of these catch on. Some may be of lengthy pedigree (like the idea that capital punishment is a bad thing and ought to be abolished), while others may be quite new and original (like the hula hoop). People sort through this market of ideas and prove receptive to some while remaining immune to others. Their receptivity may not be very predictable, but it is surely not random.

The process by which an idea becomes accepted can be quite complicated, and it does not follow that the growth in acceptance of an idea derives simply from the manipulative cleverness of its advocates. And any knowledgeable promoter will admit that no amount of promotion can guarantee that a product will sell: as impresario Sol Hurok is alleged to have put it, "If people don't want to come, nothing will stop them." If concentrated efforts at promotion and persuasion alone could assure the success of a product, we would all be driving Edsels. Careful planning and adept promotion are important, but so are happenstance and luck. Moreover, success need not be permanent: even a great triumph of promotion and persuasion may prove short-lived as tastes change for uncontrollable reasons or as the competition imitates and improves its product.

PROMOTING WAR AVERSION: THE CASE OF WORLD WAR I

Ultimately, it seems to me, the promotion concept provides the best explanation for the growth of war aversion in the developed world—and for its retreat from doomsday. The process can be examined best by evaluating the rise of war aversion at the time of World War I.

As suggested earlier, the experience of what was then known as "the Great War" was crucial since the war clearly changed attitudes toward war in the developed world. In an area where war had been accepted as a fixture for thousands of years, the idea suddenly gained substantial currency that war there was no longer an inevitable fact of life and that major efforts should be made to abandon it. The war marked, as Arnold Toynbee points out, the end of a "span of five thousand years during which war had been one of mankind's master institutions" (1969, 214). Evan Luard observes that "the First World War transformed traditional attitudes toward war. For the first time there was an almost universal sense that the deliberate launching of a war could now no longer be justified" (1986, 365). Bernard Brodie points out that "a basic historical change had taken place in the attitudes of the European (and American) peoples toward war" (1973, 30). Eric Hobsbawn concludes, "In 1914 the peoples of Europe, for however brief a moment, went lightheartedly to slaughter and to be slaughtered. After the First World War they never did so again" (1987, 326). And K. J. Holsti observes, "When it was all over, few remained to be convinced that such a war must never happen again" (1991, 175). As noted above, before World War I it is very easy to find serious people exalting war as a desirable necessity. After it, such people (for example, Benito Mussolini) become extremely rare.

Obviously, this change of attitude was not enough to prevent the cataclysm of 1939–45 or the many smaller wars that have taken place since 1918. But the existence of these wars should not be allowed to cloud an appreciation for the shift of opinion that was caused by World War I. The notion that the institution of war, particularly war in the developed world, was repulsive, uncivilized, immoral, and futile—voiced only by minorities before 1914—was an idea whose time had come.[6] As suggested earlier, it is one that has permeated most of the developed world ever since, and it has probably been an important element in the remarkably long period of freedom from international war that has enveloped the developed world since 1945.

THE UNIQUENESS OF WORLD WAR I

What made World War I so special in its impact on attitudes toward war? There seem to be four possibilities. The first is the most obvious: the war was unique in its sheer destructiveness. On evaluation, however, and in broader historical perspective, it appears that World War I was not all that unusual in its duration, destructiveness, grimness, political pointlessness, economic consequences, or breadth. In two important and somewhat related respects, however, the war

---

[6]As noted earlier, the widespread acceptance of the notion that war had become unthinkable aided Adolf Hitler, history's supreme atavism, in his astoundingly single-minded quest to bring about another war in Europe. After World War I most people paid Hitler the undue compliment of assuming that, no matter how belligerent his actions and demands, he could not seriously contemplate doing anything that might plunge the world into another cataclysmic war. Throughout the 1930s Hitler, a liar of truly monumental proportions, assiduously played on this perception. In virtually every speech he assured everyone—foreigners as well as the war-fearing German people (Kershaw 1987)—that his needs and demands were eminently limited and satisfiable, and that his fear and loathing of war was all-consuming. His arguments on this issue were agile and multifaceted. He proclaimed war to be "infinite madness" (1933), a "disaster" (1936), and "an evil" (1938). Amplifying, he argued that it was intolerably costly ("no possible profits could justify the sacrifices and sufferings that war entails"—1935), foolishly diverting, beneficial only to Communism, and potentially annihilative ("I do not believe that Europe can survive such a catastrophe"—1935). He also used his World War I experience to support his argument: "These years make me in the depths of my being wishful for peace, since I recognize the frightful horrors of war"—1939). Incredibly, he even used his *racism* to show his peaceful intentions: "Our racial theory therefore regards every war for the subjection and domination of an alien people as a proceeding which sooner or later changes and weakens the victor internally, and eventually brings about his defeat. . . . National Socialist Germany wants peace because of its fundamental convictions" (1935). (Hitler 1942, 1046, 1348, 1513, 1198, 1231, 1669, 1218–1220.) On this issue, see Mueller 1989a, 64–71; Mueller 1991d.

does seem to have been quite unique: it was the first major war in history to have been preceded by substantial, organized antiwar agitation; and it followed a century that was most peculiar in European history, one in which the continent had managed, perhaps without fully appreciating it, to savor the relative blessings of substantial periods of peace. Finally, World War I was unique in that it was the first to raise the specter that the science of warfare had so advanced that the next such war could bring world annihilation; however, this belief was probably less a cause of changed attitudes toward war than a consequence of those changes.

1. THE DESTRUCTIVENESS OF WORLD WAR I.   Norman Rich argues that World War I, "to a far greater extent" than earlier wars "nourished some of the worst qualities of the human character. For four years men were systematically trained in the use of violence, for four years hatred and slaughter were extolled as the highest human virtues, for four years men were exposed to suffering and death, their sensibilities blunted to the pain and suffering of others. The brutalizing effect of war was a common experience to the population of all belligerent powers, and it left its mark on them all" (1973). In none of these respects was World War I remotely unusual either in kind or degree. It is, in fact, difficult to imagine a war that could not be condemned for its systematic violence, intense hatred, suffering, death, and blunted sensibilities.

The Great War, as it was known for two decades, was extremely costly of course: casualties were enormous, and they were intense, suffered over what could be considered to be a rather short period of time. But in broader historical perspective, the destructiveness of the war does not seem to be all that unique.

To begin with, it was not the first war of that magnitude. The Taiping Rebellion, a civil war that raged through China between 1851 and 1864, probably caused a greater loss of life in absolute terms: over 30 million against less than 20 million in World War I.[7] If one looks at the costs of previous wars in relative terms, the uniqueness of World War I is even less obvious. There were about 430 million people in Europe in 1914 (McEvedy and Jones 1978, 19). Of these a high estimate is that some 17,860,000 Europeans died in the war—11,867,000 in the military, 5,993,000 civilians. This high estimate of the death rate, then, would suggest that about 4.1 percent of the European population perished in the war.[8] A

[7] Taiping: Ho 1959, 275. World War I: Sivard 1987, 29–31 (all Sivard's estimates are based on data gathered by William Eckhardt). Sivard estimates the Taiping total deaths at 2,000,000, a figure that is almost inconceivably low: see Ho 1959, 236–247.

[8] This estimate takes the war death figures as detailed in Sivard (1987, 29–31) for the European combatants—that is, it excludes the deaths suffered in the war by Australia (60,000), Canada (55,000), India (50,000), New Zealand (16,000), Turkey (1,450,000), and the United States (126,000). If these non-European peoples were included in the calculations, the proportion killed in the war would be lower because their populations would dramatically inflate the percentage base. McEvedy and Jones estimate that a total of 8 million military deaths were suffered in the war (1978, 34), substantially lower than Sivard's 12,599,000. A careful and widely accepted 1923 estimate of total military deaths is also lower: between 10 and 11 million (Dumas and Vedel-Petersen 1923, 144). Others estimate total battle deaths at 9,000,000: Winter 1989, 206; Small and Singer 1982, 89. Another estimate is 7,734,300: Levy 1983, 91.

war in which one in twenty-five dies is calamitous, but there had been hundreds, probably thousands, of wars previously in which far higher casualty rates were suffered.

For example, the destruction of Carthage by Rome in 146 BC was essentially total. Indeed, in ancient times it was not uncommon for victors to "consecrate" city-states to the gods by killing every person and animal in them and by destroying all property (Botterweck and Ringgren 1986, 189–198). If the Bible is to be taken as literal truth, the Israelites launched a series of such wars. God was reportedly concerned that the current occupants of the promised land might subvert the Israelites by teaching them the "abominations which they have done unto their gods" thus causing the Israelites to sin. Accordingly it was required that they kill the heretics before such damage could come about (Deuteronomy 20: 16–18), and the book of Joshua relates the consequent utter annihilation of the peoples of Jericho, Ai, Libnah, Lachisk, Eglon, Hebron, Debir, Hazor, and the areas in between (the people of Gibeon, however, cut a deal and were merely enslaved).

History is filled with examples of such slaughter. According to Thucydides, when the Athenians invaded the island of Melos in 416 BC, they "put to death all the grown men whom they took and sold the women and children for slaves, and subsequently sent out five hundred colonists and inhabited the place for themselves" (1934 ed., 337). Josephus' classic account of the Jewish War that ended in AD 79 catalogues massacre, pestilence, human sacrifice, famine, cannibalism, and the slaughter of prisoners, resulting in the death of hundreds of thousands, perhaps millions (1982 ed., 450–451). When Genghis Khan's hordes moved into Russia in the thirteenth century, whole towns "vanished"—they were smashed, burned down, and depopulated. In Riazan, the captured men, women, and children were killed with swords or arrows, thrown into fires, or bound, cut, and disemboweled (Brent 1976, 117, 120). When Constantinople fell to the Crusaders in 1204, the victors were soon "transformed into a mob driven by hate, greed, and lust," as Donald Queller puts it, and sank into a frenzy of pillage, rape, and massacre, and then, in 50 years of occupation, systematically looted the city of its treasures, reducing it to ruins (1977, 149–153).

Most appropriately, perhaps, World War I should be compared to earlier continent-wide wars fought in Europe such as the Thirty Years War of 1618–48, the Seven Years War of 1756–63, and the Napoleonic Wars that ended in 1815. In proportionate, and sometimes in absolute terms, these wars were often at least as costly as World War I for individual belligerent countries. According to Frederick the Great, Prussia lost one-ninth of its population in the Seven Years War (Luard 1986, 51), a proportion higher than almost any suffered by any combatant in the wars of the twentieth century (Small and Singer 1982, 82–99). Germany's population dropped by about 20 percent in the Thirty Years War (Parker 1984, 211), and Holsti calculates that, "if measured in terms of direct and indirect casualties as a proportion of population," it was Europe's most destructive armed conflict (1991, 313). Using a high estimate for the death rate for World War I and a low one for that of the Napoleonic Wars, it seems that, proportionately, about three times as many people died in the latter war as in the earlier one—a substantial difference, perhaps, but not clearly a revolutionary one. Using a low estimate for deaths in

World War I and a high one for deaths in the Napoleonic Wars, the death rates for the two wars are about equal.[9] Winners lost heavily in World War I, but some of the worst losses of the Napoleonic Wars were also suffered by a winner, Russia. And the expression "Pyrrhic victory" stems from a battle fought in 279 BC.

Not only were there many horribly destructive wars before World War I, but, as noted earlier, people generally believed that many of the wars had been even worse than they actually were. It seems unlikely that the utter annihilation of all those cities in Canaan as detailed in the book of Joshua actually took place, but when the authors of the Bible got around to writing the story a few centuries later, they apparently concluded that annihilation made for a good yarn. Similar exaggerations—some of them quite spectacular—characterize much other writing on war. For centuries a legend prevailed holding that Germany had suffered a 75 percent decline in population during the Thirty Years War.[10] Yet such beliefs had never brought about a widespread revulsion to war; instead war continued to be accepted as normal.[11]

Nor was World War I special in the economic devastation it caused. As noted above, within a few years after the war, most of the combating nations had substantially recovered economically. By contrast, many earlier European wars had been fought to the point of total economic exhaustion—Kaeuper's study of the devastating economic effects of war in the late Middle Ages was discussed earlier The Thirty Years War set back the German economy by decades and the Seven Years War brought Austria to virtual bankruptcy.[12] Because of war, argues Bertrand Russell, "North Africa has never regained the level of prosperity it enjoyed under the Romans" (1953, 74). And it is worth repeating Milward's observation that, "as an economic choice war, measured [as a percentage of the Gross National Product of the combatants] has not shown any discernible long-term trend towards greater costliness" (1977, 3).

---

[9]Sivard estimates 2,380,000 military and civilian deaths in the Napoleonic Wars (1987, 29) when Europe had a population of 180,000,000 (McEvedy and Jones 1978, 18), and this generates a death rate of 1.3 percent as against 4.1 percent for World War I. However, authoritative estimates of deaths in the Napoleonic Wars by nineteenth-century historians (more relevant for present purposes since these would inform the perspectives of their contemporaries) were often much higher. For example, Sivard estimates total military deaths to have been 1,380,000, but most historians held that the French alone suffered between 1,700,000 and 3,000,000; and even those who discounted that estimate argued that total military deaths in the wars were "less than 2,000,000" (Dumas and Vedel-Petersen 1923, 28). Levy's estimate of battle deaths in the war, 1,869,000, is substantially higher than Sivard's (1983, 90). For World War I estimates, see note 8.

[10]The legend is reported in Wedgwood 1938, 516.

[11]One partial caveat might be made to this argument about the loss of life in war. The moral notion about the "sanctity of life" (as opposed to the sanctity of the soul) seems to be a fairly new one, apparently arising in the course of the nineteenth century. If human life becomes more greatly treasured, the costs of war effectively rise as a consequence of such a change in perspective or values.

[12]During the Thirty Years War—when almost two-thirds of the expenditures of the city of Nordlingen were devoted to direct military demands—the average wealth declined precipitously. The city gradually recovered during the next twenty years, but then another cycle of wars left it "helpless to solve its own financial problems." It took fifty years to recover (and then only with outside intervention) at which point it was plunged once again into deep debt by the wars of the French Revolution. See Friedrichs 1979, 154, 169.

World War I toppled political regimes in Germany, Russia, and Austria-Hungary, but it was hardly unusual in this respect. And to suggest that World War I was new in the annals of warfare in its tragic futility and political pointlessness would be absurd—by most reasonable standards huge numbers of costly previous wars would rival, and often surpass, it on those dimensions. For example, there is the Trojan War which stemmed from the abduction from Greece of the beautiful Helen. The point of the war receives the following caustic analysis by a soldier in Shakespeare's *Troilus and Cressida:*

> For every false drop in her bawdy veins,
> A Grecian's life hath sunk; for every scruple
> Of her contaminated carrion weight,
> A Trojan hath been slain.
> Since she could speak,
> She hath not given so many good words breath
> As for her Greeks and Trojans suffered death.

It is true that World War I was soon viewed as a tremendous waste—enormous sacrifice for little gain. But the war could have been accepted as a noble necessity. After all, the war did appear to crush German expansionism and militarism, and initially at least it established a new order dominated by the victors—rather along the lines of the costly wars against Napoleon a century earlier. The revulsion and disillusion did not emerge because this massive war was peculiarly pointless, but because people were ready to evaluate war using new standards.

Actually, in some respects World War I could be seen to be an *improvement* over many earlier wars. Civilian loss, in the West at least, was proportionately quite low, while earlier wars had often witnessed the destruction of entire cities. Modern instances would include Magdeburg in 1631, Moscow in 1812, and Atlanta in 1864.[13] Moreover, logistics were vastly improved in World War I so that, unlike in olden days, soldiers did not have routinely to forage among the civilian population for food, sexual release, and shelter. Nor was pillage and booty-seeking, a commonplace in many wars, the standard in World War I. It was the motto even of the well-organized Gustavus Adolphus that "war must support war" (Millet and Moreland 1976, 15; see also Contamine 1984, 57). Starvation, both of soldiers and of civilians, very often found in earlier wars, was far less of a problem

---

[13]Because of this phenomenon World War I was somewhat more notably destructive compared to earlier continent-wide wars if one deals only with battle deaths. Levy calculates battle deaths as a percentage of the entire population of the continent and concludes that World War I was 3.6 times more destructive than the Napoleonic Wars by this measure and some 2.4 times more destructive than the Thirty Years War (1983, 89–91). However, if a war generates horror this should logically spring from its total destruction, not simply from the deaths it inflicts on young men in uniform. Indeed, the "unnecessary" deaths of "innocent civilians" has usually been seen to be war's chief outrage. For an able discussion, see Holmes 1989.

in World War I. An Italian writer in the 1530s observed that for over twenty years civilians had seen "nothing but scenes of infinite slaughter, plunder and destruction of multitudes of towns and cities, attended with the licentiousness of soldiers no less destructive to friends than foes" (Hale 1985, 179). Knights in the fourteenth century, observes Kaeuper, "seem to have accepted arson and pillage as normal and expected accompaniments of campaigning." As Henry V put it jauntily, "War without fire is like sausages without mustard" (1988, 84).

In World War I prisoners of war were generally well treated by many standards. In ancient warfare it was routine for the victors to slaughter the retreating enemy. After routing the Persians Alexander the Great's forces pursued and supposedly killed 100,000 in a massacre that lasted for miles and for hours. And it was Genghis Khan's motto that "the vanquished can never be the friends of the victors; the death of the former is necessary therefore for the safety of the latter," and some 18,000,000 reportedly fell victim to this policy in China alone (Montross 1944, 27, 145).[14] Nor, of course, were soldiers or civilians enslaved in World War I. In many earlier eras enslavement of the defeated was the accepted routine.

Moreover, with the successful development of modern medicine and of institutions like the Red Cross, a wounded soldier was far more likely to recover than in earlier wars where the nonambulatory wounded were characteristically abandoned on the battlefield to die in lingering agony from exposure and blood loss. Disease was also becoming far less of a scourge than in most earlier wars. In addition, the battle dead were accorded comparative respect and honor in World War I: after Waterloo the tens of thousands of corpses left on the battlefield were systematically stripped of valuables, equipment, brass, clothes, and finally of teeth, used at the time for dentures which for years thereafter were known as "Waterloo teeth" (Howarth 1968, 207). And, while regimes toppled in World War I, the political leaders who started the war, unlike Henry V, Frederick the Great, Gustavus Adolphus, or Napoleon, did not have to be concerned about being killed in battle.

World War I is often seen to be unusual because it was so unromantic. As Roland Stromberg observes, "romantic illusions vanished in the grimness of trench warfare and mass slaughter. . . . [This war] was to destroy forever the heroic image of war" (1982, 152; see also Fussell 1975, ch. 1). But if that is so, it is because people were ready to see, and to be repulsed by, the grimness of warfare.[15] Mud, filth, and leeches were not invented in 1914, but are standard accom-

---

[14]To Genghis Khan "the greatest pleasure in life is to defeat your enemies, to chase them before you, to rob them of their wealth, to see those dear to them bathed in tears, to ride their horses, and to clasp to your breast their wives and daughters" (Kellet 1982, 292–293).

[15]Conceivably this receptivity was heightened by the hothouse romanticism, glorifying war, death, annihilation, and destruction for their redemptive and cleansing qualities, that was so fashionable among intellectuals before 1914. For example, in "Peace," a poem written as the war began, Rupert Brooke thanks God for having "matched us with His hour," compares the entry into war "as swimmers into cleanness leaping," and finds "release" in war where "the worst friend and enemy is but Death." (For a superb discussion, see Stromberg 1982.) Because of this phenomenon, it seems possible Europeans were peculiarly ripe for disillusionment. However, romanticism about war goes back to the origins of the institution. And the famous and pathetic demise of the quintessential romantic, Lord Byron, in the Greek war of independence in 1824 seems to have had no lasting impact on war romanticism.

paniments of warfare, and "mass slaughter" is its whole point. Because of improvements in sanitation it is probable that the average soldier in the trenches was
less afflicted by dysentery than was the average knight encased in shining armor;
but this perennial wartime affliction somehow was taken to give evidence of war's
degradation and repulsiveness only in the modern case.

In World War I as in every war before it, men met in swarms and attempted
to annihilate one another with projectiles and by hacking and slashing with sharp
or blunt instruments. Why the 1914 method should somehow be seen to be worse
than earlier is not at all clear. The machine gun was an innovation, but the air of
battle had been filled with showers of deadly lead since firearms had been invented. Tanks and long range artillery (like the long bow before them) may have
made some aspects of battle more "impersonal," but men generally tend to find
killing each other at long range less repugnant than up close—consider the repel-
lant impact of the phrases "hand to hand combat" and "killing in cold blood."
Thus, technological advances could have been taken to be a psychic improvement,
making warfare less crude and dirty, more nearly immaculate. People found gas to
be a repulsive form of warfare, but in fact gas was not a great killer: among
Americans, for example, only 2 percent of those wounded by gas died as compared to 24 percent of those wounded by bullets or shrapnel; for the British the
comparison was gas fatalities, 3 percent and 37 percent from gunfire; for the
Germans it was 3 percent and 43 percent, respectively (Gilchrist 1928, 48; see also
McNaugher 1990). Therefore it would have been entirely possible to embrace gas
as a more humane form of warfare—one allowing battles to be decided with minimal loss of life.[16] And it is far from obvious why a man wearing a gas mask is held
to be foolish, inhuman, and monstrous, but not one whose head is encased in a
knight's helmet.[17] Ugliness, as the poet did not say, lies in the eye of the beholder.

A most instructive comparison can be made with the American Civil War of
1861–65, which is often called the first modern war. There are quite a few similar-
ities between the two wars. Both were triggered by incidents that, in historical
perspective, were quite trivial. Both initially inspired great enthusiasm. And both
came to rely on conscription and degenerated into four years of combat characterized by grindingly inconclusive battles, appalling bloodshed, and rising bitterness.
Thus, in its own terms the American Civil War was as brutal and horrible as World
War I. Yet the experience did not bring about a rejection of war among the
American people—indeed quite soon Americans were romanticizing about war
just like Europeans who had not yet undergone the experience of modern war

---

[16]Some people, in fact, did draw this lesson. H. L. Gilchrist, the U.S. Army's leading expert on the
medical effects of chemical warfare, concluded that gas "is the most humane method of warfare ever
applied on the battlefield" (1928, 47). In 1925, the British defense analyst, Basil Liddell Hart, specu-
lated that "gas may well prove the salvation of civilization from otherwise inevitable collapse in case of
another world war" (Mearsheimer 1988, 90). See also Stockton 1932, 536–539.

[17]Interestingly, in Serge Eisenstein's classic 1938 film, *Alexander Nevsky,* invading Teutonic knights
are made to appear menacing and inhuman precisely because of their helmets.

(Linderman 1987, 266–297; Mueller 1989a, 30–32, 38–39).[18] Clearly, the war's massive destructiveness was not enough, alone, to discredit the time-honored institution. Like previous wars, the Civil War came too early historically to have a lasting impact on war attitudes, even among Americans. The notion that war should be eliminated from the course of human affairs was an idea whose time had yet to come.

2. THE EXISTENCE OF THE PREWAR ANTIWAR MOVEMENT.

While the costs and horrors of World War I may not have been notably unusual in historical perspective, the war seems to have been truly unique in that it was the first in history to have been preceded by substantial antiwar agitation.

Given the general disrepute to which the institution of war has generally sunk in much of the world, it may be surprising to learn that the idea that war is a bad thing is, as a political issue, really only about 100 years old (even as the idea that slavery is a bad thing is only about 200 years old).[19] There have been individual war opponents throughout history, but organized peace groups appeared for the first time only in 1815 and they achieved significant public notice and momentum only by the 1880s or so. For some thirty years before 1914, then, there had been bodies of idea entrepreneurs in European and American politics who were urging that war was repulsive, immoral, uncivilized, and futile (Beales 1931; Hinsley 1963; Chickering 1975, ch. 1; Howard 1978, ch. 2; Mueller 1989a, ch. 1; Cooper 1991).

Constructed on arguments that had been around for centuries and sometimes related to other growing thought patterns of the era, like liberalism and the idea of progress, the antiwar movement of the late nineteenth century was a shifting, and sometimes uncomfortable, coalition of voices calling for the elimination of war. There were the moralists, the Quakers eminently, who found war, like other forms of killing, to be immoral. There were those whose objections were essentially aesthetic: they found the carnage and destruction of war to be disgusting and repulsive. There were those who felt war to be uncivilized, a throwback to a barbaric past that the progressive, cultured sophisticates of nineteenth-century Europe ought now to reject. There were those whose objections were primarily practical: war and conquest, they had come to believe, were futile and counterproductive, particularly from an economic standpoint, and, as an institution of international contest, war ought now to be replaced by trade and the commercial spirit. These war opponents were joined by socialists and others who had concluded that war

---

[18]Paul Fussell argues that World War I was the first literary war (1975, 157). However, as Edmund Wilson points out, much the same could be said about the American Civil War (1962, ix). J. M. Winter observes that the difference was that the World War I writings became "vastly popular," producing such spectacular bestsellers as Erich Maria Remarque's *All Quiet on the Western Front* (also a huge success as a film, as was King Vidor's antiwar *The Big Parade* of 1925 which became the highest grossing silent movie ever). Such literature, Winter argues, "emphatically and repeatedly touched a chord in public taste and popular memory" (1989, 826). That is, the war was not new because it affected the writers, but because it touched the postwar readers.

[19]In a recent book, for example, Terrence Cook assumes that war aversion has always been the dominant view: "With possible exceptions such as Genghis Khan, Hitler, or the Marquis de Sade, few have defended wars between peoples . . . as if good in themselves" (1991, 4).

was essentially a mechanism through which the capitalist class carried out its disputes, using the working classes as cannon fodder. Among their activities, the various elements of the antiwar movement were devoted to exploring alternatives to war such as arbitration and international law and organization, and to developing mechanisms, like disarmament, that might reduce its frequency or consequences. These people were quite similar to the "transnational moral entrepreneurs," identified by Ethan Nadelmann, who had previously successfully campaigned against piracy, privateering, and slavery, and who today rail against the international drug trade, pollution, and the killing of whales and elephants (1990). They were also similar to those entrepreneurs Neta Crawford (1993) identifies (indeed, they were often the same people) who have successfully worked in the last century to promote decolonization as an international norm for the first time in human history.

The antiwar movement was growing substantially at the turn of the century, but it was still very much a minority movement. Its voice was largely drowned out by those who still held war to be a method for resolving international disputes that was natural, inevitable, honorable, thrilling, manly, invigorating, necessary, and often progressive, glorious, and desirable (see Mueller 1989a, ch. 2).

But while the antiwar people were often ridiculed, their gadfly arguments were persistent and unavoidable, and the existence of the movement probably helped Europeans and Americans to look at the institution of war in a new way when the massive conflict of 1914–18 entered their experience. World War I served, therefore, essentially as a catalyst. It was not the first horrible war in history, but because of the exertions of the prewar antiwar movement it was the first in which people were widely capable of recognizing and being thoroughly repulsed by those horrors and in which they were substantially aware that viable alternatives existed.

3. THE PECULIARITY OF THE 1815–1914 EXPERIENCE. Another unique aspect of World War I derives from its historical setting: for Europeans, the war followed a century characterized by peace and by wars that had proved to be small and manageable. Between 1815 and 1854 there was an era of near-total peace within Europe, something that was utterly unprecedented in its history. There were several significant wars in Europe between 1854 and 1871, but these were all short and, in their own terms, efficient—goals were accomplished at costs that were quite small by most historical standards. Then, from 1871 until 1914 Europe lapsed into another period of near-total peace that was even longer than the first (although it was marred by small wars on the fringes of Europe, by colonial wars, and by a distant Great Power war between Russia and Japan in 1904). The uniqueness of these peaceful periods in French and British history is indicated by the data in Table 9.1.

Before 1815 there were no prolonged periods of peace on the continent, and for the most part war was a regular, expected part of the rhythm of events. As Luard observes, the two long stretches in the nineteenth century in which all major European countries "were at peace with each other, both in Europe and outside, despite many disputes and much competition for territory," represent "a dramatic change from the pattern of war in the preceding age, when major powers

TABLE 9.1

Soldiers killed or wounded in battle,
as a percentage of the population, by decades, 1630–1919

Decade	France	Great Britain
1630–39	0.09	—
1640–49	0.32	0.45
1650–59	0.05	0.70
1660–69	0.01	0.16
1670–79	0.21	0.13
1680–89	0.01	—
1690–99	0.31	0.35
1700–09	0.58	0.58
1710–19	0.26	0.12
1720–29	—	—
1730–39	0.10	—
1740–49	0.36	0.33
1750–59	0.14	0.17
1760–69	0.07	0.06
1770–79	0.01	0.05
1780–89	0.03	0.09
1790–99	1.48	0.23
1800–09	1.19	0.13
1810–19	1.54	0.37
1820–29	°	°
1830–39	—	—
1840–49	—	°
1850–59	0.13	0.10
1860–69	—	—
1870–79	0.43	—
1880–89	—	—
1890–99	—	0.01
1900–09	—	0.01
1910–19	5.63	2.61

°0.001 or less

Source: Wright 1942, 658, 660.

were in recurrent warfare against each other" (1986, 58–59). Partly because of this remarkable new phenomenon, economic and demographic growth in Europe exploded.[20]

---

[20]Between 1700 and 1800 the population of Europe had increased by 50 per cent; between 1800 and 1900, it increased 117 percent (McEvedy and Jones 1978, 18). In the 120 years between 1700 and 1820 the real gross domestic product per capita of Britain increased 52 percent; in the 93 years from 1820 to 1913, it rose 229 percent. For France the comparable figures were 37 per cent and 213 percent (Maddison 1983, 30). In the 80 years from 1750 to 1830 the real gross national product per capita for developed countries rose 30 per cent; in the 83 years between 1830 and 1913, it grew 179 percent (Bairoch 1981, 7). In 1850, 10 countries had adult illiteracy rates of less than 30 percent; in 1913, 17 had adult illiteracy rates of less than 10 per cent. In the 60 years between 1780 and 1840 world trade increased 245 percent; in the 60 years between 1840 and 1900 it increased 1241 percent (Hobsbawm 1987, 345, 349).

These developments were used by members of the antiwar movement to argue that peace was a blessed condition and that war was a barbarism that people in civilized Europe ought now to put behind them. But the warlessness and the economic and social progress of nineteenth-century Europe did not by themselves lead to a broad rejection of war. As noted, most people still found war to be thrilling and many argued that it was progressive and desirable, a point of view that if anything became *more* popular and trendy at the end of the century.[21] Nonetheless, the inhabitants of nineteenth-century Europe, perhaps without fully noticing, enjoyed the benefits of peace even as they continued to assume war to be a normal fact of life and even as most continued to thrill at the thought of it. Accordingly when they plunged into the cataclysm of World War I the experience came as a special shock.

Moreover, the peculiarities of the 1815–1914 period even seem to have affected many war advocates who had come to operate under the assumption that war would be not only heroic and decisive, but also minimally inconvenient. Quintessential war glorifiers like Heinrich von Treitschke idealized war in considerable part because they believed "wars will become rarer and shorter, but at the same time far more sanguinary" (1916, vol. 2, 443).[22] In their experience, long, continent-wide conflicts like the Napoleonic Wars or the Seven Years War were a thing of the past. All the midcentury wars in Europe had been brief and, as noted earlier, this was new. War advocates deftly ignored the contemporary long wars in other parts of the world—including the American Civil War which one German general dismissed as "armed mobs chasing each other around the country, from whom nothing can be learned" (Mueller 1989a, 48). And they assumed that a war in Europe would be "brisk and merry," as one German diplomat put it in 1914 (Lebow 1981, 251).

Thus, although there were a few war advocates who even welcomed the prospect of a long war,[23] much of the prewar enthusiasm for war was based on the assumption that any future war would be brief and bearable.[24] As Sigmund Freud reflected in a 1915 essay, "We pictured it [war] as a chivalrous passage of arms, which would limit itself to establishing the superiority of one side in the struggle, while as far as possible avoiding acute suffering that could contribute nothing to the decision." While they disagreed with war opponents about the value of war,

---

[21]See note 15 and Mueller 1989a, 38–46.

[22]In England, the Reverend Father H. I. D. Ryder was observing that war "is calculated to evoke some of the best qualities of human nature, giving the spirit a predominance over the flesh." And he reminded his readers that "under the touch of civilisation war has lost some of its most offensive features." In particular, he felt, noncombatants could now be regarded "as henceforth excluded from the casualties of civilised warfare" (1899, 726–727).

[23]The German general, Friedrich von Bernhardi thought that another seven years war "will unify and elevate the people and destroy the diseases which threaten the national health" (1914, 233). Some other Germans agreed: see Chickering 1975, 390–391.

[24]On the short war illusion, see Mueller 1989a, 46–51; Farrar 1973; Snyder 1984; Van Evera 1984, 58–107. Stanley Engerman suggests a sort of parallel in the history of boxing where rule changes have fended off the moralists and kept the sport alive by introducing rounds, shortening the duration of matches, and creating the technical knockout.

most war enthusiasts would agree that a long war of attrition was singularly undesirable. When a war of that sort eventually materialized, the premise upon which their romanticism rested was shattered. The war brought "disillusionment," observed Freud. "Not only is it more bloody and more destructive than any war of other days . . . ; it is at least as cruel, as embittered, as implacable as any that preceded it. . . . Moreover, it has brought to light an almost incredible phenomenon: the civilized nations know and understand one another so little that one can turn against the other with hate and loathing" (1957, vol. 14, 278–279).

In this regard, one other consideration might be mentioned. Kaeuper has observed that war became "an essential and characteristic function of medieval states" not only because the medieval chivalric code glorified "war as the greatest test and expression of manhood," but also because war was seen to be economically profitable: "making a profit, and looking forward to it eagerly, was entirely compatible with the chivalric ethos; only post-Medieval adaptations of the ideas of chivalry have considered profit-making a strain and debasement of pure ideals" (1988, 11–14). It is not particularly clear when this change took place, but the nineteenth-century historian, H. T. Buckle, gives much of the credit for initiating it to Adam Smith's *Wealth of Nations* of 1776, which Buckle calls "probably the most important book that has ever been written." The book helped to undermine the "warlike spirit," Buckle suggests, because it convincingly demonstrated that the best path to prosperity was in the free trade of commodities, not, as previously supposed, in the accumulation of gold which tended to be played, to use jargon not then in vogue, as a zero sum game (1862, 151–158).

Whatever the process, the notion that war could be economically profitable had been substantially undermined by the late nineteenth century (Mueller 1989a, 28). War advocate von Treitschke, in fact, was disgusted by the notion that something as sublime as a war should be fought for mere "material advantage." "Modern wars," he urged, "are not fought for the sake of booty" (1916, vol. 1, 15). Homer Lea, an American military analyst, determined that commercialism was a "debased" form of strife because it lacks "honor or heroism" (1909, 45).

Accordingly where earlier war enthusiasts had celebrated war both for its nobility *and* for its profitability, those in 1914 restricted themselves primarily to its nobility alone.[25] To that degree, war enthusiasm had already been undermined when the war came about, and it was therefore easier to shatter.

4. PREMONITIONS OF APOCALYPSE. Finally, it is possible that World War I is unique because it raised the specter that through some combination of aerial bombardment and gas or bacteriological poisoning the next

---

[25]In 1910 William James concluded that war "in ancient times" was "profitable, as well as the most exciting, way of living," while "modern war is so expensive that we feel trade to be a better avenue to plunder." War persists, he felt, not for economic reasons but because "modern man inherits all the innate pugnacity and all the love of glory of his ancestors. . . . Without any exception known to me, militarist authors take a highly mystical view of their subject" (1911, 268–269, 277). On James, see also Chapter 8.

large war could lead to world annihilation—the destruction of winner and loser alike.

This view was rather widely held after the war. In 1925 Winston Churchill observed that war was now "the potential destroyer of the human race. . . . Mankind has never been in this position before. Without having improved appreciably in virtue or enjoying wiser guidance, it has got into its own hands for the first time the tools by which it can unfailingly accomplish its own extermination" (1932, 248). And Freud concludes his 1930 book, *Civilization and Its Discontents,* by declaring, "Men have brought their powers of subduing nature to such a pitch that by using them they could now very easily exterminate one another to the last man" (1930, 144).

As these statements suggest, it was largely the impressive achievements of science that were inspiring these apocalyptic visions, and it is true, of course, that during the war science had fabricated effective new methods for killing large numbers of people. With the development of long range artillery and particularly the bomber, it was reasonable to anticipate that these methods of slaughter might well be visited directly upon the civilian population in the next great war. And in fact, of course, they were—though not to the point of extermination.

There are at least two reasons for discounting this phenomenon as an important cause of the shift of opinion on war, however. First, as indicated earlier, wars of annihilation and wars in which civilians were slaughtered were hardly new: history is filled with examples. The fact that annihilation could now be *mutual* was new perhaps, but this distinction may be a bit delicate. In eras in which wars of annihilation were common, the fact that winner and loser were not simultaneously destroyed was more a matter of sequencing than anything else. Side A might annihilate B, but unless A could then dominate all others it stood a significant risk that in the next war with side C it would itself be annihilated. A war syndrome with stakes like that had not led to substantial efforts to abolish war in the past.

Second, it seems likely that this phenomenon was more a result of antiwar feeling than its cause: that is, people opposed to war in a sense *wanted* to believe it would be cataclysmic in the desperate hope that this would make it less likely to occur. This is suggested by the timing of the apocalyptic literature: for the most part this came late, in the 1930s, when the danger of another war was growing, not in the 1920s as a direct result of World War I.

Among the fiction of the era, a few stories and novels depicting the next war as a worldwide cataclysm did appear shortly after World War I. But, as I. F. Clarke notes in his study of the fiction of the era, "it is noteworthy that the large-scale production of tales of the future did not begin until 1931." And his observation that "the authors all described war in order to teach peace" seems especially apt (1966, 169–170). It was less that the anticipated horrors of the next Great War created the yearning for peace than that the yearning for peace caused people to anticipate that the next war would be cataclysmic.

A similar pattern is found in the official discussions in Britain about the future danger of aerial bombardment. As early as 1917 the Cabinet was informed that "the day may not be far off when aerial operations with their devastation of enemy towns and destruction of industrial and populous centres on a vast scale may become the *principal* operation of war" (Bialer 1980, 1–2). But this fear seems to have become general only in the 1930s when another war began to loom as a distinct possibility (and when, of course, the airplane had been developed much more fully). It was, as one military analyst put it at the time, "a brain child born in the early years of the century and turned into a Frankenstein in the early 1930s" (Bialer 1980, 12, also 2).[26]

THE MECHANISMS OF ATTITUDE CHANGE

Before World War I, the idea that war ought to be abolished had received considerable notice, but it appears that this idea was boosted to ascendance by the end of the war largely because of two key phenomena relating to the victors: (1) permanent peace became a central British war aim from the start of the war, and (2) the promise of a war to end war became important to entice the Americans into the conflict. The groundwork for this had been laid by the prewar peace movement.

PEACE AS A BRITISH WAR AIM.   Most of the belligerents—France, Russia, Germany, Austria-Hungary—were fighting for motives that were rather old-fashioned and easily understood: they were locked into mortal combat over issues of turf and continental hegemony. The British, on the other hand, were fighting for more ephemeral reasons to a substantial degree. Although such tangible issues as their naval arms race with Germany and strategic calculations about comparative military relationships on the continent were hardly irrelevant, their entrance into the war was triggered when Germany brutally invaded neutral Belgium and Luxembourg, and it was this circumstance, more than any other, that impelled the remarkable outcry in Britain against Germany as the war broke out in August 1914. As David Lloyd George recalls, the war "leapt into popularity" with "the threatened invasion of Belgium" which "set the nation on fire from sea to sea" (1933, 65–66).[27] Thus, Britain was fighting in part for a rather pacifistic principle: small countries which wish to avoid being engulfed by conflicts among larger countries, and in fact wish to drop out of the war system entirely, should be allowed to do so.

As early as the second month of the war, Britian's Liberal Prime Minister, H. H. Asquith, was not only making this clear (the smaller countries "must be recognized as having exactly as good a title as their more powerful neighbors . . . to a place in the sun"), but he was also broadening the principle, calling for "the definite repudiation of militarism as the governing factor in the relations of states and in the future molding of the European world" and for "the substitution for

---

[26]It is also noteworthy in this regard that those few in Europe who still wanted war—Adolf Hitler in particular—correctly assumed that the doomsday theorists were wrong (Bialer 1980, 133–134). For nonapocalyptic visions in the 1930s of a future war, see Stockton 1932, 501–549; and Dupuy and Eliot 1937.

[27]For the impact of the invasion of Belgium in turning pacifist and neutralist factions in Britain into war supporters, see Robbins 1976, 30–32.

force . . . of a real European partnership based on the recognition of equal rights and established and enforced by a common will" (Rappard 1940, 20).[28] This is impressive because, although Britain had been a hotbed of antiwar agitation before 1914, Asquith had not been in those ranks—although he had supported, somewhat self-servingly, efforts to dampen the costly prewar international arms competition (Robbins 1976, 11). Accordingly, in his 1914 speech he appears to be rather startled to hear himself suddenly making noises similar to those made by the most idealistic members of the antiwar movement: "A year ago," he observed, his proposals "would have sounded like a Utopian idea." But, he argued, "if and when this war is decided in favor of the allies it will at once come within the range and before long the grasp of European statesmanship" (Rappard 1940, 20).[29] Thus, for the British at least, peace early on became a war aim—not merely victorious peace but, if at all possible, perpetual, permanent, enforced peace.

THE AMERICANS.   The United States also played an important role in the growth of this idea. In an illuminating study of this process published in 1940, the Swiss political scientist William Rappard observes (with flourish) that, while the "seed" of the idea may largely have been developed in Britain, it "fructified in America, where it was transplanted with assiduous care by British gardeners and whence it was later carried back to Europe in countless specimens upon the wings of President Wilson's eloquence" (1940, 21).

From the beginning the British took a considerable interest in American opinion on the war, and of course they were fully aware that American military participation on their side could help substantially to achieve victory. As David Lloyd George, who became Prime Minister in 1916, frankly recalled later, "Allied statesmen were all conscious of the fact that a time would come when America could intervene with irresistible effect." Accordingly "peace aims were framed in such a way as to convince America, and especially the pacific and anti-Imperialist American President, that their objectives were fundamentally just" (1938, 22; see also Rappard 1940, 46–47; Herman 1969, 195).

During his tenure in office, that President, Woodrow Wilson, twice ordered American troops into Mexico and rather half-heartedly even sent some to Russia during the civil war that followed the 1917 revolution there. Accordingly it would certainly not be accurate to characterize him as the purest of pacifists. Nonetheless, as the British were well aware, his inclinations were strongly in that direction: his "distaste for war," observes Russell Weigley, was "so acute that it verged on pacifism" (1976, 62). As Arno Mayer has put it, Wilson "had a pro-

---

[28]For a similar statement by the Labour Party on October 14, see Mayer 1959, 143.

[29]Before the year was out H. G. Wells, also no particular friend of the prewar peace movement, had penned a book on the issue of war aims in which he apparently created the slogan later to be recalled with such bitterness and irony: "The War That Will End War." The immediate cause of the war, Wells observed, was the invasion of Luxembourg and Belgium, but the war had quickly become not one of "nations but of mankind" and its object should be to "exorcise a world-madness and end an age." It was, he urged, "a war for peace" (1914, 9, 12, 14).

nounced horror of war" (1959, 347). Alexander and Juliette George discuss his "antipathy to violence" (1956, 173).[30]

To play on Wilson's proclivities and to entice him into the war on their side, the British emphasized arguments to which they were naturally inclined anyway and which, further, were sensible for maintaining the morale of their own troops. First, they stressed the attractive nobility of their cause: as Asquith put it in 1917, they were "waging, not only a war for peace, but a war against war" (Rappard 1940, 46). Second, to portray the Germans as the bad guys, they exaggerated stories about atrocities committed by German soldiers against Belgian civilians, and they embellished the fiendishness of chemical warfare which had been introduced into combat by the Germans in 1915—for example, for dramatic effect they quintupled their gas casualty figures from the first German attack (Brown 1968, 14). As part of this creative act of international libel, they condemned the Germans from the start for their addiction to "militarism." A result of this was to further associate militarism with badness.[31]

Gradually, Wilson and the American people came around. There were many reasons for the American entry into the war, but high among them, as Arthur Link stresses, was Wilson's desire that the "United States fulfill its mission to insure a just and lasting peace of reconciliation" (1957, 88–89).

WAS WILSON NECESSARY?   At the end of the war in 1918 President Wilson was quite probably the most famous, the most influential, and the most revered man in the world. Although this aura dissipated in the acrimony of the peace talks and as the U.S. Senate refused to ratify his cherished League of Nations treaty, Wilson, more than anyone else, had established perpetual peace as a primary goal for the international system.

But it does not seem that the idea that war ought to be abolished in the "civilized" world required Wilson to be its entrepreneur. It was already common currency by 1914 and had plenty of supporters in Britain and France—and, for that

---

[30]Wilson had long been an enthusiastic supporter of such devices promoted by the antiwar movement as arbitration and free trade, he had joined the American Peace Society in 1908, had addressed the Universal Peace Union in 1912, and had appointed a man strongly hostile to war, William Jennings Bryan, as his first secretary of state. He was no tool of the antiwar movement, but much of his idealistic thinking about foreign affairs was consonant with its point of view (Patterson 1976, 205-209; see also Herman 1969, ch. 7). A desire to make his mark in world history was also not entirely absent from his motives: as one of his principal advisors, Colonel Edward M. House, wrote strokingly to him in 1918, "The sentiment is growing rapidly everywhere in favor of some organized opposition to war and I think it essential that you should guide the movement. . . . It is one of the things with which your name should be linked during the ages" (Rappard 1940, 33; see also George and George 1956, chs. 9–11). Wilson's famous desire to "make the world safe for democracy" was in large part a pacifist motivation. He and many others in Britain, France, and the United States had become convinced that, as Lloyd George put it later, "Freedom is the only warranty of Peace" (Rappard 1940, 42–44).

[31]See Hofstadter 1959, 196–198. For an official American depiction of the connection, see Notestein and Stoll 1917. For a discussion of the destruction of Prussian militarism as an important British war aim, see Gooch 1981, ch. 7. On the effectiveness of British propaganda, see Squires 1935.

matter, in Germany and Austria.[32] And, as noted earlier, the idea was quickly embraced and promulgated by prominent British decision makers and intellectuals as
soon as the war broke out.

In the United States peace societies had, as Charles Chatfield observes, "acquired unprecedented strength and reputation" in the decade before the war
(1971, 8; see also Patterson 1976, ch. 7; Kuehl 1969, 172). When war erupted, the
American groups grew enormously in number and activity, and their ranks soon
included not only prominent members of Wilson's own Democratic party, but also
hard-nosed leading Republicans, like Theodore Roosevelt and William Howard
Taft—the two men who had split their party's vote in 1912, allowing Wilson to win
the presidency (Chatfield 1971, 15–87). Even if someone else had been President,
the idea that this ought to be the last war would in all probability have been
American policy—as it was British policy.

Wilson may deserve credit for some of the special characteristics of the
League of Nations and of the peace settlement, and the impact (however short-
lived) of his eloquence and international stature should not be underestimated.
But the basic idea of constructing an international organization to enhance the
prospects for peace had been around for centuries and had been actively promoted (especially in the United States) for decades (see Patterson 1976, ch. 6).
After the war began the idea was urged in the United States by many prominent
politicians and intellectuals well before Wilson got on board.[33]

Furthermore almost any American president would have enjoyed an especially influential place at the peace table. In fact it could be argued that a more
pragmatic and less Messianic politician might have been more effective than
Wilson, whose unwillingness to compromise with the Senate substantially caused
the failure of the League treaty in the United States.[34]

WAS WORLD WAR I NECESSARY?   It is tempting to push this line of
reasoning one step farther. If Wilson was not clearly necessary to bring about the
idea that war ought to be abolished as a way of doing business in the developed
world, was the Great War itself necessary?

A strong case could be made that the idea was rapidly growing before the war
and that it would soon have caught on generally anyway. As noted, the peace idea
had begun to take off late in the nineteenth century, and it really gained ground
after 1900. Peace societies were proliferating, famous businessmen like Alfred
Nobel and Andrew Carnegie were joining the fray, various international peace
congresses were being held and governments were beginning to take notice and
to participate, political Liberals and feminist leaders were accepting war opposi-

---

[32]On the German and Austrian prewar peace movement, see Wank 1988; Chickering 1975; Chickering
1988.

[33]In 1915 Norman Angell observed that any talk of five minutes with an American pacifist would find
him drawing "from his pocket a complete scheme for the federation of the world" (Kuehl 1969, 239).
Ray Stannard Baker concludes that "practically nothing—not a single idea—in the Covenant of the
League was original with the President" (cited in George and George 1956, 210).

[34]On this point, see George and George 1956, ch. 15. For discussion, see Kuehl 1969, ch. 14.

tion as part of their intellectual baggage, and many Socialists were making it central to their ideology and had agitated impressively and effectively against the Italo-Turkish war of 1911–12 and the Balkan wars of 1912–13, helping to prevent escalation of those conflicts (see Wank 1988, 48–52).[35]

Because of developments like these, peace advocates were beginning to sense progress and to feel a not entirely unjustified sense of optimism. As the distinguished British historian, G. P. Gooch, concluded in 1911, "We can now look forward with something like confidence to the time when war between civilized nations will be considered as antiquated as the duel" (1911, 248–249).

World War I, of course, shattered the optimism of the peace advocates even as it gave them new credibility and caused them to redouble their efforts. But even in retrospect some of its members remember the prewar era with satisfaction and one of them, Norman Angell, whose famous antiwar book, *The Great Illusion,* became a colossal international bestseller after 1909, argues in his memoirs that if the war could have been delayed a few years, "Western Europe might have acquired a mood" which would have enabled it to "avoid the war" (1951, 178).

In the long run it is possible that Angell might be right: the antiwar movement may have been in the process of gathering an unstoppable momentum like the antislavery movement during the century earlier. Ultimately, however, it seems likely that for their idea to carry the day it was necessary, first, for war to discredit itself: the Great War, or something like it, may have been required for the antiwar impetus to become accepted.

The central problem was that before 1914 the institution of war still carried with it much of the glamour and the sense of inevitability it had acquired over the millennia. Despite the remarkable and unprecedented century of semi-peace in Europe, war still appealed not only to wooly militarists, but, as noted earlier, also to popular opinion and to romantic intellectuals as something that was sometimes desirable and ennobling, often useful and progressive, and always thrilling.[36] The antiwar movement was assiduously seeking to undermine those perceptions, and was making real progress at doing so. But before 1914 the movement was still being discredited as a flaky fringe: Angell recalls that friends advised him to "avoid that stuff or you will be classed with cranks and faddists, with devotees of Higher Thought who go about in sandals and long beards, live on nuts" and that men who advocated peace were apt to be suspected of lacking "manliness, virility" (1951, 146–147, 159–160). "War continues to exist," wrote Bertha von Suttner, another famous and bestselling peace advocate, in 1912, "not because there is evil in the

---

[35]The National Arbitration and Peace Conference which packed Carnegie Hall in New York in 1907 was supported by 8 cabinet officers, 2 former presidential candidates, 10 Senators, 4 Supreme Court justices, 9 governors, 10 mayors, 27 millionaires, 18 college presidents, 30 labor leaders, 40 bishops, 60 newspaper editors, and representatives of 166 businesses (Patterson 1976, 129).

[36]The war, of course, substantially disillusioned the nineteenth-century Meliorists who held that Europe was becoming progressively more civilized; but that was nothing compared to what it did to those who held that *war* was progressive. On the shattering of the Meliorist myth, see Fussell 1957, 8. Fussell also argues that the war "reversed the Idea of Progress." In his classic, *The Idea of Progress* (1920), J. B. Bury suggests that the idea continued to develop after the war.

world, but because people still hold war to be a good thing" (cited in Chickering 1975, 91). Or as William James, the author of the famous tract, "The Moral Equivalent of War," pointed out in 1904, "The plain truth is that people *want* war" (1911, 304).

PROMOTING WAR AVERSION

As this analysis suggests, for the last hundred years or so, a lot of people have been trying to promote the notion that war is a bad idea—very much in the way people like them had, a century earlier, tried to promote the notion that slavery ought to be abolished. There have been several components to their strategy.

First, idea entrepreneurs needed to undermine the competition, to seize upon and to bring out its defects. Antiwar agitation stressed the vulgarity, futility, brutality, and repulsiveness of warfare, and ridiculed its claims of nobility and grandeur.

Second, war's opponents sought to create demand for values which, if embraced, would rather automatically help their product to be accepted—in much the way that promoters of diet pills or corsets are aided if people generally come to embrace the belief that being thin is desirable or that promoters of nuclear power are aided by the clean air movement. For example, war opponents stressed that prosperity and economic growth are extremely important. This argument would not do well with people who think war brings wealth, but, as noted above, by the end of the nineteenth century few people thought that it did: by that time war advocates were stressing the exhilarating qualities of war, not its economic benefits. Thus if a promoter could get across the idea that material wealth is a high good, the cause of peace would be advanced.

Third, the product—peace—was effectively demonstrated to be viable and attractive. Once Europe had lived without large-scale war for a substantial period of time in the nineteenth century, it became clear to many that one could live quite well without the bracing benefits of war.

Finally, there is the matter of luck and timing. Good promoters always stand ready to use fortuitous events and circumstances to advance their product, and successful promotion is often less a matter of artful manipulation than a matter of cashing in on the tides of history or of being in the right place at the right time: one must be there when opportunity knocks, and one must be prepared to lurch into action while the sound of the knock is still reverberating. Thus, although antiwar advocates were able to show as time went by that peace is markedly superior in several important respects to the competition, this was not enough to assure success: they apparently needed a cataclysmic event—World War I—to help in their persuasive efforts.

In brief, the process by which attitudes toward war changed at the time of World War I seems to have been as follows. In the decades before 1914 antiwar entrepreneurs were preparing international thought to be receptive to their notions, and they were assiduously developing the blueprints for institutions that might be viable substitutes for war should the desire for such plans become general. Furthermore, in the century before 1914 Europeans gradually became, perhaps without quite noticing it, accustomed to the benefits of peace.[37] Nevertheless, the traditional appeals of war persisted. For the abolition of war to become an accepted commodity, it was probably necessary for there to be one more vivid example of how appalling the hoary, time-honored institution really was. World War I may not have been all that much worse than some earlier wars, but it destroyed the comforting notion that wars in Europe would necessarily be long on dashing derring-do and short on bloodshed, and it reminded Europeans of how bad wars on their continent could become. Thanks to the prewar fulminations of the peace movement and thanks to the experience with an unprecedented century of comparative warlessness, people in the developed world were at last ready to begin to accept the message.

As suggested earlier, the approach used here also suggests that the demise of an institution need not be permanent. If war is merely an idea and makes use of natural proclivities, it can never be made impossible (see Chapter 8). Therefore, even if a succession of inventive entrepreneurs are able to push it into apparent extinction, another set might be able to revive the idea with the right kind of dedicated promotional strategy. Nonetheless, institutions do become obsolete. Slavery seems quite dead (although if Hitler had triumphed, he might have revived it in some form). So do dueling, eunuchism, human sacrifice, and the bustle. And it seems that ancient and once ubiquitous institutions like monarchy, colonialism, and perhaps even religion are in the process of dying out. I think war is probably destined eventually to join this list, but while the approach used here supplies an explanation for the process, it furnishes no guarantee that the process will be permanently successful.

---

[37]The experience of the peaceful nineteenth century in Europe suggests that, while trade and interdependence may not lead inexorably to peace, peace leads to, or at any rate facilitates, trade and economic growth. That is, peace ought to be seen not as a dependent, but rather as an independent, variable in such considerations. Thus the growing economic unity of Europe and the building of a long-envisioned channel tunnel are the consequences of peace, not its cause.

The Historical Movement of Ideas: The Rise of Democracy

Despite several major setbacks and despite severe, dedicated competition, democracy has gradually grown in acceptance over the last 200 years until it presently dominates the developed world and seems on a clear upswing in most other areas as well—it has been in especially rapid rise since 1975. Most amazing of all, of course, was the way a set of countries at the time of the quiet cataclysm—first in eastern Europe and then in the disintegrating Soviet Union—quickly, almost casually, and with little or no notable or formal preparation, moved from authoritarianism to (or toward) democracy.

In many respects, the growth of democracy is quite surprising because, as an idea abstracted from practice, democracy once seemed quite absurd and dangerous to objective evaluators—and quite understandably so. If one looks at what many theoretical formulators have had to say, it would appear that democracy would bring about a vast leveling and require that government be run by demagogues and the incompetent.

At the start, therefore, democracy was mostly something one read about in books, particularly ones that dealt with the tiny city-states of ancient Greece. The notion that such a system for governance should or could be established in large, diverse countries seemed quite preposterous to those who troubled to think about it at all. As Robert Dahl has put it, "Most people took it as a matter of self-evident good sense that the idea of applying the democratic process to the government of the nation-state was foolish and unrealistic" (1989, 328).

The success of the idea of democracy, then, was by no means predestined or inevitable. As with the rise in acceptance of war aversion, people had to be persuaded to accept the idea of democracy. A great help in this process came when democracy actually began to be put into practice: it proved to be not nearly as terrible as most people had anticipated. It actually worked rather well, it did not require an absurd leveling, it mostly eschewed demagogues, and in general it managed, somehow, to select leaders that were often rather capable.

In this chapter I make three arguments about democracy in an effort to help explain its remarkable growth—and its often rather easy acceptance, particularly lately. I argue, first, that democracy is really a simple idea, that it can come into existence quite naturally, and that even elections are not necessary for it to take effect. Second, I hold that democracy has been able to become established and accepted in part because, despite the assertions of many of its advocates, in practice it has very little to do with political equality—indeed, effectively it relies on, and celebrates, political inequality. And, third, I suggest that one of democracy's great strengths is that it does not demand much of people and that it can function quite well with the minimal human being.

The chapter then outlines a mechanism that seeks to explain how the idea of democracy came to be accepted. As with the rise in the acceptance of war aversion discussed in the previous chapter, the most satisfactory explanation for democracy's rise, it seems to me, stresses the promotional efforts of idea entrepreneurs, not objective changes in social or economic phenomena. The chapter concludes with the suggestion that the oft-noted connection between democracy and war aversion may be substantially spurious.

DEMOCRACY, RESPONSIVE GOVERNMENT, AND ELECTIONS

The crucial element in most definitions of democracy is that the government be responsive—that it be, in Abraham Lincoln's classic phrase, "government of the people, by the people, for the people." Thus Robert Dahl says, "I assume that a key characteristic of a democracy is the continued responsiveness of the government to the preferences of its citizens, considered as political equals" (1971, 1), and William Riker concludes that "democracy is a form of government in which the rulers are fully responsible to the ruled in order to realize self-respect for everybody" (1965, 31). Or in H. L. Mencken's irreverent words, democracy is "the theory that the common people know what they want, and deserve to get it good and hard" (1920b, 203). Authoritarian governments can sometimes be responsive as well. But their responsiveness depends on the will and the mindset of the leadership. By contrast, democracy is *routinely, necessarily* responsive: because people are free to develop and use peaceful methods to criticize, pressure, and replace the leadership, the leaders must pay attention.[1]

Most discussions of democracy, including Dahl's and Riker's, emphasize elections as a device to make this responsiveness happen—indeed, Riker argues that "the essential democratic institution is the ballot box and all that goes with it" (1965, 25). Some, like Samuel Huntington, assert elections into their very definition of democracy.[2] But it really does seem that if citizens have the right to complain, to petition, to organize, to protest, to demonstrate, to strike, to threaten to emigrate, to shout, to publish, to express a lack of confidence, to bribe, and to wheedle in back corridors, government will tend to respond to the sounds of the shouters and the importunings of the wheedlers: that is, it will necessarily become responsive whether there are elections or not.

Essentially, *democracy—government that is necessarily and routinely responsive—takes effect when people agree not to use violence to overthrow the government and when the government leaves them free to criticize, to pressure, and to try to replace it by any other means.* And there are, in fact, plenty of nonviolent methods for removing officeholders besides elections. Governments often topple or are effectively threatened by scandal, legal challenge, street protest, embarrassment, bribery, economic boycott or slowdown, threats to emigrate, and loss of confidence.

The addition of elections to this panoply of devices may sometimes change policy outcomes, and it probably makes the enterprise more efficient because elections furnish a specific, clearly visible, and direct method for replacing officeholders. Elections—fair and free ones, at any rate—also make the process more just, at least by some standards, because they extend participation to those who only care enough about what is going on to bother to go to the polls every few years to pull a few levers or make a few X's (though the weight of an individual's vote on policymaking is so small that the act of voting is scarcely a rational use of

---

[1]In my view, the formal and informal institutional mechanisms used to facilitate this core relationship are secondary and vary from democracy to democracy—though this does not mean that all institutions are equally fair or efficient. Others may wish to add other considerations to this core definition, embellishing it with concerns about ethos, way of life, social culture, shared goals, economic correlates, common purposes, customs, preferred policy outcomes, norms, patriotism, shared traditions, and the like (see Lienesch 1992). I think these issues are interesting, but they do not seem to me to be as essential to the functioning of democracy. (For a similar approach, see for example Linz 1978, 5–6.) This is suggested, I think, by the remarkable ease with which traditional nondemocracies (indeed, antidemocracies) like Portugal and Paraguay have latched onto democracy in recent years: they just did it, without, it appears, very much in the way of cultural or psychic preparation, a phenomenon that is discussed more fully below.

[2]Following what he calls "Schumpeterian tradition," Huntington (1991b, 7) defines "a twentieth-century political system as democratic to the extent that its most powerful collective decision-makers are selected through fair, honest, and periodic elections in which candidates freely compete for votes and in which virtually all the adult population is eligible to vote." (At other places (1991b, 16), however, he uses as a democratic criterion the requirement that 50 percent of adult males be eligible to vote.) As discussed more fully below, this definition, with its entangling obsession with elections and mass suffrage, is very demanding and would exclude everything known as a democracy before the twentieth century, as he suggests, as well as very many putative democracies during it.

one's time), and because they give a bit of potential clout to those who do not vote but could if sufficiently riled or inspired.

But most of what democratic governments actually do on a day by day basis is the result of pressure and petition—lobbying, it's called—not of elections whose policy message is almost always ambiguous and often utterly undecipherable.[3] Petitioners can sometimes use the threat of elections, implied or otherwise, to influence officeholders. And in some democracies contributions toward campaign expenses can help petitioners to facilitate access or to affect policy—a phenomenon that many see as a perversion. But the essential interaction between government and citizenry would take place without elections if the right of petition is viable and if people have the right to organize and to devise methods to pressure officials.

In fact, there are many cases where people excluded from participation in elections have nevertheless profoundly affected policy if they had the right to petition and protest. The nineteenth-century feminist movement, for example, achieved many of its goals—including eventually votes for women—even though the vast majority of its members were excluded from the electorate. Similarly, people between the ages of 18 and 21 were active and successful in a movement to get the voting age lowered in the United States. As these experiences demonstrate, it is absurd to suggest that people who are not allowed to vote can have no impact on public policy.

Moreover, there exist cases of what might be called democracies without elections: Mexico and Hong Kong. People go to the polls in Mexico, of course, but the ruling party carefully counts the ballots and for decades, curiously enough, never lost an election. In Hong Kong, the government is appointed from afar. Yet in both places people are free to petition and protest, and the governments can be said in a quite meaningful sense to be responsive to the will and needs of the population.[4] Elections might shade or reshape policy in one way or another (particularly in Hong Kong over the issue of reunification with China), and democrats would undoubtedly deem the result to be more just, but the essential responsiveness is already there.[5]

---

[3]Thus, the free competitive play of "special interests" is fundamental; to reform them out of existence would be uncomprehending and profoundly antidemocratic.

[4]Although they are fully aware of Mexico's electoral defects and although they document the fact that Mexicans are equally aware of these defects, Almond and Verba have no difficulty accepting Mexico as a functioning democracy in a classic study (1963).

[5]In Hong Kong, rulers have traditionally been sensitive to vigilant and entrenched business elites who, in turn, helped to keep the rest of the population docile, reasonably content, and politically apathetic. When the government signed a treaty in 1984 promising to hand the colony over to China in 1997, however, much of this traditional apathy was shrugged off as treaty opponents screamed loudly, organized pressure groups, signed petitions, staged mass demonstrations, and pointedly threatened to emigrate. An authoritarian government would have responded by suppressing the protest and jailing its leaders. In Hong Kong the rulers acted like democrats: they listened, and they tried to mollify and coopt the protest movement by giving in to some of its demands and by letting it compete for some previously appointed leadership positions. When the opponents did well in this competition, the government further responded by replacing some of its hardline appointees with apolitical professionals. See Scott 1989; Mosher 1991.

Looked at this way, democracy is at base a fairly simple thing—even a rather natural one. And this perspective accordingly helps to explain why democracy has been so easy to institute in so many places lately. If people feel something is wrong, they will complain about it; and some of the complainers will naturally be led to organize and to try to convert others to their point of view. People do not need to be encouraged or coaxed; nor do they first need to be imbued with the democratic spirit or achieve a high degree of development or literacy. They will just *do* it. This is suggested by the way the Bill of Rights is worded in the American Constitution. Nowhere does it admonish citizens to complain or to lobby: rather, it restrains the government from restricting their ability to do so. The framers were well aware that complaint and pressure would emerge naturally, without any encouragement from the government.

Unless this natural tendency is artificially stifled, and unless the complainers resort to violence to get their point of view across, democracy will take effect. What seems unnatural is to try to *stop* people from complaining. This requires a lot of work: thought police and informers and dossiers and organized social pressure.

The argument can be put another way. If the freedom to speak, organize, and petition is respected, responsiveness happens and democracy comes into view even without elections. But if one has elections—even competitive ones—without the freedom to speak, organize, and petition, few would call the resulting enterprise democratic.

Stressing petition, rather than elections, as the essence of democracy, leads, I think, to a cleaner definitional view of the subject. By insisting on the importance of elections, one is almost automatically forced to consider the scope of suffrage, and one can be led in absurd consequence to conclude that, because of the exclusion of women and other adults from the electorate, democracy did not exist before this century anywhere in the world and that it did not emerge in Switzerland until 1971. But countries with limited suffrage have clearly often acted and felt like democracies as have places like Mexico and Hong Kong where elections have been fraudulent or nonexistent. At the same time, severe restrictions on the rights of speech and petition (as well as the vote) of blacks in the American South for much of its history and in South Africa for almost all of its, suggest that those areas could not be considered democracies by either standard.

DEMOCRACY AND POLITICAL INEQUALITY

Throughout history most democrats have accepted the notion that all people are created equal as an essential part of their intellectual baggage. Some have done so with such vigor and passion that antidemocrats have been thoroughly justified in concluding that democrats not only believe in equality, but that equality is truly central to the democratic system. As Plato put it mockingly long ago, democracy is "a pleasant constitution . . . distributing its peculiar kind of equality to equals and unequals impartially" (1957 ed., 316).

Antidemocrats have burlesqued the equality theme because it seems to suggest that democracy would require an enormous and ridiculous leveling—indeed, some of the earliest democratic activists were called Levellers. Plato (and many Greek democrats) envisioned democracy as a rather random affair in which people "share citizenship and office on equal terms" and office is "given by lot" (1957 ed., 314; Dahl 1989, 19). In the comic opera, *The Gondoliers*, W. S. Gilbert lets a couple of democrats jointly inherit a kingdom. Unwilling to abandon their "Republican fallacies," they determine that in their kingdom "all shall equal be," whether they be the Lord High Bishop Orthodox, the Lord High Coachman on the box, or the Lord High Vagabond in the stocks. Accordingly they establish "a despotism strict combined with absolute equality," in which as monarchs they spend their day variously making proclamations, polishing the plate, receiving deputations, and running little errands for the ministers of state.

In modern practice, however, democracy has not looked anything like that. It came to be associated with a special, and perhaps rather minimal, form of political equality, the kind usually called equality of opportunity. In a democracy all people are free—that is, equally unfettered as far as the government is concerned—to develop their own potential, to speak their minds, and to organize to promote their interests peacefully. As Riker concludes, "Equality is simply insistence that liberty be democratic, not the privilege of a class" (1965, 20). And when John Locke concludes that "all men by nature are equal," he defines equality as "that equal right that every man hath, to his natural freedom, without being subjected to the will or authority of any other man" and goes out of his way to point out that such attributes as age, virtue, and merit might give some a "just precedency" (1970 ed., 322). Thus *political equality is something that evolves without much further ado when people are free—it is subsumed by, dependent upon, and indistinguishable from, liberty*.[6] That is, if people are free, they are, as far as democracy is concerned, politically equal as well.

It is true that each member of the electorate in modern democracies has more or less the same voting strength at the ballot box.[7] However, as noted in the previous section, the political importance of an individual is not very significantly determined by this circumstance, and therefore political inequality effectively prospers: some people are, in fact, more equal than others. A store clerk has the same weight in an election as the head of a big corporation or a columnist for the Washington Post, but it would be absurd to suggest they are remotely equal in their ability to affect and influence government policy.

Initially, this freedom (and hence equality) of opportunity focused on class

---

[6]On this issue, see also Riker 1982, 7–8. Sometimes it simply means equality before the law (see Riker 1982, 14–15). Thus an aristocrat who killed someone in a drunken brawl would be held as accountable as a commoner who did so. But it seems entirely feasible to have that sort of legal equality under an authoritarian system—it might have been achieved as much in Nazi Germany or Communist Russia as in democratic England or America.

[7]Technically this is not always accurate even in advanced democracies. A resident of an underpopulated state like Wyoming has a substantially greater voting weight in national elections than a resident of New York or California.

distinction, and it made democracy subversive of hereditary class as it relates to politics: the pool from which leaders are chosen is widened to include everybody, and all are free to participate if they choose to do so. As the author of the American Declaration of Independence, Thomas Jefferson is responsible for the most famous expression of the notion that "all men are created equal." But in other writings he made it clear that, far from supplanting distinction, democracy merely replaces one form of distinction with another. Rather than having "an artificial aristocracy, founded on wealth and birth," he pointed out, a democracy would be ruled by "a natural aristocracy" based on "virtue and talents" (1939 ed., 126–127). Or as Pericles put it in ancient Greece, in a democracy "advancement in public life falls to reputation for capacity, class considerations not being allowed to interfere with merit" (Thucydides 1934 ed., 104).

Unlike authoritarian systems, therefore, the political weight of individuals in a democracy is not rigidly bifurcated by class or by ideological test. One is free to try to increase one's political importance by working in politics or by supplying money in appropriate places, or one can reduce it by succumbing to apathy and neglecting even to vote.

In practice, then, *democracy is a form of government in which the individual is left free to become politically unequal.* That is, the actual working out of the process encourages people to explore, develop, and express their differences, not to suppress them—democratic individualism, in fact, is in many respects the antithesis of the kind of equality that Plato and Gilbert ridiculed. The implications of the noises made by some democratic enthusiasts, therefore, have not been borne out in practice. Indeed, as E. M. Forster has suggested, one of the great appeals of democracy as it has actually been practiced is that, far from assuming everyone is alike or equally capable, it admits, and even celebrates, variety: people are different and thus unequal (1951). Democracy does not level—it has proved to be remarkably tolerant of differences, diversity, inequality, and even of studied eccentricity. It is among the least conformist and least uniform of systems: it not only tolerates inequality, it fairly revels in it.

Another way to look at all this would be as follows. Opposition and petitioning cost time and money. Democracy takes effect when the government does not increase this cost by harassing or jailing the petitioners and the opposition, or by imposing additional economic or other sanctions on them. The costs of opposition and petition are not equal because some people have more time, money, or relevant skills than others. Elections do have something of an equalizing effect because the cost of this form of political expression is much the same for everybody. However the political impact of a single vote is so small that, unless one gets a psychological charge out of the act, it makes little sense to go through the exercise.

Political inequality, in fact, has enabled democracy to survive a defect that many thought would be devastating if ever the system were put into practice on a large scale. Opponents of democracy have historically viewed the institution as one in which demagogues mesmerize and bribe the masses and then rule as bloody tyrants. Assuming that numbers were all that mattered in a democracy, Plato concluded that in a democracy the dominant class, because largest in numbers, would be a group of "idle and dissolute men," some of whom would become leaders, while the remainder would be their ignorant and cowardly followers. He anticipated that the leaders would use their clout to "plunder the propertied classes, divide the spoil among the people, and yet keep the biggest share for themselves" (1957 ed., 325–327).

By and large this has not come about for at least two reasons. First, while it is true that the rich form a minority of the electorate, their money and status can be parlayed into substantial political influence. As suggested, the simple arithmetic of the ballot box is only a portion of the democratic effect—and perhaps not even a necessary one. Elsewhere, a sort of weighted voting takes place, and the rich enjoy influence far out of proportion to their numbers.

And second, as will be discussed more fully in the next section, the poor, the idle, and the dissolute in practice have not shown all the short-sighted stupidity that Plato posited. Resentment of the wealthy may have some short-run demagogic appeal, but voters have often shown a rough appreciation for the fact that a systematic dismemberment of the propertied class is not all that good for the poor either—or even for the idle.[8]

The result has been that in order *really* to plunder the propertied it has been necessary to abandon democracy—as in China, the Soviet Union, Cuba, Nicaragua, Burma, Iran, Vietnam, revolutionary France, Cambodia. Where the would-be plunderers have remained democratic—as in Sweden—the propertied have been able to hang on to much of their assets and have not felt it necessary to flee.[9]

There is a somewhat more subtle and general effect as well. In practice, if not in Plato's imaginings, democracy gives to property owners a certain confidence that they can protect themselves from arbitrary seizure of their property—or at any rate that they will have recourse if such seizure does take place.[10] Insofar as that confidence is necessary to encourage capitalism and its effects such as economic growth and efficiency, democracy will have an economic leg up on authoritarian regimes—or at least on those of the more absolutist sort.

---

[8]On this issue, see also Popkin 1991, 21. Reviewing several recent studies about transitions to democracy, Nancy Bermeo observes, to her dismay, that "in every enduring case, dramatic redistributions of property were postponed, circumscribed, or rolled back" (1990, 365). Marxists and others argue that the working classes support the rich because their minds have been skillfully manipulated such that they have developed a "false consciousness" about their true interests (see Cook 1991, 248-256).

[9]A most extreme test of this seems to be on the horizon in South Africa where a massive expansion of political freedom is likely soon to put those who once ran the system very much into the minority. If the system remains democratic, experience suggests they should be able to hang on to many of their privileges.

[10]The U.S. constitution, of course, has a specific guarantee against unreasonable seizures of property, but Plato would undoubtedly dismiss such paper provisions, since in a democracy they could easily be overridden at whim by a majority that was sufficiently large and determined—as in fact happened to Japanese-American property owners in the United States during World War II. What is impressive is how comparatively rare such arbitrary seizures have been in democracies.

Democracy and the Minimal Human Being

John F. Kennedy once proclaimed that "democracy is a difficult kind of government. It requires the highest qualities of self-discipline, restraint, a willingness to make commitments and sacrifices for the general interest, and it also requires knowledge" (1964, 539). From time immemorial statements like this have raised derisive hoots from antidemocrats, and modern polling data quantitatively confirm their argument: when it comes to either the grand or the narrow issues of politics, the average voter hardly displays such qualities. If Kennedy were right, democracy would be impossible.

As it happens, however, democracy is really quite easy—any dimwit can do it—and it can function remarkably well even when people exhibit little in the way of self-discipline, restraint, commitment, knowledge, or, certainly, sacrifice for the general interest: a system built on perpetual self-sacrifice, in fact, is doomed to eventual failure. Democracy's genius in practice is that it can work even if people rarely, if ever, rise above the selfishness and ignorance with which they have been so richly endowed by their creator.[11]

Assessing the Minimal Human Being

One important reason that democracy has succeeded is that, as developed and modified over the course of the last 200 years, it has been demonstrated that democracy can function quite well with the minimal human being. In a democracy, people do not need to be good or noble, nor do they need to be deeply imbued with the democratic spirit, whatever that may be. They need merely to calculate their own best interests and, if so moved, to express them.

One useful perspective on this derives from the British writer and essayist, Sydney Smith. In 1823, eight years after the end of the Napoleonic Wars, he penned a letter railing exhaustedly against war in all its vigor, absurdity, and "eloquence." In the process he expressed a yearning for four qualities of a more basic, even mundane, nature: "For God's sake, do not drag me into another war! I am worn down and worn out, with crusading and defending Europe, and protecting mankind; I must think a little of myself. . . . No war, dear Lady Grey!—no eloquence; but apathy, selfishness, common sense, arithmetic" (1956 ed., 323–324).

---

[11]Riker's perspective on this seems sound: democracy is characterized not by "popular rule" but by a device which provides for "an intermittent, sometimes random, even perverse, popular veto" which "has at least the potential of preventing tyranny and rendering officials responsive." Riker concedes that this is "a minimal sort of democracy," but he contends that it "is the only kind of democracy actually attainable" (1982, 244–246). (However, he does argue, somewhat in passing, that "democratic ideals depend on a vigilant citizenry.") Actually, as suggested earlier, Riker may not be minimal enough: the potential for rendering officials responsive and for preventing tyranny is already in operation whenever the natural proclivity to complain and to petition for redress goes unstifled or uncurbed.

In this perspective people are not incapable of such admirable qualities as compassion, eloquence, nobility, grandeur, altruism, self-sacrifice, and unblinkered obedience. But Smith seems to suggest that these virtues can become excessive and that we might well be better off, more secure, less likely to go astray, if we take it a bit easy: it is possible to rise above apathy, selfishness, common sense, and arithmetic, but it is not necessarily wise to do so. For laid-back liberals of the Smith ilk, human beings are a flawed bunch, and it seems wiser, and certainly less tiring, to work with human imperfections rather than to seek zealously to reform the race into impossible perfection.[12]

This perspective holds that, in general, people have in them a strong streak of apathy and will not be readily roused into action. In other words, they will tend to pursue concerns that matter to them personally rather than ones that other people think *should* matter to them. Some people, as it happens, will be quite content to spend their time taking naps, watching television, hanging out on street corners, boozing away the evening, or reading trashy novels rather than pursuing high culture, changing the world, or saving souls.[13] Relatedly, they will be selfish—guided more reliably by their own interests than by perceptions of the general good.

At the same time, however, people do not act randomly but rather apply common sense and arithmetic.[14] That is, they have a canny, if perhaps not terribly sophisticated, ability to assess reality and their own interests and to relate things in a fairly logical and sensible way.[15]

An institution is likely to prove particularly effective if it can be fabricated so that it will function properly even when people exhibit qualities no more exalted than those which emerge in the Smith perspective. Over the last 200 years or so democracy has worked its way into wide acceptance in the world in part because it has proved to be fundamentally sound in the sense that it does not require more from the human spirit than apathy, selfishness, common sense, and arithmetic. Indeed, in some respects it exalts and revels in these qualities.

This embellishes the conclusion above that democracy is not terribly difficult to institute and that no elaborate prerequisites are necessary for it to emerge,

---

[12]For a discussion of this trait in Greek liberalism, see Havelock 1957, 123. "Don't expect too much from human life," admonishes Smith. Rather, have "short views of life—not further than dinner or tea," "keep good blazing fires," and "be as much as you can in the open air without fatigue." His definition of "a nice person" suggests that he was not overtaxed by a quest for perfection: "A nice person is clear of little, trumpery passions, acknowledges superiority, delights in talent, shelters humility, pardons adversity, forgives deficiency, respects all men's rights, never stops the bottle, is never long and never wrong, always knows the day of the month, the name of every body at table, and never gives pain to any human being. . . . A nice person never knocks over wine or melted butter, does not tread upon the dog's foot, or molest the family cat, eats soup without noise, laughs in the right place, and has a watchful and attentive eye" (1956, 201–202).

[13]Sir John Falstaff, who might be seen as a sort of quintessential caricature of the Smith liberal, mutters at one point, "I were better to be eaten to death with a rust than to be scour'd to nothing with perpetual motion."

[14]Smith could work up quite a bit of enthusiasm for arithmetic. As he put it in a letter to a child in 1835: "Lucy, dear child, mind your arithmetic. You know, in the first sum of yours I ever saw, there was a mistake. You had carried two (as a cab is licensed to do) and you ought, dear Lucy, to have carried but one. Is this a trifle? What would life be without arithmetic but a scene of horrors?" (1956, xiii).

[15]On this issue, see the discussion of "low-information rationality" in Popkin 1991.

something that is suggested by the remarkable ease with which various peoples—many of them utterly innocent of democratic experience—took to democracy when it was offered to them in the last two decades. It seems likely that democracy can come about rather naturally, almost by default, unless devices and gimmicks are fabricated to suppress it.[16]

THE MINIMAL HUMAN BEING AND THE DEMAGOGUE

For millennia antidemocratic theorists and philosophers argued that this is not enough. Democracy, as a method of arranging a government and selecting leaders, is inherently defective, they have insisted, because ordinary people will base their choices on their selfish, shortsighted interests rather than on an informed concern for the general welfare. In particular, the critics have argued that the process is inherently unstable and will generally lead to capricious mob rule often focused on the persecution of the rich, the intellectually superior, and other minorities as dictated by whichever demagogue happens to prove the most seductive at the moment. Even Voltaire, who loved liberty, was unable to believe that ordinary people were capable of making sensible selections. He yearned for rule by enlightened philosopher-kings (preferably witty ones), not by the people, who were dismissed by him as "stupid and barbarous" and in need of "a yoke, a cattle prod, and hay" (Chodorow and Knox 1989, 609).

Similarly, Plato believed that the only people who ought to rule were those whose "earliest years were given to noble games" and who now give themselves over "wholly to noble pursuits." He anticipated that in a democracy the voters would not share his passion for noble games and, indeed, would be "supremely indifferent as to what life a man has led before he enters politics." Instead all a politician need do is assert "his zeal for the multitude" and they would be "ready to honor him" (1957 ed., 316). Mencken argued that "the most popular man under a democracy is not the most democratic man, but the most despotic man. The common folk delight in the exactions of such a man. They like him to boss them. Their natural gait is the goose-step" (1920a, 221).

As noted earlier, Plato anticipated that the leaders would use their clout to "plunder the propertied classes, divide the spoil among the people, and yet keep the biggest share for themselves." Bloody tyranny would soon emerge, he felt, because "he who is the president of the people finds a mob more than ready to obey him, and does not keep his hands from the blood of his kindred. He heaps unjust accusations on them—a favorite device—hales them before the courts, and murders them" (1957 ed., 326–328). In *Coriolanus,* set in at least semi-democratic Rome, Shakespeare vividly depicts such a process. A natural leader (whose noble games have included victorious war) is at first honored by the mob. But he is un-

---

[16]For the argument that for millennia democracy may have been the "natural" and standard form of government among tribes of hunter-gatherers, see Dahl 1989 p. 232; Glassman 1986.

able to bring himself hypocritically to grovel before them, and soon the people, manipulated by wily demagogues, turn on him and crush him.

That these grim scenarios were not entirely fanciful was demonstrated in the years after the French Revolution of 1789. Democracy there soon degenerated, under Robespierre, into the sort of tyrannical, murderous mobocracy that Plato had envisioned two millennia earlier, and it eventually became associated with an expansionary ideology, with war, and, under Napoleon, with aggressive, continent-wide military conquest.

Thus the concern has been eminently sensible, and it has been among the key reasons why democracy has been rejected for thousands of years in almost all societies above the village level. Some 200 years ago, however, large democracies came into existence, and it has been found that, in practice, these concerns, so devastating on paper, are, despite the traumatic French example, substantially overdrawn.

It is noteworthy in this regard, that once in authority, the tyrants in France, as well as later ones who came into authority more or less democratically, like Hitler and Mussolini, felt it necessary to abandon democracy in order to maintain control. Wiser than Plato about mobs, they knew that if they left the field free to other rivals, the people might well come to honor a competitor (maybe even one who played noble games in his youth). That is, the notion that masses of people are readily, predictably, and consistently manipulable proved to be naive. As such would-be manipulators as advertisers, public relations specialists, and political candidates could assure Plato, Mencken, or Shakespeare, putting out a product that a free public will buy is uncertain at best.

The agile demagogue/tyrant is aware of the essential validity of a famous, and quite cynical, observation about democracy that has been variously attributed to Abraham Lincoln and to that great showman and prince of ballyhoo and humbug, Phineas T. Barnum. It is perhaps the most profound thing ever said about the institution and the key to an explanation about why, despite its patent defects, democracy more or less works. The observation concludes first that Plato, Mencken, and Shakespeare were right: people in general are so addled that they can *all* sometimes be faked out: "you can fool all the people some of the time." Moreover, some people are so stupid that they will *never* get it right: you can fool "some of the people all the time." What makes anything work, however, is that people, in fact, are *not* equal: somewhere there are a few people at least who will eventually figure it out: "you can't fool all the people all the time."[17]

Of Sydney Smith's minimal virtues—apathy, selfishness, common sense, and arithmetic—Plato and Shakespeare include only one in their characterizations of the masses: selfishness. But while people may be selfish, it turns out they are not

---

[17]On the absence of any conclusive evidence that Lincoln ever said this, see Woldman 1950, 74. The connection with Barnum, who is also alleged to have said, "There's a sucker born every minute" (and probably didn't—see Saxon 1989, 334–337), could be considered plausible because the two statements are quite congruent and might be seen to spring from the same mentality. In tandem they make up a cautionary tale: there are a lot of suckers who can be fooled all the time, they suggest, but be careful—there are a lot of nonsuckers out there too, and eventually, if left free, they'll see through the most artful of frauds and humbugs.

simple bundles of erratic passions yearning to break loose at a deft signal from a skilled demagogue. Rather, they retain a basic, if less than masterful, facility for common sense and arithmetic—for thoughtful, if sometimes slow-witted, deliberation, and for relating things in a logical way. They can not—all of them, anyway—be fooled all the time.

Moreover, they are not necessarily incapable of considering their own long-term interests, rather than just their immediate ones. If they are left free to discuss and argue among themselves, therefore, there is a good chance that they will eventually see through even the most effusive flatteries and the most exquisite fabrications of the most dazzling illusionists.[18] At any rate, as suggested, successful illusionists have been aware of the danger: once in political control they have quickly moved to destroy democracy before it destroys them.

Apathy also plays an important role in making democracy function. It is no easy task to persuade people to agree with one's point of view, but as any experienced demagogue is likely to point out with some exasperation, what is most difficult of all is to get them to listen in the first place. People, particularly those in a free, open society, are regularly barraged by shysters and schemers, by people with new angles and neglected remedies, by purveyors of panaceas and palliatives. And all of them, *all* of them, use flattery and assert their "zeal for the multitude," in Plato's words. Very few are successful—and even those who do succeed, including Adolf Hitler, owe their success as much to luck as to skill.

One of the great, neglected aspects of free speech is the freedom not to listen. When the stormy Aleksandr Solzhenitsyn was forced to leave the Soviet Union for the West, he may have been gratified finally to be in a society where he could freely speak his mind. But he was soon appalled to discover that when he eloquently promulgated his message of warning and deliverance, huge numbers of people were fully prepared, after getting over the novelty of his abrupt appearance in their midst, to fail to heed his song and story (1981). Solzhenitsyn's message—that Communism was a great, menacing evil—was one his audiences in the West were generally predisposed to agree with. But to his intense frustration they were not all that anxious to get off their duffs and *do* something about it.

THE TYRANNY OF THE MAJORITY

Apathy helps not only with the demagogue problem in democracy, but also with the related problem of the tyranny of the majority. It is not difficult to find a place where the majority harbors a considerable hatred for a minority—indeed, it may be difficult to find one where this is *not* the case. Polls in the United States regularly have found plenty of people who would cheerily restrict homosexuals,

---

[18]Niccolò Machiavelli, not commonly known as an ardent democrat, was quite confident of this ability: "As to the people's capacity of judging things, it is exceedingly rare that, when they hear two orators of equal talents advocate different measures, they do not decide in favor of the best of the two; which proves their ability to discern the truth of what they hear." In another place he approvingly quotes Cicero: "The people, although ignorant, yet are capable of appreciating the truth, and yield to it readily when it is presented to them by a man whom they esteem worthy of confidence" (1950 ed., 263, 120).

atheists, accused Communists, Nazi paraders, flag-burners, and people who like to shout unpleasant words and perpetrate unconventional messages. But it is not easy to get this majority to do anything about it—after all, that would require a certain amount of work.

Mostly, people do not seem to be all that moved by questions of civil liberties, whether the issue is expanding or suppressing them. For example, public opinion data suggest that it is scarcely justified to use the word "hysteria" to characterize the McCarthy era. One poll of the time asked "What kinds of things worry you most?" Less than 1 percent mentioned the threat of domestic Communism. Another asked for "some of the things" the president should do "for the good of the country" and only 4 percent included cleaning out domestic Communism on their list (Mueller 1988a, 21). It almost seems that the only time many people even consider the issue is when they are being queried about it in public opinion surveys.

This can be unsettling to intellectuals who study such issues and to philosophers who muse about them. Such pundits have a strong interest in free inquiry, as do members of the democratic political elite who may have concluded that free speech helps preserve their right to speak their minds when out of office and therefore facilitates their potential political resurrection. But most people never say anything that anyone else—even the most paranoid of dictators—would want to suppress. And they really do have other things to worry about, many of them quite pressing from their point of view.

Thus as a result of apathy and selfishness, people in an important sense are in effect remarkably tolerant—not only of free speech but of efforts to restrict it. For democracies the danger is not so much that agile demagogues will play on hatreds and weaknesses to fabricate a vindictive moblike tyranny of the majority: the perversions of the French Revolution have proved unusual. More to be feared is the tyranny of a few who obtain bland acquiescence from the uninterested, and essentially unaffected, many. That is the path through which democracy is more likely to be subverted.

THE MINIMAL HUMAN BEING CHOOSES AND CHECKS LEADERS

Thus, it seems, rule by demagogues and mobs proved essentially inconsistent with democracy. Moreover thanks to apathy and to the political inequality that characterizes actual (as opposed to theoretical) democracy, minorities, if allowed democratic freedoms, have generally been able to protect themselves and to pursue their interests, a quality, as suggested in Chapter 1, that may help in the nationalist quarrels that have become so visible in Europe and elsewhere in the aftermath of the quiet cataclysm. But it still does not follow that ordinary people will be effective at judging leaders. They may be wily about demagogues, but it could certainly be anticipated that they would tend to promote fellow mediocrities to run things. Democracy has an advantage over monarchy and other authoritarian forms of government in that political and opinion leaders can emerge from anywhere in the population, not simply from a selected class or group. And it also chooses these leaders competitively and subjects them to review. But this process would be of little value if the judges were incompetent.

The amazing thing about democracy is that the selectors and reviewers *are* substantially incompetent, but the process nevertheless generates able, even superior, leaders and tends to keep them responsive and responsible. The system seems to work for the same reason that demagogues are kept in check: you cannot fool all the people all the time. If people remain free to use whatever common sense they choose to muster at the moment to discuss and to argue among themselves, and if they are free to generate competing ideas, there is a good chance they will get it more or less right eventually.[19]

Petitioners and voters may not, on average, exhibit much in the way of nobility of spirit or rich philosophical knowledge, they may often succumb to fits of apathy, and they may tend most reliably to be motivated, at best, by narrow self-interest. Nevertheless, the democratic process seems not only to have kept governments more or less alert and responsive, but for the most part it has tended to select good—or pretty good—leaders. There have been mistakes and exasperations and sometimes even disasters. But it can be plausibly argued that democracies on the whole have done rather well at managing their affairs and at choosing leaders, and that governments so instituted have been responsive to the will, if any, of the people—or at any rate to that of those who choose to organize and to complain.[20]

In addition, once democracy was tried out it became clear that voters were inclined, rather surprisingly perhaps, to identify (in Jefferson's terms) "virtue and talents" with "wealth and birth." This could be seen in the earliest competitive elections in the American colonies 100 years before the Declaration of Independence. As Edmund Morgan observes, "The men whom people elected to represent them in their assemblies, especially in the colonies to the south of New England, were generally those whose birth and wealth placed them a little or even a lot above their neighbors. Even in New England, where most seats were filled by comparatively ordinary men, those who stood highest socially and economically seem to have been deferred to by the other representatives and appointed to the committees that directed legislative action" (1988, 147–148).

Democracy opens up the competition for leadership positions to people who would have previously been barred for genetic or ideological reasons. Nevertheless

---

[19]Similarly, the device of using ordinary people—usually chosen from the voting rolls—as members of trial juries has, on the whole, worked rather well, as has the device of referendum.

[20]In addition democracy furnishes a safety valve for discontent. Those with complaints may or may not ever see relief of their grievances, but rather than wallowing in frustration, they are allowed to express themselves and to seek to change things in a direction they prefer. Democracy also rather automatically comes accompanied by certain values that many find congenial for their own sake: a permissiveness and tolerance, for example, or an openness and absence of cant and mendacity. E. M. Forster likes democracy because it "admits variety" and because it "permits criticism." Those are his "two cheers" for democracy (1951, 70). For some the act of voting or of participating in public discussion carries with it a sense of belonging that can be quite satisfying psychologically. And among those who believe in the democratic myth, the voting act can be taken to bestow a certain legitimacy upon the government so chosen (those who believe that only God can choose leaders, on the other hand, will remain unimpressed).

the system was fairly easy to accept because changes in leadership have not usually been terribly revolutionary: by and large, the same people, or sorts of people, remain in office. They are often virtuous and talented, *and* wealthy and well-born—like Jefferson himself. Thus in practice democracy proved not necessarily to be destructive of aristocratic dominance because voters tended to support many of the same patricians who would have been in office if unalloyed monarchy had still been the order of the day.[21] Democracies, like monarchies, have largely been run by the well-born, although democratic myth-builders, particularly in the United States, have usually chosen to emphasize the occasional political success of upstarts raised in log cabins (see Pessen 1984).[22]

Nor have the masses proved volatile or mercurial or capricious—abruptly abandoning one champion to follow another with a more seductive line of banter. Where democracy has been most fully established, in fact, voters have proved constant to the point of tediousness. The shift of a few seats in a Scandinavian parliament is a major event; in American legislatures most incumbents are regularly returned. Some of this can be attributed to a broad tolerance born of apathy—if things are going ahead more or less congenially, why bother to take the time to reassess them? But it does keep things measured, even staid, in most democracies. Caprice, it seems, is more likely to be found in tyrannies, dictatorships, and monarchies.[23]

PARTICIPATION

Some analysts have argued that "democratic states require . . . participation in order to flourish" (Lienesch 1992, 1011). Such a conclusion, it seems to me, succumbs to the "I theorize therefore it must be so" school. We now have over 200 years of experience with living, breathing, messy democracy. If any sort of significant participation and/or responsibility were required for it to flourish, we would still be living in an age of queens and kings and eunuchs.

The empirical reality, of course, is that democracies have been flourishing like crazy even while huge numbers of their citizens decline not only to participate and to be responsible, but even to spend much time trying to figure out what is going on. Recent surveys find that around half the citizens of that venerable democracy, the United States, do not have the foggiest idea which party controls the Senate or what the first 10 amendments of the Constitution are called or what the Fifth Amendment does or who their congressional representative or senators are—and this lack of knowledge has generally increased (particularly when educa-

---

[21]Interestingly, much the same thing has happened when authoritarian governments have converted to democracy. After the change to democracy in eastern Europe and the former Soviet Union, many of the same people (now professing their ardent affection for democracy) have remained in charge and have been elected to office.

[22]Snobs, too, have been quite safe because social and class distinctions remained substantially unruffled. Thus, Gilbert's witty slander against equality, "If everybody is somebody, then nobody is anybody," has not been borne out.

[23]That was certainly Machiavelli's belief: "As regards prudence and stability, I say that the people are more prudent and stable, and have better judgment than a prince" (1950 ed., p. 263).

tion is controlled for) since the 1940s during which time the United States has championed and presided over a spectacular growth in democracy in most areas of the world (Delli Carpini and Keeter 1991). Moreover, nearly half fail to vote even in high visibility elections and only a few percent ever actively participate in politics (see Conway 1991, ch. 1).

Such statistics characteristically inspire a great deal of tongue clucking, but it may be more useful to reshape democratic theories and ideals to take cognizance of such elemental and widely-known data: clearly, democracy works despite the fact that it often fails to inspire (or require) very much in the way of participation and responsibility and knowledge from its citizenry.[24] And why, one might ask, is this a bad thing—except that it embarrasses some theorists? Why should we expect people to spend a lot of time worrying about politics when democracy not only leaves them free to choose other ways to get their kicks but in its seemingly infinite quest for variety is constantly developing seductive distractions? A world-renowned physicist was once asked how he was going to vote in an upcoming election. His response was, "Who's running?" Democratic theorists and idealists may be intensely interested in government and its processes, but it verges on the arrogant to suggest that other people are somehow inadequate or derelict unless they share the same curious passion. Also, as argued earlier, this apathy (that is, interest in things other than politics) has probably helped democracy work and become accepted.

—

THE RISE OF DEMOCRACY:
MECHANISMS OF CHANGE

To explain the rise of democracy, one approach is to try to trace the totality of the historical process in rich historical detail, tacitly assuming that everything that accompanied democracy's rise somehow contributed to the phenomenon. Another approach is to assume that the rise is the result of other, "deeper" social and economic changes, ones that are easier to measure and to deal with.

By contrast, as suggested earlier, it seems to me that about all that is required for a country to become a democracy is the more or less general desire to do so. That is, for a country to become a democracy it is a necessary and sufficient condition that the country—or perhaps only its political elite—find the idea attractive, that it catch the bug.[25]

---

[24]For the romantic view that "one way of defining democracy would be to call it a political system in which people actively attend to what is significant," see Bellah et al. 1991, 273. For the amazing, and perhaps desperate, argument (by a lecturer at Harvard's Kennedy School of Government) that America will get back on the road to the democratic ideal "only when we have figured out how to use television to teach the essence of citizenship, the virtues of individual sacrifice in the common good and the nobility necessary to make democracy work," see Squires 1990.

[25]On the issue of elite transformations, see Higley and Gunther 1992.

A problem in viewing democracy in all its exquisite complexity is that it can lead one to conclude that the system is difficult to institute, particularly if one comes to believe that all sorts of attitudinal, cultural, economic, and atmospheric developments are necessary before democracy can function. This perspective has led to considerable pessimism about the pace of democratization in the world (see, for example, Dahl 1971, 45, 47; Moynihan 1975; Huntington 1984; Dahl 1989, 264). Experiences in places like Portugal, Spain, eastern Europe, and the former Soviet Union suggest that such pessimism is overdrawn, that democracy is really quite an easy thing to institute, and that it need not necessarily come accompanied with the social, economic, and cultural clutter that some favor.[26]

But, while there seem to be no necessary prerequisites or preconditions except for the catching of the bug or the buying of the idea, it must be acknowledged that there are plenty of *correlates* of democracy. As Dahl has pointed out, democracy has been "strongly associated" with a whole series of social and economic characteristics: "a relatively high level of income and wealth per capita, long-run growth in per capita income and wealth, a high level of urbanization, a rapidly declining or relatively small agricultural population, great occupational diversity, extensive literacy, a comparatively large number of persons who have attended institutions of higher education, an economic order in which production is mainly carried on by relatively autonomous firms whose decisions are strongly oriented toward national and international markets, and relatively high levels of conventional measures of well-being" (1989, 251; see also Huntington 1991b).

That such characteristics are merely correlates, not causes, Dahl observes, is suggested by the case of India where political leaders were able to establish a viable democracy "when the population was overwhelmingly agricultural, illiterate . . . and highly traditional and rule-bound in behavior and beliefs." Or "even more tellingly" there is the case of the United States which took to democracy when it was still "overwhelmingly rural and agricultural" (1989, 253; Dahl 1971, 186; Fukuyama 1992, 221).

So it goes with the other supposed causes. Democracy may have been established earlier in Protestant countries than in Catholic ones, but once Catholic countries like Italy or Portugal or Spain took a notion to become democratic, their

---

[26]Surely the most spectacular case of a new, instant democracy is Paraguay, a country that had never known any government except Jesuit theocracy or rigid military dictatorship. In 1989 Paraguay's guiding autocrat, entrenched since 1954, was overthrown by a man who had been one of his chief henchmen and who had become fabulously wealthy in the process. The new leader was sensitive to the fact that democracy is what everyone is wearing nowadays—that "despots have gone out of style," as a reporter from the *Economist* puts it (16 May 1991, 48). Accordingly he held fair elections and promised that, if elected president, he would guide the country to full democracy in four years. Paraguayans, in the first free election in their grim history, took him at his word and something that looked suspiciously like democracy quickly broke out: as the reporter cheerfully observed, "newspaper, television, and radio reports are filled with mud-slinging worthy of the most mature democracy." Then in 1993, on schedule, another election was held and another man became president (Brooke 1993). Huntington argues, "Political leaders cannot through will and skill create democracy where preconditions are absent. In the late 1980s, the obstacles to democracy in Haiti were such as to confound even the most skilled and committed democratic leader" (1991b, 108). But a few years earlier, some might have said the same thing about Paraguay. In my view, the obstacle to democracy in Haiti has been a group of thugs with guns, not the absence of "preconditions."

religious tradition did not seem to cramp their style very much. If economic development is associated with democracy, it has *also* been associated with antidemocratic Communism.[27] Although he maintains that economic development is the most "pervasive force" for democratization in recent decades, Samuel Huntington has pointed out that countries "transit to democracy at widely varying levels of development" (1984, 200; 1991b, 85).[28]

Moreover, modern methods of transportation and communication do not seem to be required even in large democracies: the United States became democratic before the development of the steamboat, the railroad, and the telegraph— that is, when things and information moved scarcely faster overland than in the days of ancient Athens. And democracy has lately been established in large, undeveloped, illiterate countries like Papua New Guinea and Namibia while it remains neglected in such technologically sophisticated societies as Saudi Arabia.

Some analysts have held that a sizeable middle class is necessary for democracy: as Barrington Moore put it, "No bourgeois, no democracy" (1966, 418; Huntington 1984, 204). The cases of India and quite a few other places call that generalization into question, and the recent experience of the eastern Europeans seems to shatter it. Similar damage is done by the eastern European events to Charles Lindblom's previously unassailable observation that to become a democracy a country must have a market-oriented economy (1977, 116, 161–169; Huntington 1984, 204-205, 214; Riker 1982, 7). The nations in eastern Europe and the former Soviet Union have become democracies even though the vast majority of the people in those countries still work for the government and even though most property is still state owned. (They are working to change that, but only because the old economic system has become discredited, not because the process of democracy mandates it.) While capitalists (contrary to Plato's fears) have generally been able to use democracy to keep confiscation of their property to a bearable level, there does not seem to be a necessary link between democracy and market capitalism (see also Fukuyama 1992, 122–123).

Much of the history of democratic development, particularly since 1975, also calls into question time-honored notions about the process by which a country becomes a democracy. Dankwart Rustow envisioned this as a slow, gradual process in which national unity leads to prolonged and inconclusive struggle which leads in turn to a conscious decision to adopt democratic rules followed by habituation to these rules. These "ingredients," says Rustow "must be assembled one at a time" (1970, 361). Writing shortly before the developments in eastern Europe took place, Dahl presciently concluded that "the democratic ideal is likely to maintain a strong attraction for people in nondemocratic countries" and "their authoritarian governments will find it increasingly difficult to resist the pressures for

---

[27]As Huntington observes, in 1981 almost all countries with per capita gross national products over $4220 were *either* democratic *or* Communist (1984, 202).

[28]Elsewhere Huntington concludes, however, that "economic development makes democracy possible" (1991b, 316), implying, it would seem, that despite the cases of India, Paraguay, Papua New Guinea, much of the Caribbean, Botswana, and eighteenth-century America, democracy is impossible without economic development.

greater democratization." Yet he anticipated that "it would be surprising" if the proportion of the countries in the world that are democratic "were to change greatly over the next twenty years" (1989, 264).[29] The experience in such places as Portugal, Spain, and especially eastern Europe suggests that gradualism is hardly required, at least not anymore. The experience since 1975 also severely tests Huntington's previously unexceptionable observation that "democratic regimes that last have seldom, if ever, been instituted by mass popular action" (1984, 212).

To be sure, over the last two centuries the developed world has experienced great changes that accompanied democracy's rise: the Industrial Revolution, enormous economic growth, the rise of a middle class, a vast improvement in transportation and communication, surging literacy rates, and massive increases in international trade. But if these developments "caused" the growth of democracy, they also stimulated their direct opposites: Nazism, Fascism, Bolshevism. Moreover, the process of development was often wildly out of synchronization. Democracy and the Industrial Revolution may have flowered together in England in the late eighteenth century, but firm democracy did not come to industrial Germany until 1945 (and then it had to be imposed from the outside), and it is only now being developed in industrial Russia. Moreover, by the end of the twentieth century it is quite easy to find democracy comfortably accepted in places that are very poor, have yet to develop much of a middle class, and are still quite backward in industry, literacy, communications, transportation, and trade.

Although democracy does happen to correlate with various social and economic characteristics—wealth, capitalism, literacy, and so forth—these connections are, in my view, essentially spurious. The McDonald hamburger sold first, and continues to sell best, in rich capitalistic, literate, Protestant countries, but it does not follow that you have to be rich or capitalistic or literate or Protestant or well-prepared or sophisticated or middle class or industrialized or cosmopolitan or uncontentious to buy one. All you have to do is decide you want one. You can even get one now (along with elections and almost too much free speech) in Moscow.

THE PROMOTION OF DEMOCRACY

Thus it seems that democracy, like war aversion, is essentially a state of mind, not a logical or empirical consequence of other factors (see also Muravchik 1992). As Dahl points out, the role of beliefs in the rise of democracy is "pivotal" (1989, 260): it is difficult to see, he notes, how democracy could exist if political elites "believed strongly that a hegemonic regime was more desirable" (1971, 126). By the same token, if elites generally come to believe that democracy is the way

---

[29]Earlier, he had concluded that, "In the future as in the past," democracy is "more likely to result from rather slow evolutionary processes than from the revolutionary overthrow of existing hegemonies" and "the transformation of hegemonic regimes" into democracies "is likely to remain a slow process, measured in generations" (1971, 45, 47).

things ought to be done and if they are not physically intimidated or held in check by authoritarian thugs, the country can quite easily become democratic without any special historical preparation and whatever the state of its social or economic development.[30]

As with the rise of war aversion discussed in the previous chapter, the key element in explaining the increasing appeal and attractiveness of democracy derives from the activities of idea entrepreneurs. Democracy, it seems to me, is an intellectual construct that has an intrinsic appeal, has proved in practice to be notably better (or less bad) than the competition, and, despite some occasional overeager and inflated claims, has been rather well promoted by its advocates who, after several lucky breaks and after 200 years of patient, persistent salesmanship, are now cashing in.

As suggested in Chapter 9, the process by which an idea is successfully promoted can be quite complicated. And, although democracy advocates have been successful, it does not follow that their triumph derives simply from their own manipulative cleverness. There appear to have been several components to explain their success, and some suggestions about the process are sketched below.[31]

DEMONSTRATION

First, because of the understandable bias against democracy, it was essential that the product be demonstrated—put into practice somewhere, altering the theories where necessary to make them work better and to increase their appeal. As suggested above, when democracy was tried out in large countries some 200 years ago it proved, despite the prophesies of wise doomsayers, to work rather well. Although notably less than perfect, it was clearly not as unrealistic and difficult to institute and maintain as it often appeared on paper; it did not necessarily deliver the government into the hands of mobs, incompetents, and demagogues; it can function with real, flawed human beings; it does not characteristically lead to persecution of the rich and other minorities; it does not precipitate a vast social leveling; it can be a rather effective method for choosing and reviewing leaders and for keeping them alert and responsive; and it creates a style of life that is entirely bearable, even admirable at times.

---

[30]At one point, Huntington does acknowledge "the beliefs and actions of political elites" as "probably the most immediate and significant explanatory variable" in the current wave of democratization. He concludes, however, that, while this may be "a powerful explanatory variable, it is not a satisfying one. Democracy can be created even if people do not want it. So it is not perhaps tautological to say that democracy will be created if people want democracy, but it is close to that. An explanation, someone has observed, is the place at which the mind comes to rest. Why do the relevant political elites want democracy? Inevitably, the mind wants to move further along the causal chain" (1991b, 36). As he moves further along, he clings to the concept of economic preconditions, but his other explanations for the recent democracy wave stress, as do the arguments that follow, persuasion and promotion phenomena: democracy's stylishness and the influence of fashion leaders, changes of doctrine in the Catholic Church, the role of key converts like Gorbachev, the failures of the competition, and patterns of imitation (1991b, 45–46).

[31]For a further discussion of some of these issues, see Mueller 1990.

Since concerns about the competence of ordinary people to review the policies and activities of their leaders have been raised for thousands of years, those promoting democracy had a simple experimental solution. Initially they restricted the vote to the best and the brightest. When that proved to work out pretty well, they gradually broadened the electorate to see if special problems would emerge as suffrage was expanded. It seems likely that those in authority soon learned that political clout was only imperfectly measured by the strict, simple arithmetic of the ballot box: as argued earlier, those in the minority can very often generate substantial influence through position, money, and organization. Thus suffrage expansion rarely was the end of the world for anybody as long as the system remained democratic. Moreover, the democratic experiment strongly suggested that the extension of the electorate to embrace ever larger proportions of what Lincoln allegedly called "the great unwashed" did not obviously lower (or raise) the average quality of the chosen leaders.

UNDERMINING THE COMPETITION

In seeking to persuade people to accept democracy its advocates needed not only to demonstrate that the institution was sound, but also that it was superior to the competition. Thus, they needed to undermine the competition, to seize upon, and to bring out its defects.

When democracy emerged it had first to contend with the ancient institution of hereditary monarchy, a remarkably defective form of government whose amazing longevity can probably be attributed as much to the absence of well-promoted competition as anything else (and perhaps as well to its often-ingenious association with religion). Once formidable alternatives were fabricated, it faded out in rather short order—over a century or so—particularly in the developed world. Later, democracy was confronted with new, often dynamic, forms of authoritarianism—Fascism, Nazism, and Communism—as well as with assorted forms of nonmonarchical dictatorships. These variously self-destructed in war and in economic and social failure.

These competitors promised to deliver superior competence in decision making, and sometimes they also promised to supply certain durable values that seemed unachievable with democracy.

COMPETENCE IN DECISION MAKING. The notion that authoritarian regimes are inherently more competent at making and carrying out decisions is a common one, and, indeed, decision making in democracies is often muddled and incoherent, and the results are sometimes foolish, shortsighted, and irrational. As Alexis de Tocqueville observed in the 1830s, "a democracy can only with great difficulty regulate the details of an important undertaking, persevere in a fixed design, and work out its execution in spite of serious obstacles. It cannot combine its measures with secrecy or await their consequences with patience" (1990 ed., 235).

However, Tocqueville's implication that monarchies and other authoritarian regimes are superior at getting things done, would be difficult to demonstrate. In the nineteenth century it was probably the British experiment, not the American one, that was most influential in suggesting that democracies could be effective. During that time democratic Britain became the strongest and most important country in the world. It ruled the seas, developed the world's dominant economy, established a vast and impressive overseas empire, and was the scene of a substantial intellectual renaissance in philosophy, literature, and science. It was led in these endeavors by democratically selected politicians, such as Benjamin Disraeli and William Gladstone, who would be considered exceptional by the standards of most any age. Even more to the point, it was difficult to imagine that Britain could have attained this if all power had resided, as in days of old, in its monarch, the fussy and simple Queen Victoria.[32] Among democracy's postmonarchy competitors, Communism and various forms of military dictatorship often proved to be thunderingly incompetent, while Nazism and Fascism, capable, perhaps, at getting trains to run on time, led their peoples into self-destructive wars.[33]

HIGHER VALUES, TRUE EQUALITY, ORDER, AND THE RALPH'S GROCERY EFFECT.   Some of democracy's competitors have also variously promised to deliver certain higher social and ethical values, true social equality, and a more orderly society.

For centuries, as Francis Fukuyama has pointed out, people who aspire to grander goals, who have higher visions, have criticized "the emptiness at the core of liberalism" (1989, 14). There is, it often seems, no *there* there. Liberal democracy, at least in the form suggested by the perspective of Sydney Smith, has little to say about some of the great philosophical issues: What is truth? What is good?

---

[32]It is entirely possible, of course, to have a king who is effective, humane, responsive, decisive, and wise, but even if genetic favor is enhanced with all sorts of clever princely training, it is perverse to think that these qualities will necessarily be passed on to his son. Like his contemporaries, William Shakespeare appears to have had a great deal of enthusiasm for Henry V, "this star of England" who achieved "the world's best garden." Regrettably, Henry left the garden in charge of his son who had no aptitude for the task the institution of monarchy forced upon him. Through incompetence and mismanagement he soon lost his father's gains and "made his England bleed." Louis XIV of France, the longest-reigning monarch in European history and one of the most ardent exemplars of the monarchical system, was fully aware of its defects: "I have often wondered how it could be that love for work being a quality so necessary to sovereigns should yet be one that is so rarely found in them." When he died, the throne went to his great-grandson, aged five, who grew into an indolent adult and reigned ineffectually for over fifty years (Chodorow and Knox 1989, 561, 625). Things can be even worse if the king leaves no obvious heir, a conundrum that often sets off vicious intrigue or is resolved by principles that find justice in blood lines, not competence. In 645 years of rule the Hapsburg family, in Rebecca West's estimation, produced "no genius, only two rulers of ability. . . , countless dullards, and not a few imbeciles and lunatics" (1941, 1097). Saudi Arabia is the very model of a modern monarchy. Yet its king is said to be a "master of indecision." The Saudis "could spend days and weeks arguing among themselves. Royal family deliberations could make the American Congress seem fast" (Woodward 1991, 265).

[33]Democracy may not be all that easy to maintain, and indeed many democracies have often reverted to authoritarian rule. Moreover, it is reasonable to expect that some of the new democracies in the current wave will collapse. But democracy may not be peculiarly fragile. Any government can be overthrown by a sufficiently large and dedicated group of thugs with guns. And it is not at all clear that authoritarian governments—fraught with histories of coups and countercoups, and with endless battles for succession—are any less fragile. The problem seems to be one of definition. When a democracy gets overthrown we say it has failed, but when one dictator topples another we sometimes see this as persistence of form and a kind of stability.

What is the meaning of life? And, why are we all here, anyway? In contrast, some of the competitors of democracy have seemed to offer admirable—even sublime—qualities that are not attainable with democracy. Some cater to the desire for security, certainty, and community, and they seductively proclaim the existence of a general will supplied by God, by temporal authority, or by a cosmic populist sense, thus relieving individuals of the task of determining their own self-interest in matters of governance. They often offer to manage individual idiosyncracies for the greater good and to give security to all by arranging to have the collective or an overseer protect the individual against the traumas of risk and failure. And they authoritatively supply truth through comforting revelation, freeing people from the uncertainties of individual error.[34]

In addition, while democracy destroys the automatic political relevance of some political and class differences, in practice it has proven to be incapable of delivering certain kinds of social and economic equality. In fact, as argued earlier, it has in part grown in acceptance precisely because privileged people have generally been able to preserve their advantages under it.

Moreover, democracy can be quite disorderly. It is inherently and distressingly messy and contentious, and people are permitted loudly and irritatingly to voice opinions that are clearly erroneous and even dangerous.

In getting people to reject competitors which promise to do better in these respects, democrats have, it seems to me, essentially persuaded them to accept the Ralph's Grocery philosophy. Ralph's Pretty Good Grocery in Lake Wobegon, a Minnesota town invented by humorist Garrison Keillor, operates under a sensible but unexhilarating slogan: "If you can't get it at Ralph's, you can probably get along without it." (The opposite slogan, hopelessly unrealistic and utopian, advertises Alice's Restaurant—in some other town—where "you can get anything you want.") Democrats of the Smith variety have come to embrace Ralph's point of view in general form: if you can't get it with democracy, they suggest, you can probably get along without it.

It may be possible to create a society where comforting truth is supplied from on high, where strict social equality is attained, or where order reigns supreme, but experience suggests that society in the process loses flexibility, responsiveness, and intellectual growth. On the whole, democrats have decided, it is better to get along without the blessings an orderly and sternly equal society can bring.

As an institution, then, democracy is at once effective and defective: it works, but it is incapable of delivering certain goods. Beginning about 200 years ago people in the developed world have increasingly come to conclude that it is not only easier to attain the pretty good than the really terrific, it is also wiser.

In an essay first published in 1939, E. M. Forster recommended that we raise "two cheers for democracy" in a perspective that the folks at Ralph's Grocery can

---

[34]One classic, if extreme, expression of this perspective is the Grand Inquisitor in Dostoyevsky's *The Brothers Karamazov*. As he sees it, people are terrified of the freedom and individualism of democracy, and they are willing, indeed anxious, to surrender it for bread, security, miracle, mystery, authority, and the warmth of communal unity. "All that man seeks on earth," he explains, is "some one to worship, some one to keep his conscience, and some means of uniting all in one unanimous and harmonious ant-heap" (1945 ed., 305–306). It would seem, however, that if the Grand Inquisitor were right, prisons and slavery would be more popular.

readily relate to: in a sentiment later echoed by Winston Churchill, Forster observed that democracy "is less hateful than other contemporary forms of government" (1951, 69). Or, as it is usually put: democracy is the worst form of government except for all the rest.[35]

Admittedly, this unromantic, even antiromantic, view of democracy does not lend itself to glowing slogans. Romantic democrats have banners that proclaim "liberté, égalité, fraternité!"[36] and romantic antidemocrats have slogans like "Workers of the world, unite! You have nothing to lose but your chains!" or "Ein Reich, Ein Volk, Ein Führer!" Democrats of the Smith/Lincoln/Barnum/Forster/Churchill persuasion, by contrast, proclaim only, and in small letters, "you can't fool all of us all the time..." But they can shrug quizzically, point to 200 years of experience, and mutter quietly, "Well, it seems to work." As a form of government, democracy may be messy, but to try to make it perfect would be absurd, potentially dangerous, and oxymoronic.

CREATION OF DEMAND FOR CONGENIAL VALUES

Democracy's advocates also created demand for values which, if embraced, would help their product to be accepted. For example, democracy will be aided (but its success will not necessarily be assured) if the notion becomes accepted that the government should be visualized as the creation of ordinary people, and that it ought to be routinely responsive to their will and preferences; or that a rigid class system is a bad thing; or that liberty is a good one.

As noted above, Voltaire was a great propagandist for liberty, but he was not a democrat. In time democrats were able to demonstrate that liberty can be obtained best with their system; that, as Huntington puts it, "liberty is, in a sense, the peculiar virtue of democracy. If one is concerned with liberty as an ultimate social value, one should also be concerned with the fate of democracy" (1991b, 28). To that degree, Voltaire was playing into the hands of democracy's promoters.

Something similar has happened in the current democratic wave. In the 1960s the Catholic Church adopted the notion that the church ought to seek to promote "social change" and to protect "basic personal rights" (Huntington 1991b, 78). These dictates did not particularly stem from a newfound love for democracy, but from a need to respond to various then-fashionable forms of "liberation theology," some of which were totalitarian (and violent) in origin. By the late 1980s, however, the Pope, while specifically denying he was an "evangelizer of democracy," argued that, since he was "the evangelizer of the Gospel" to which "of course, belong all the problems of human rights," it followed that democracy "belongs to the message of the Church" because, he now had come to believe, "democracy means human rights" (Huntington 1991b, 84).

---

[35]Winston Churchill, referring perhaps to Forster, observed in a House of Commons speech in November 1947 that "it has been said that democracy is the worst form of government except all those other forms that have been tried from time to time" (1950, 200). Twenty years before Forster, William Ralph Inge had put it this way: "Democracy is a form of government which may be rationally defended, not as good, but as being less bad than any other" (1919, 5).

[36]In my view, liberté is essential to democracy, while a quest for égalité and fraternité only complicate matters.

DEVELOPING FASHION MODELS

Democracy soon developed admirable fashion leaders or role models. The idea of democracy took hold first in modern times primarily in Britain, the United States, and northern Europe, areas that have proved in many respects over the last two centuries to be fashion leaders—watched, admired, and then imitated. The wealth and vigor of these countries have not been irrelevant to the appeal of their ideas: advertisers always picture admirable, attractive people using or modeling their products. But the message is not that you must *be* admirable and attractive in order to buy the product, but rather that you will *become* admirable and attractive *if* you buy it.[37]

LUCK AND TIMING

Finally, there was, as in the case of the promotion of war aversion, the matter of luck and timing. Although democrats were able to show as time went by that democracy is inherently a good—pretty good—product, and also that it is markedly superior in several important respects to the competition, this was not enough to assure success: inherent superiority has never guaranteed that a product will come to dominate a market. Most objective experts agree that Beta is superior to VHS for home video recording; yet, VHS captured an overwhelming share of the market. We all now agree that photocopying is better than carbon paper, but when Xerox started out its chief problem was convincing people that they had any need for their machines. To be sure, it is easier to peddle a pretty good product than a pretty bad one, but products rarely sell themselves: they need to become available at the right time and to be pushed in the right way.

Democratic promoters were lucky that they first tested their product in Britain and the United States because, in the process, democracy came to be associated with countries which were held to be admirable—that is, which became fashion leaders or role models—for reasons that were often quite irrelevant to the institution itself. Moreover, they were lucky that the French Revolution, with all its democratic excesses, came *after*, rather than before, the substantial establishment of democracy in the United States and Britain. Had France stood as the only example of democracy, the experience might have permanently discredited the

---

[37]Huntington points to a similar phenomenon which he calls "demonstration effects" or "snowballing." He concludes, however, that "snowballing alone is a weak cause of democratization" (1991b, 100–106, 288). Fashion leadership relates to the correlation between democracy and economic development. Consider an analogy. At one time Paris was the center of fashion for women's clothes. Designs shown there soon filtered to other areas in the world in a fairly predictable pattern: cities and areas that were with it copied Paris quickly, those less with it took longer or avoided infection entirely. For the most part, Paris was imitated most quickly by people in other large urban areas in the developed world. Paris fashions did well in New York not because New York is a large city like Paris, but because New Yorkers were more anxious to be with it than people in rural areas—or indeed than people in other large cities like Los Angeles or Atlanta. There is a strong, if imperfect, correlation between Paris fashion and urbanization. But the essential determinant, the one that explains the diffusion best, is not city size, but rather the degree to which people are tuned in to fashion cues coming out of Paris.

product.[38] They were also lucky that the spectacular, if temporary, failure of democracy in America—the Civil War—did not happen earlier. In addition, the progress of democracy has sometimes been importantly propelled by unforeseen events, particularly World Wars I and II, which substantially discredited some of its chief competitors.

By the same token, however, the triumph of democracy has been by no means inevitable. If the British and American democratic experiments had become negative role models by degenerating into the mob violence and expansionary war that characterized France after its democratic revolution of 1789, the world might never have adopted democracy at all and could easily have remained mired in what Ernest Gellner calls "the dreadful regiment of kings and priests" (1988, 3–4). Or Hitler's dynamic alternative to democracy—highly attractive at the time to many—might have flourished if he had not had expansionary, and ultimately self-destructive, war secretly on his agenda.[39] On the other hand, since literacy and modern communications do not seem to be required for a country to become democratic, the world—or substantial portions of it—could have become democratic centuries earlier if the right people at the right time had gotten the idea, had deftly promoted and demonstrated it, and been graced by the right kind of luck. And the process can perhaps be reversed or superseded without notable social or economic change if other ideas come along which seem, or can be made to seem, superior.

DEMOCRACY AND PEACE:
A SPURIOUS CONNECTION?

It seems to me that some areas of the world can productively be considered "advanced" and that, in general, ideas move from more advanced areas to the rest of the world. This observation may be somewhat tautological since we are likely to

[38]Thomas Jefferson, one of democracy's most adept promoters, was fully aware of the danger posed by the disastrous French example. As he wrote in 1795, "What a tremendous obstacle to the future attempts at liberty will be the atrocities of Robespierre!" (1939 ed., 279).

[39]In France, democracy degenerated into chaos, the rise of a dictatorship, and then aggressive, continent-wide military expansion. In the wake of the Napoleonic Wars, most European leaders blamed democracy for this development and sought to suppress it—quite possibly setting its progress back substantially just as Jefferson had feared. According to a recent biographer, Metternich "was determined that a French revolution and a Napoleon should never plague Europe again. The former was 'the volcano which must be extinguished, the gangrene which must be burnt out, the hydra with jaws open to swallow the social order'. He had seen it arouse hysterical expectations drowned in blood, and the ensuing 'saviour' turn into a tyrant whose ambition had caused the death of millions" (Seward 1991, 85). In Germany a century later, democracy also degenerated into chaos, the rise of a dictatorship, and then aggressive, continent-wide military expansion. In the wake of Hitler's aggressions, however, most Western leaders blamed *chaos* (particularly economic chaos) for this development and sought to encourage democracy as a remedy. As the Truman doctrine of 1947 puts it, "The seeds of totalitarian regimes . . . spread and grow in the evil soil of poverty and strife. . . . The free peoples of the world look to us for support in maintaining their freedoms. If we falter in our leadership, we may endanger the peace of the world."

determine which areas are "advanced" by observing that new ideas tend to origi-nate there. But it does seem that when ideas have filtered throughout the world in recent centuries, they have tended to do so in one direction, with what Europeans would a century ago have called the "civilized world" at the lead. Without prejudg-ing the quality or value of the ideas so transmitted, it does seem that, for better or worse, there has been a long and fairly steady process of what is often called "Westernization": Taiwan has become more like Canada than Canada has become like Taiwan; Gabon has become more like Belgium than Belgium has become like Gabon (on this issue, see also Nadelmann 1990, 484).

In recent centuries, major ideas that have gone from the developed world to the less developed world include Christianity, the abolition of slavery, the accep-tance of democratic institutions and Western economic and social forms, and the application of the scientific method. Not all of these have been fully or readily ac-cepted, but the point is that the process has largely been unidirectional: there has so far been little in the way of a reverse flow of ideas. Sometimes ideas which have had a vogue and become passé in the West can still be seen to be playing them-selves out in the less advanced world: the romance about violent class revolution, largely a nineteenth-century Western idea, has been mostly discredited in the West, but it continues to inspire a few of revolutionaries in less developed lands.

As suggested above, the growth in acceptance of the idea of democracy seems best explained by this sort of analysis (see also Mueller 1990). After a long process, democracy has been selling well, particularly lately, even in such isolated and un-derdeveloped places as Burma and Madagascar. Like soccer and Shakespeare and fast food and the cotton gin and the airplane and the machine gun and the com-puter and the Beatles, it caught on first in one corner of the world and is in the process, except where halted by dedicated forces, of spreading worldwide. Eventually, I suppose, it could fall from fashion, but for now things look pretty good.

In the last few years there has been a burgeoning and intriguing discussion about the connection between democracy and war aversion (see for example, Doyle 1986; Russett 1990; Singer and Wildavsky 1993). Most notable has been the empirical observation that no two democracies have ever gotten into a war with each other. This relationship may be substantially spurious. The idea that war is undesirable and inefficacious and the idea that democracy is a good form of gov-ernment have largely followed the same trajectory: they were accepted first in northern Europe and in North America and then gradually, with a number of traumatic setbacks, became more accepted elsewhere. In this view, the rise of democracy not only is associated with the rise of war aversion, but also with the decline of slavery, religion, capital punishment, and cigarette smoking, and with the growing acceptance of capitalism, scientific methodology, women's rights, en-vironmentalism, abortion, and the string quartet.

Although these ideas all have followed the same trajectory, they have been substantially out of synchronization with each other: they have followed parallel trends, but not coterminous ones. The movement toward democracy began some 200 years ago, but the movement against war really began only 100 years ago. Critics of the democracy/peace connection often cite examples of wars or near-wars between democracies. Most of these took place before World War I—that is, before war aversion had been bought as an idea by large numbers of people in the "advanced" world.

If democracy, as Mencken put it, is "the theory that the common people know what they want, and deserve to get it good and hard" (1920b, 203), the people will get war if they want it. Before 1914, democracies were often poised for war, even with other democracies: France and England certainly neared war in the Fashoda crisis, and both the War of 1812 and World War I could be considered to have democrats on both sides. Moreover, if Cuba had been as brutally run by democratic Belgium in 1898 as it was by undemocratic Spain, the resentment triggered in the United States is unlikely to have been much less. Belgium and Holland, democracies by some standards, got into a war in 1830, and Switzerland in 1847 and the United States in 1861 tumbled into civil wars in which the two sides remained essentially democratic.[40]

Since World War I, the democracies have been in the lead in rejecting war as a methodology. As discussed in Chapter 9, this has not necessarily caused them to adopt a pacifist approach, and many of them have found themselves in wars, usually deriving from colonial commitments or from participation in the Cold War against threatening Communism. But they have taken the lead in promoting the ideas that war is a bad thing and that democracy is a good one.

However, while democracy and war aversion have often been promoted by the same advocates, the relationship may not be a causal one. And when the two trends are substantially out of sync today, democracies will fight one another. Jordan's elected parliament likes to scream for war with Israel. It is not at all clear that telling the hawks in the Jordanian parliament that Israel is a democracy will dampen their ardor in the slightest. The same phenomenon, it seems, has been found in the various elected parliaments in the former Yugoslavia. A necessary, logical connection between democracy and war aversion, accordingly, is far from clear.

---

[40]The South was democratic, of course, only among the white population. Huntington argues, "Democracies are often unruly, but they are not often politically violent. In the modern world democratic systems tend to be less subject to civil violence than are non-democratic systems" (1991b, 28). This is probably generally true for the "modern world," but less so for the nineteenth century.

ANTICIPATED CATACLYSMS:
PREDICTIONS ABOUT ENDLESS
PEACE, TERMINAL WAR,
AND OTHER CALAMITIES

In a book published in 1623, the religious writer and peace advocate, Eméric Crucé, observed that, "the ancient theologians promised [that] after 6,000 years have lapsed . . . the world will live happily and at peace." Crucé was alluding to two widely accepted notions. The first held that a day for God takes up 1,000 human years and was based on two biblical passages: "For a thousand years in your sight are like a day that has just gone by" (Psalm 90:4) and "With the Lord a day is like a thousand years" (2 Peter 3:8). The second held that the life of mankind, following the pattern of the creation week, would therefore encompass 6,000 years of toil followed by 1,000 years of rest.

"Now it happens," suggested Crucé hopefully, "that this period will soon be over" (1972, 146). In this judgment he was, however, somewhat premature.

There is, regrettably, some disagreement about the age of the earth, and therefore about when its 6,001st year will begin. But many theologians of Crucé's era had spent much time trying to dope it out. Easily the most famous of these was the Archbishop of Armagh, James Ussher (1581–1656). He worked chiefly from biblical information but added both extrabiblical and astronomical data to develop a complete chronology of the history of the earth.

His findings, written in Latin, cover exactly 2,000 pages of his "Whole Works," and they conclude that God created heaven and earth at 6 PM on Saturday, October 22, 4004 B.C. and that light was created on Sunday, October 23, at high noon (Barr 1985, 591–593; Knox 1967, 105–106). Ussher worked with great care and does not seem to have forced the data to fit preconceived notions, although because of the ambiguity of some of the biblical material it was necessary from time to time to make assumptions that might make even a rational choice theorist blush: for example, to make things come out sensibly, he finds it useful to conclude that when Genesis 11:26 says "when Terah had lived seventy years, he became the father of Abram, Nahor and Haran," it means that Terah became the father of Nahor and Haran when he was seventy, but that he did not become the father of Abram for another sixty years (Barr 1985, 586).

Despite such occasional infelicities (he also ignored the stopping of the sun in the days of Joshua and its brief reverse perambulation in the days of Hezekiah), Ussher's chronology gained substantial acceptance, and for our purposes it clearly forms a useful first approximation.[1] However, an adjustment is necessary if one is to adapt his dating system to ours. Although Pope Gregory XIII had introduced the calendar we use today in 1582, Ussher kept to the old Julian system and, partly because of his agitation, the British did not adopt the Gregorian calendar until 1752 (Barr 1985, 584; 1987, 10). Accordingly, Ussher's datings are ten days out of sync with ours.

Putting this all together and adjusting dates appropriately, we have an empirical test. If everybody has everything right, we can expect the earth's 6,001st year to begin—and therefore peace and happiness to break out—on Friday, November 1, 1996, at 6 PM local (that is, Iraq) time.

Should war still abound on that day, we could abandon Ussher and test the estimations of some of the other biblical chronologists. By the calculations of the Jesuit thinker, Petavius (1583–1652), the earth's 6,001st year will not begin until 2017 (on October 26); by those of Martin Luther (1483–1546), it will come in 2040; by those of the eleventh-century Anglo-Norman historian, Orderic Vitalis (and several earlier scholars), it will come in 2048; by those of the great classicist, Joseph Justus Scalinger (1540–1609), it will come in 2050; by those of Calvisius (1556–1615), it will come in 2056; by those published by Bishop John Lightfoot in 1658, it will come in 2072; and by those of Jewish tradition, it will be delayed until 2239 (Barr 1985, 582, 590; 1987, 3, 9; Young 1982, 24; Lightfoot 1989, 26). In all, we have, perhaps, something to look forward to.

———

VARIOUS SHAPES OF THINGS TO COME

Crucé was far from the last person to see light at the end of the tunnel. Others, however, have envisioned a dark tunnel at the end of the light.

HAMLET: What news?
ROSENCRANTZ: None, my lord, but that the world's grown honest.
HAMLET: Then is doomsday near.

— *WILLIAM SHAKESPEARE*, HAMLET, *1602–1603.*

---

[1]Ussher's chronology had several tidy benchmarks. By his reckoning Jesus was born precisely in the year 4000 A.M. (anno mundi) and the Temple of Solomon was completed precisely in the year 3000 A.M. Moreover, although he could not possibly appreciate the significance of the finding, he was able to deduce that Noah's infamous flood had began on Sunday, December 7. Barr 1985, 594, 607.

The guarantee of perpetual peace is nothing less than that great artist, nature. In her mechanical course we see that her aim is to produce a harmony among men, against their will and indeed through their discord. . . . The spirit of commerce, which is incompatible with war, sooner or later gains the upper hand in every state. As the power of money is perhaps the most dependable of all the powers included under the state power, states see themselves forced, without any moral urge, to promote honorable peace and by mediation to prevent war wherever it threatens to break out.

—IMMANUEL KANT, 1795. (KANT 1957 ED., 24)

The present is distinguished from every preceding age by an universal ardour of enterprise in arts and manufactures. Nations, convinced at length that war is always a losing game, have converted their swords and muskets into factory implements, and now contend with each other in the bloodless but still formidable strife of trade. They no longer send troops to fight on distant fields, but fabrics to drive before them those of their old adversaries in arms, and to take possession of a foreign mart. To impair the resources of a rival at home, by underselling his wares abroad, is the new belligerent system, in pursuance of which every nerve and sinew of the people are put upon the strain.

—ANDREW URE, 1835. (URE 1835)

War is on its last legs; and a universal peace is as sure as is the prevalence of civilization over barbarism, of liberal government over feudal forms. The question for us is only How soon?

—RALPH WALDO EMERSON, 1849
(EMERSON 1904 ED., 161, EMPHASIS IN THE ORIGINAL)

The second greatest evil known to mankind—the one by which, with the exception of religious persecution, most suffering has been caused—is, unquestionably, the practice of war. That this barbarous pursuit is, in the progress of society, steadily declining, must be evident, even to the most hasty reader of European history.

—HENRY THOMAS BUCKLE, 1855. (BUCKLE 1862, 137)

There thus seems reason for believing that all the leading currents of modern civilisation are setting steadily and rapidly towards the formation of a body of international opinion which . . . may ultimately, and at no remote date, become an effective check on the conduct of nations.

—J. E. CAIRNES, 1865. (CAIRNES 1865, 649)

Perpetual peace is a dream, and not a pleasant one at that; and war is part of God's ordering of the world. . . . Without war, the world would wallow in materialism.

—COUNT HELMUTH VON MOLTKE, 1880. (CITED IN CHICKERING 1975, 392–393)

Savagery, with its idols and weapons—these are already repelling people. If we are still closer to barbarism than most people think, we are perhaps also closer to ennoblement than many hope. The prince or statesman is perhaps already alive who will accomplish what will be regarded in the future as the most glorious and brilliant of all deeds—who will bring about general disarmament.

—BARONESS BERTHA VON SUTTNER, 1889. (CITED IN CHICKERING 1975, 90,
EMPHASIS BY VON SUTTNER)

My hope was that the terrible effects of dynamite would keep men from war, but now I see to my utter dismay that my life work amounts to nothing. Everywhere inventors are bent on the adaptation of high explosives to the aims of mutual destruction. . . . I greatly fear that the perpetual peace of which Kant has spoken will be preceded by the peace of the cemetery. . . . The twentieth century will be an epoch of great unrest; . . . I am pessimistic about mankind. The only thing that will ever prevent them from waging war is terror.

—ALFRED NOBEL, 1890. (NOBEL 1925, 194-198)

The outward and visible sign of the end of war was the introduction of the magazine rifle. . . . [I]t is impossible for the modern State to carry on war under the modern conditions with any prospect of being able to carry that war to a conclusion by defeating its adversary by force of arms on the battlefield. No decisive war is possible. Neither is any war possible . . . that will not entail, even upon the victorious Power, the destruction of its resources and the break-up of society. War therefore has become impossible, except at the price of suicide.

—JEAN DE BLOCH, 1899. (BLOCH 1914, XVII, XXXI)

There is only one thing to be rationally expected, and that is a frightful effusion of blood in revolution and war during the century now opening.

— WILLIAM GRAHAM SUMNER, 1899. (SUMNER 1899, 333)

[I]t must be remembered that under the touch of civilisation war has lost some of its most offensive features. The condition of non-combatants is immensely relieved, and we may regard the sack which gave defenceless women and children to the mercy of a maddened soldiery, and the bombardment of unfortified towns and harbours, as henceforth excluded from the casualties of civilised warfare. I believe that the state of war is not only by no means the greatest of all evils, but that it is calculated to evoke some of the best qualities of human nature, giving the spirit a predominance over the flesh.

—THE REVEREND FATHER H. I. D. RYDER, 1899. (RYDER 1899, 726–727)

It is by conflict alone that life realizes itself. . . . War may change its shape, the struggle here intensifying, there abating; it may be uplifted by ever loftier purposes and nobler causes—but cease? How shall it cease? Indeed, in the light of History, universal peace appears less as a dream than as a nightmare which shall be realized only when the ice has crept to the heart of the sun, and the stars, left black and trackless, start from their orbits.

—J. A. CRAMB, 1900. (CRAMB 1915, 146)

We are dashing towards the precipice, cannot stop, and we are approaching its edge.

—LEO TOLSTOY, 1904. (TOLSTOY 1904, 23)

ïïEven a successful conflict between modern States can bring no material gain. We can now look forward with something like confidence to the time when war between civilized nations will be considered as antiquated as the duel, and when the peacemakers shall be called the children of God.

—G. P. GOOCH, 1911. (GOOCH 1911, 248–249)

The hope seems warranted that, in no distant future, life among nations will become still more closely assimilated to life among citizens of the same nation, with legislation, administration, reform all tending to the one great object of law, order and peace among men.

—SIR THOMAS BARCLAY, 1911. (BARCLAY 1911, 16)

What shall we say of the Great War of Europe, ever threatening, ever impending, and which never comes? We shall say that it will never come. Humanly speaking, it is impossible. . . . The bankers will not find the money for such a fight, the industries of Europe will not maintain it, the statesmen cannot. So whatever the bluster or apparent provocation, it comes to the same thing at the end. There will be no general war until the masters direct the fighters to fight. The masters have much to gain, but vastly more to lose, and their signal will not be given.

—DAVID STARR JORDAN, 1913. (JORDAN 1913, 173, 178)

History shows that war is a powerful instrument of civilization. . . . As wars were necessary for human progress in the past, we may conclude that they will also be necessary to progress in the future. . . . War is not only a biological necessity, but under certain circumstances a moral necessity, and is an indispensable instrument of civilization.

—GENERAL FRIEDRICH VON BERNHARDI, 1914. (BERNHARDI 1914, 111, 114; EMPHASIS IN THE ORIGINAL)

[T]o the normal vision of most of us war is almost unimaginable; even in Europe none of the great civilized nations has seen war within its boundaries for more than forty years. . . . The signs seems to indicate that the world is losing both its imagination and its taste for war. . . . The fact can no longer be blinked at; the military game is up.

—RANDOLPH S. BOURNE, 1914. (BOURNE 1914, 12–13)

The end of war, for all time, is now definitely in sight. . . . Mars has already received his deathblow. . . . A world emancipated from the thrall of war, long only the speculation of philosophers, is growing real and tangible.

— GEORGE A. ENGLAND, 1914. (ENGLAND 1914, 12–14)

In Europe the epoch of conquest is over, and save in the Balkans and perhaps on the fringes of the Austrian and Russian Empires, it is as certain as anything in politics can be, that the frontiers of our modern national states are finally drawn. My own belief is that there will be no more wars among the six Great Powers.

—Henry Noel Brailsford, 1914. (Brailsford 1914, 35)

This, the greatest of all wars, is not just another war—it is the last war!

—H. G. Wells, 1914. (Wells 1914, 14)

He [John Maynard Keynes] told me that he was quite certain that the war could not last much more than a year and that the belligerent countries could not be ruined by it. The world, he explained, was enormously rich, but its wealth was, fortunately, of a kind which could not be rapidly realised for war purposes: it was in the form of capital equipment for making things which were useless for waging war. When all the available wealth had been used up—which, he thought would take about a year—the Powers would have to make peace. . . . These views were stated with extraordinary clarity and absolute conviction and I unhesitatingly believed them. . . . He embraced me with emotion when I said that I should not enlist since the war would be over before I could take part in it. It was a great relief for us all to have Maynard's assurance on this point.

—David Garnett, recalling a conversation from 1914. (Garnett 1954, 271–272).

In September 1914 Maynard . . . rebuked me sharply...for surmising that the war would not soon be over. . . . Maynard was the cleverest man I ever met.

—Clive Bell. (Bell 1956, 45, 52)

The existence of the Soviet Republic side by side with imperialist states for a long time is unthinkable. One or the other must triumph in the end. And before that end supervenes, a series of frightful collisions between the Soviet Republic and the bourgeois states will be inevitable.

—Vladimir I. Lenin, 1919. (cited in Burin 1963, 337)

[Today] is witnessing the dawn of universal peace. . . . Public opinion is now turning against war . . . as a just and desirable method of settling disputes between civilized people.

—Mary Scrugham, 1921. (Scrugham 1921, 81, 124)

To the multitude who now preach that we are entering an era of peace, I can only say: my dear fellows, you have badly misinterpreted the horoscope of the age, for it points not to peace, but to war as never before.

—Adolf Hitler, November 5, 1930. (cited in Knox 1990)

Men have brought their powers of subduing nature to such a pitch that by using them they could now very easily exterminate one another to the last man.

—SIGMUND FREUD, 1930. (FREUD 1930, 144)

When the next war comes . . . European civilization [will be] wiped out.

— STANLEY BALDWIN, 1930s. (CITED IN KAGAN 1987)

If it rests with Germany war will not come again. This country has a more profound impression than any other of the evil that war causes. . . . It is the disciplined conviction of the Nazi Movement that war can benefit no one, but only bring general ruin in its train.

—ADOLF HITLER, AUGUST 5, 1934. (HITLER 1942, 1181)

If we don't end war, war will end us.

—H. G. WELLS, 1936. (CHARACTER IN THE 1936 FILM,
THINGS TO COME, SCREENPLAY BY WELLS)

The end of everything we call life is close at hand and cannot be evaded.

—H. G. WELLS, 1945. (WELLS 1968, 67)

The war shall soon be over. We shall recover in fifteen or twenty years, and then we'll have another go at it.

—JOSEPH STALIN, APRIL 1945. (CITED IN DJILAS 1962, 114-115)

A future war with the Soviet Union is as certain as anything in this world.

—JOSEPH G. GREW, 1945. (CITED IN GADDIS 1987, 218n)

In our recent Western history war has been following war in an ascending order of intensity; and today it is already apparent that the War of 1939–45 was not the climax of this crescendo movement.

—ARNOLD J. TOYNBEE, 1950. (TOYNBEE 1950, 4)

Unless we are able, in the near future, to abolish the mutual fear of military aggression, we are doomed.

—ALBERT EINSTEIN, 1950. (EINSTEIN 1960, 533)

We are faced with an either-or, and we haven't much time. The either is acceptance of a restriction of nuclear armaments. . . . The or is not a risk but a certainty. It is this. There is no agreement on tests. The nuclear arms race between the United States and the U.S.S.R. not only continues but accelerates. Other countries join in. Within, at the most, six years, China and several other states have a stock of nuclear bombs. Within, at the most, ten years, some of those bombs are going off. I am saying this as responsibly as I can. That is the certainty.

—C. P. SNOW, 1960. (SNOW 1961, 259)

I have a firm belief that unless we have more serious and sober thought on various aspects of the strategic problem . . . we are not going to reach the year 2000—and maybe not even the year 1965—without a cataclysm.

—HERMAN KAHN, 1961. (KAHN 1961, x)

There will be liberation wars as long as imperialism exists. . . . Such wars are not only justified, they are inevitable . . . The victory of socialism on a world scale, inevitable by virtue of the laws of history, is no longer far off.

—NIKITA S. KHRUSHCHEV, 1960. (CITED IN HUDSON ET AL., 1961, 212–214)

[L]iberal democracy on the American model increasingly tends to the condition of monarchy in the 19th century: a holdover form of government, one which persists in isolated or peculiar places here and there, and may even serve well enough for special circumstances, but which has simply no relevance to the future. It is where the world was, not where it is going. In this respect American institutions reached their apogee in 1919.

—DANIEL PATRICK MOYNIHAN, 1975. (MOYNIHAN 1975, 6)

In my opinion the world is moving ineluctably towards a third world war—a strategic nuclear war. I do not believe that anything can be done to prevent it. The international system is simply too unstable to survive for long.

—HANS J. MORGENTHAU, 1979. (CITED IN BOYLE 1985, 73)

The Soviet Union is a seriously troubled, even sick society. The indices of economic stagnation and even decline are extraordinary. The indices of social disorder—social pathology is not too strong a term—are even more so. The defining event of the decade might well be the break-up of the Soviet Empire. But that . . . could also be the defining danger of the decade.

—DANIEL PATRICK MOYNIHAN, 1980. (MOYNIHAN 1992, 19)

I believe that the Soviet system has no internal potential for change, just as Soviet imperialism cannot stop of its own will. In theory, the only possibility of change in the Soviet Union lies in the creation of some kind of enlightened absolutism which could initiate reforms, but even then bureaucratic repression can strangle the process of democratization. Even for such an enlightened autocrat to emerge, it is imperative that there be some sort of a national crisis: *a military crisis or a revolutionary crisis, or both at the same time.*

—MILOVAN DJILAS, 1980. (CITED IN PIPES 1984, 203)

One day—and it is hard to believe that it will not be soon—we will make our choice. Either we will sink into the final coma and end it all or, as I trust and believe, we will awaken to the truth of our peril . . . and rise up to cleanse the earth of nuclear weapons.

—JONATHAN SCHELL, 1982. (SCHELL 1982, 231)

The nomenklatura *[the Soviet elite] will resist changes as long as it can and that means, in effect, as long as it is able to compensate for internal failures with triumphs abroad. It will always find the pursuit of an aggressive foreign policy preferable to coping with internal problems, because in the former case it can buy time with tactical maneuvers of all sorts, whereas internal problems call for structural changes which are far more difficult to undo. . . . This conceded, it is nevertheless true that the Stalinist system now prevailing in the Soviet Union has outlived it usefulness and that the forces making for change are becoming well-nigh irresistible.*

—RICHARD PIPES, 1984. (PIPES 1984, 279–280)

This book is based on a central proposition: the American-Soviet conflict is not some temporary aberration but a historical rivalry that will long endure.

—ZBIGNIEW BRZEZINSKI, 1986. (BRZEZINSKI 1986, xiii)

Russian culture, geography, and the dynamics of imperial rule all militate against the radical transformation of the Soviet Union as a player in world politics. Of course, states have changed their roles quite dramatically in response to altered circumstances. . . . But it is virtually inconceivable that a Soviet empire at the peak of its relative military prowess would choose quite voluntarily to attempt to settle permanently for a comfortably semiretired status from the rough and tumble of world politics. Even though severe economic problems may well invite and require severe solutions, the Russian culture, which is the product of a half-millennium of national experience, is not going to be cast off and replaced at the policy convenience of a reforming czar.

—COLIN S. GRAY, 1991. (GRAY 1991, 73).

REFERENCES

Adomeit, Hannes. 1986. Soviet Crisis Prevention and Management: Why and When Do Soviet Leaders Take Risks? *Orbis* 30 (1, Spring): 42–64.

Aird, John S. 1990. *Slaughter of the Innocents*. Washington, DC: AEI Press.

Alden, John. 1961. Up from the Ashes—The Saga of *Cassin* and *Downes*. *United States Naval Institute Proceedings* 87 (1, January): 33–41.

Allison, Graham T. 1971. *Essence of Decision: Explaining the Cuban Missile Crisis*. Boston: Little, Brown.

Almond, Gabriel A., and Sidney Verba. 1963. *The Civic Culture: Political Attitudes and Democracy in Five Nations*. Princeton: Princeton University Press.

Ambrose, Stephen E. 1990. Secrets of the Cold War. *New York Times,* 27 December, A19.

Angell, Norman. 1951. *After All: An Autobiography*. New York: Farrar, Straus and Young.

Arnett, Peter. 1972. Close-Up of North Vietnam at War: Everything Moves by Night. *New York Times,* 3 October, 4.

Art, Robert J., and Kenneth N. Waltz. 1983. Technology, Strategy, and the Uses of Force. In *The Use of Force,* ed. Robert J. Art and Kenneth N. Waltz. Lanham, Md.: University Press of America.

Ashton, Basil, Kenneth Hill, Alan Piazza, and Robin Zeitz. 1984. Famine in China. *Population and Development Review* 10 (4, December): 613–645.

Bairoch, Paul. 1981. The Main Trends in National Economic Disparities since the Industrial Revolution. In *Disparities in Economic Development since the Industrial Revolution,* ed. Paul Bairoch and M. Levy-Lebager. London: Macmillan.

Baldick, Robert. 1965. *The Duel: A History of Dueling*. New York: Potter.

Baldwin, Hanson W. 1950. War of Prevention: Perils of Proposed Attack on Soviet Now Are Weighed Against Alleged Advantage. *New York Times,* 1 September, 4.

Baldwin, David A. 1971. The Power of Positive Sanctions. *World Politics* 24 (1, October): 19–38.

Barclay, Thomas. 1911. Peace. In *Encyclopedia Britannica,* 11th ed., vol. 21, 4–16.

Barnhart, Michael A. 1987. *Japan Prepares for Total War: The Search for Economic Security, 1919–1941*. Ithaca: Cornell University Press.

Barr, James. 1985. Why the World Was Created in 4004 B.C.: Archbishop Ussher and Biblical Chronology. *Bulletin of the John Rylands University Library* 67 (2, Spring): 575–608.

———. 1987. Biblical Chronology: Legend or Science? Ethel M. Wood Lecture. Senate House. University of London, 4 March.

Barrett, David M. 1993. *Uncertain Warriors: Lyndon Johnson and His Vietnam Advisers*. Lawrence: University Press of Kansas.

Beales, A.F. 1931. *The History of Peace: A Short Account of the Organised Movements for International Peace*. New York: Dial.

Bell, Clive. 1956. *Old Friends: Personal Recollections*. London: Chatto & Windus.

Bell-Fialkoff, Andrew. 1993. A Brief History of Ethnic Cleansing. *Foreign Affairs* 72 (3, Summer): 110–121.

Bellah, Robert N., Richard Madsen, William M. Sullivan, Ann Swidler, and Steven M. Tipton. 1991. *The Good Society*. New York: Knopf.

Benthem van dem Bergh, Godfried van. 1992. *The Nuclear Revolution and the End of the Cold War*. London: Macmillan.

Berger, Thomas U. 1993. From Sword to Chrysanthemum: Japan's Culture of Anti-Militarism. *International Security* 17 (4, Spring): 119–150.

Berkowitz, Bruce D. 1987. *Calculated Risks*. New York: Simon and Schuster.

Berkowitz, Leonard. 1989. Situational Influences on Aggression. In *Aggression and War: Their Biological and Social Bases*, ed. Jo Groebel and Robert A. Hinde, 91–100. Cambridge: Cambridge University Press.

Bermeo, Nancy. 1990. Rethinking Regime Change. *Comparative Politics* 22 (3, April): 359–377.

Bernhardi, Friedrich von. 1914. *Germany and the Next War*. New York: Longmans, Green.

Bettmann, Otto L. 1974. *The Good Old Days—They Were Terrible!*. New York: Random House.

Betts, Richard K. 1987. *Nuclear Blackmail and Nuclear Balance*. Washington: Brookings.

Bialer, Uri. 1980. *Shadow of the Bomber: The Fear of Air Attack and British Politics, 1932–1939*. London: Royal Historical Society.

Bialer, Seweryn, and Michael Mandelbaum. 1988. *The Global Rivals*. New York: Knopf.

Binder, David. 1988. Soviet and Allies Shift on Doctrine. *New York Times*, 25 May, A13.

Blacker, Coit D. 1987. *Reluctant Warriors*. New York: Freeman.

Blainey, Geoffrey. 1973. *The Causes of Wars*. New York: Free Press.

Bloch, Jean de. 1914. *The Future of War in Its Technical, Economic and Political Relations*. Boston: World Peace Foundation.

Botterweck, G. Johannes, and Helmer Ringgren. 1986. *Theological Dictionary of the Old Testament*. Grand Rapids, Mich.: Eerdmans.

Boulding, Kenneth E. 1978. *Stable Peace*. Austin: University of Texas Press.

Bourne, Randolph S. 1914. The Tradition of War. *International Conciliation* (June).

Boyle, Francis Anthony. 1985. *World Politics and International Law*. Durham, NC: Duke University Press.

Bradley, Omar. 1949. This Way Lies Peace (as told to Beverly Smith). *Saturday Evening Post*, 15 October, 33ff.

Brailsford, Henry Noel. 1914. *The War of Steel and Gold*. London: G. Bell and Sons.

Brent, Peter. 1976. *Genghis Khan*. New York: McGraw-Hill.

Brodie, Bernard. 1966. *Escalation and the Nuclear Option*. Princeton: Princeton University Press.

————. 1973. *War and Politics.* New York: Macmillan.

Brooke, James. 1993. Governing Party's Candidate Wins Paraguay's Presidential Election. *New York Times,* 11 May, A10.

Brown, Frederic J. 1968. *Chemical Warfare: A Study in Restraints.* Princeton: Princeton University Press.

Brown, Seyom. 1987. *The Causes and Prevention of War.* New York: St. Martin's Press.

Broyles, William, Jr. 1984. Why Men Love War. *Esquire,* November, 55–65.

Brzezinski, Zbigniew. 1986. *Game Plan: A Geostrategic Framework for the Conduct of the U.S.-Soviet Contest.* Boston: Atlantic Monthly Press.

————. 1993. *Out of Control: Global Turmoil on the Eve of the 21st Century.* New York: Scribner's.

Buckle, Henry Thomas. 1862. *History of Civilization in England.* New York: Appleton.

Bueno de Mesquita, Bruce. 1981. *The War Trap.* New Haven: Yale University Press.

————. 1990. Pride of Place: The Origins of German Hegemony. *World Politics* 43 (1, October): 28–52.

Bundy, McGeorge. 1984. The Unimpressive Record of Atomic Diplomacy. In *The Nuclear Crisis Reader,* ed. Gwyn Prins, 42–54. New York: Vantage.

————. 1988. *Danger and Survival: Choices about the Bomb in the First Fifty Years.* New York: Random House.

Burin, Frederic S. 1963. The Communist Doctrine of the Inevitability of War. *American Political Science Review* 57 (2, June): 334–354.

Bury, J.B. 1920. *The Idea of Progress.* London: Macmillan.

Bush, George. 1989. Excerpts From Bush's Address on Foreign Policy at Coast Guard Academy. *New York Times,* 25 May, A8.

————. 1991. The Liberation of Kuwait Has Begun. In *The Gulf War Reader: History, Documents, Opinions,* ed. Micah L. Sifry and Christopher Cerf, 311–314. New York: Times Books/Random House. Speech of January 16, 1991.

Butow, Robert J.C. 1961. *Tojo and the Coming of the War.* Stanford: Stanford University Press.

Cairnes, J.E. 1865. International Law. *Fortnightly Review* 2 (1 November): 641–650.

Campbell, John C. 1967. *Tito's Separate Road: America and Yugoslavia in World Politics.* New York: Harper and Row.

Cannon, Walter B. 1929. *Bodily Changes in Pain, Hunger, Fear and Rage: An Account of Recent Researches into the Function of Emotional Excitement.* New York: Appleton-Century.

Carney, Robert B. 1981. Air Raid: Pearl Harbor! Reflections on a Day of Infamy. In *The Navy Was Not Ready for War,* ed. Paul Stillwell. Annapolis, Md.: Naval Institute Press.

Carr, E.H. 1946. *The Twenty Years' Crisis, 1919–1939.* New York: Harper and Row.

Carrington, Lord. 1988. East-West Relations: A Time of Far-Reaching Change. *NATO Review,* June.

Chatfield, Charles. 1971. *For Peace and Justice.* Knoxville: University of Tennessee Press.

Chickering, Roger. 1975. *Imperial Germany and a World Without War: The Peace Movement and German Society, 1892–1914.* Princeton: Princeton University Press.

————. 1988. War, Peace, and Social Mobilization in Imperial Germany: Patriotic Societies, the Peace Movement, and Socialist Labor. In *Peace Movements and Political Cultures,* ed. Charles Chatfield and Peter van den Dungen, 3–22. Knoxville: University of Tennessee Press.

Chodorow, Stanley, and MacGregor Knox. 1989. *The Mainstream of Civilization,* 5th ed. New York: Harcourt, Brace, Jovanovich.

Churchill, Winston S. 1932. *Amid These Storms: Thoughts and Adventures.* New York: Scribner's.

———. 1950. *Europe United: Speeches 1947 and 1948.* Ed. Randolph S. Churchill. Boston: Houghton Mifflin.

Civilian Production Administration. 1947. *Industrial Mobilization for War, Vol. I, Program and Administration.* Washington, DC: Bureau of Demobilization.

Claiborne, William, and Caryle Murphy. 1991. Retreat Down Highway of Doom: U.S. Warplanes Turned Iraqis' Escape Route Into Deathtrap. *Washington Post,* 2 March, A1.

Clarke, I.F. 1966. *Voices Prophesying War, 1763–1984.* London: Oxford University Press.

Clausewitz, Carl Von. 1976. *On War.* Trans. Michael Howard and Peter Paret. Princeton: Princeton University Press.

Clinton, William Jefferson. 1993. Inaugural Address. 20 January.

Cochran, Hamilton. 1963. *Noted American Duels and Hostile Encounters.* Philadelphia: Chilton.

Colton, Timothy J. 1986. *The Dilemma of Reform in the Soviet Union,* revised ed. New York: Council on Foreign Relations.

Contamine, Philippe. 1984. *War in the Middle Ages.* Oxford: Basil Blackwell.

Conway, M. Margaret. 1991. *Political Participation in the United States,* 2nd ed. Washington, DC: CQ Press.

Cook, Terrence. 1991. *The Great Alternatives of Social Thought.* Savage, Md.: Rowman & Littlefield.

Cooper, Sandi E. 1991. *Patriotic Pacifism: Waging War on War in Europe, 1815–1914.* New York: Oxford University Press.

Cramb, J.A. 1915. *The Origins and Destiny of Imperial Britain.* London: Murray.

Crawford, Neta C. 1993. Decolonization as an International Norm: The Evolution of Practices, Arguments, and Beliefs. In *Emerging Norms of Justified Intervention,* ed. Laura W. Reed and Carl Kaysen, 37–61. Cambridge, Mass.: American Academy of Arts and Sciences.

Crucé, Eméric. [1623] 1972. *The New Cineas.* New York: Garland.

Cushman, John F., Jr. 1992. Senate Endorses Pact to Reduce Strategic Arms. *New York Times,* 2 October, A1.

Dahl, Robert A. 1971. *Polyarchy.* New Haven: Yale University Press.

———. 1989. *Democracy and Its Critics.* New Haven: Yale University Press.

Darlin, Damon. 1990. And the New Champ In 1-Finger Chin-Ups Is Korea's Mr. Kim: Record-Happy Nation Is First In Many Guinness Entries, In Bid to Outdo Japan. *Wall Street Journal,* 17 May, A1.

Deane, John R. 1947. *The Strange Alliance.* New York: Viking.

Delli Carpini, Michael X., and Scott Keeter. 1991. Stability and Change in the U.S. Public's Knowledge of Politics. *Public Opinion Quarterly* 55 (4, Winter): 583–612.

Deudney, Daniel, and John Ikenberry. 1992. Who Won the Cold War? *Foreign Policy,* Summer, 123–138.

Djilas, Milovan. 1962. *Conversations with Stalin.* New York: Harcourt, Brace.

Dostoyevsky, Fyodor. [1879–1880] 1945. *The Brothers Karamazov.* Trans. Constance Garnett. New York: Random House.

Dower, John. 1986. *War Without Mercy: Race and Power in the Pacific War.* New York: Pantheon.

Doyle, Michael W. 1983. Kant, Liberal Legacies, and Foreign Affairs. *Philosophy and Public Affairs* 12 (Summer and Fall): 205–235, 323–353.

————. 1986. Liberalism and World Politics. *American Political Science Review* 80 (4, December): 1151–1169.

Drescher, Seymour. 1987. *Capitalism and Antislavery: British Mobilization in Comparative Perspective.* New York: Oxford University Press.

Drogin, Bob. 1991. On Forgotten Kuwait Road, 60 Miles of Wounds of War. *Los Angeles Times,* 10 March, A1.

Dumas, Samuel, and K.O. Vedel-Petersen. 1923. *Losses of Life Caused by War.* London: Oxford University Press.

Dupuy, R. Ernest, and George Fielding Eliot. 1937. *If War Comes.* New York: Macmillan.

Einstein, Albert. 1960. *Einstein on Peace.* Ed. Otto Nathan and Heinz Norden. New York: Simon and Schuster.

Eltis, David. 1987. *Economic Growth and the Ending of the Transatlantic Slave Trade.* New York: Oxford University Press.

Emerson, Ralph Waldo. 1904. War. In *The Complete Works of Ralph Waldo Emerson: Vol. 11, Miscellanies,* 148–176. Boston and New York: Houghton Mifflin.

Engerman, Stanley L. 1986. Slavery and Emancipation in Comparative Perspective: A Look at Some Recent Debates. *Journal of Economic History* 46 (2, June): 317–339.

England, George Allan. 1914. Fiat Pax. *International Conciliation,* August.

Evangelista, Matthew A. 1982/83. Stalin's Postwar Army Reappraised. *International Security* 7 (3, Winter): 110–138.

Falk, Stanley L. 1961. Disarmament on the Great Lakes: Myth or Reality? *U.S. Naval Institute Proceedings* 87 (2, December): 69–73.

Farrar, L.L., Jr. 1973. *The Short-War Illusion: German Policy, Strategy and Domestic Affairs, August-December 1914.* Santa Barbara, Calif: ABC-Clio.

Fearon, James D. 1991. Counterfactuals and Hypothesis Testing in Political Science. *World Politics* 43 (2, January): 169–195.

Fineman, Mark. 1993. Somalia Role Assessed as U.S. Flag Is Lowered. *Los Angeles Times,* 5 May, A1.

Fitzgerald, Frances. 1972. *Fire in the Lake: The Vietnamese and Americans in Vietnam.* New York: Vintage.

Foote, Peter G., and David M. Wilson. 1970. *The Viking Achievement.* New York: Praeger.

Forster, E.M. 1951. *Two Cheers for Democracy.* New York: Harcourt, Brace & World.

Freud, Sigmund. 1930. *Civilization and Its Discontents.* London: Hogarth.

————. 1957. *The Standard Edition of the Complete Psychological Works of Sigmund Freud.* Ed. James Strachey. London: Hogarth.

Friedman, Thomas L. 1992a. It's Harder Now to Figure Out Compelling National Interests. *New York Times,* 31 May, E5.

Friedman, Thomas L. 1992b. As Some Nations Build, the Past Devours Others. *New York Times,* 12 July, 4–1.

Friedrichs, Christopher R. 1979. *Urban Society in an Age of War.* Princeton: Princeton University Press.

Fujiwara, Akira. 1990. The Road to Pearl Harbor. In *Pearl Harbor Reexamined: Prologue to the Pacific War,* ed. Hilary Conroy and Harry Wray. Honolulu: University of Hawaii Press.

Fukuyama, Francis. 1987. Patterns of Soviet Third World Policy. *Problems of Communism* 36 (5, September-October): 1–13.

————. 1989. The End of History? *National Interest,* Summer, 3–18.

————. 1992. *The End of History and the Last Man.* New York: Free Press.

Fussell, Paul. 1975. *The Great War and Modern Memory*. New York: Oxford University Press.

Gaddis, John Lewis. 1974. Was the Truman Doctrine a Real Turning Point? *Foreign Affairs* 52 (2, January): 386–401.

———. 1982. *Strategies of Containment*. New York: Oxford University Press.

———. 1987. *The Long Peace: Inquiries Into the History of the Cold War*. New York: Oxford University Press.

———. 1992. *The United States and the Cold War: Implications, Reconsiderations, Provocations*. New York: Oxford University Press.

Garnett, David. 1954. *The Golden Echo*. New York: Harcourt, Brace.

Garthoff, Raymond L. 1992. Why Did the Cold War Arise, and Why Did It End? *Diplomatic History* 16 (2, Spring): 287–293.

Gates, Robert M. 1993. No Time to Disarm. *Wall Street Journal*, 23 August, A10.

Gellman, Barton. 1984. *Contending with Kennan: Toward a Philosophy of American Power*. New York: Praeger.

Gellner, Ernest. 1988. Introduction. In *Europe and the Rise of Capitalism*, ed. Jean Baechler, John A. Hall, and Michael Mann. London: Basil Blackwell.

George, Alexander, and Juliette L. George. 1956. *Woodrow Wilson and Colonel House: A Personality Study*. New York: John Day.

George, Alexander L., and Richard Smoke. 1974. *Deterrence in American Foreign Policy: Theory and Practice*. New York: Columbia University Press.

Gilchrist, H. L. 1928. *A Comparative Study of World War Casualties from Gas and Other Weapons*. Edgewood Arsenal, Md.: Chemical Warfare School.

Gilpin, Robert. 1981. *War and Change in World Politics*. New York: Cambridge University Press.

Glassman, Ronald M. 1986. *Democracy and Despotism in Primitive Societies*. Port Washington, N.Y.: Association Faculties Press.

Gleason, Alan H. 1965. Economic Growth and Consumption in Japan. In *The State and Economic Enterprise in Japan*, ed. William W. Lockwood. Princeton: Princeton University Press.

Goertz, Gary, and Paul F. Diehl. 1993. Enduring Rivalries: Theoretical Constructs and Empirical Patterns. *International Studies Quarterly* 37 (2, June): 147–171.

Goldstein, Donald M., Katherine V. Dillon, and J. Michael Wenger. 1991. *The Way It Was: Pearl Harbor—The Original Photographs*. McLean, Va.: Brassey's (U.S.).

Gooch, G.P. 1911. *History of Our Time, 1885–1911*. London: Williams and Norgate.

Gooch, John. 1981. *The Prospect of War: Studies in British Defense Policy, 1847–1942*. London: Frank Cass.

Gordon, Michael R. 1989. Kissinger Expects a United Germany. *New York Times*, 16 November, A21.

Graham, Thomas W. 1991. Winning the Nonproliferation Battle. *Arms Control Today*, September, 8–13.

Gray, J. Glenn. 1959. *The Warriors: Reflections on Men in Battle*. New York: Harper and Row.

Gray, Colin S. 1991. Do the Changes Within the Soviet Union Provide a Basis for Eased Soviet-American Relations? A Skeptical View. In *Soviet-American Relations After the Cold War*, ed. Robert Jervis and Seweryn Bialer, 61–75. Durham: Duke University Press.

———. 1992. Strategic Sense, Strategic Nonsense. *National Interest*, Fall, 11–19.

Greenfield, Meg. 1993. Reinventing the World. *Newsweek*, 20 December, 128.

Hale, J.R. 1985. *War and Society in Renaissance Europe 1450–1620*. New York: St. Martin's.

Halperin, Morton H. 1987. *Nuclear Fallacy: Dispelling the Myth of Nuclear Strategy*. Cambridge, Mass.: Ballinger.

Harries, Owen. 1989. Is the Cold War Really Over? *National Review*, 10 November, 40–45.

Hauser, William L. 1980. The Will to Fight. In *Combat Effectiveness: Cohesion, Stress, and the Voluntary Military*, ed. Sam C. Sarkesian, 186–211. Beverly Hills, Calif.: Sage.

Havelock, Eric A. 1957. *The Liberal Temper in Greek Politics*. New Haven: Yale University Press.

Healey, Denis. 1960. *The Race Against the H-Bomb*. London: Fabian Tract 322.

Herman, Sondra R. 1969. *Eleven Against War: Studies in American International Thought, 1898–1921*. Stanford, Calif: Hoover Institution Press.

Higley, John, and Richard Gunther, eds. 1992. *Elites and Democratic Consolidation in Latin America and Southern Europe*. Cambridge: Cambridge University Press.

Hinsley, F. H. 1963. *Power and the Pursuit of Peace: Theory and Practice in the History of Relations Between States*. London: Cambridge University Press.

———. 1987. Peace and War in Modern Times. In *The Quest for Peace*, ed. Raimo Väyrynen, 63–79. Beverly Hills, Calif.: Sage.

Historicus [George Allen Morgan]. 1949. Stalin on Revolution. *Foreign Affairs* 27 (2, January): 175–214.

Hitler, Adolf. 1942. *The Speeches of Adolf Hitler, April 1922–August 1939*. London: Oxford University Press.

Ho Ping-ti. 1959. *Studies on the Population of China, 1368–1953*. Cambridge: Harvard University Press.

Hobsbawm, Eric. 1987. *The Age of Empire 1875–1914*. New York: Vintage.

Hoffmann, Stanley. 1992. Delusions of World Order. *New York Review of Books,* 9 April, 37–43.

Hofstadter, Richard. 1959. *Social Darwinism in American Thought*. New York: Braziller.

Holmes, Robert L. 1989. *On War and Morality*. Princeton: Princeton University Press.

Holst, Johan Jørgen. 1992. European and Atlantic security in a period of ambiguity. *The World Today,* December, 218–221.

Holsti, Kalevi J. 1991. *Peace and War: Armed Conflicts and International Order 1648–1989*. Cambridge: Cambridge University Press.

Hone, Thomas. 1977. The Destruction of the Battle Line at Pearl Harbor. *United States Naval Institute Proceedings* 103 (12, December).

Hosmer, Stephen T., and Thomas W. Wolfe. 1983. *Soviet Policy and Practice toward Third World Countries*. Lexington, Mass.: Lexington.

House, Karen Elliott. 1992. We Need a Foreign Policy President. *Wall Street Journal*, 3 November, A16.

Howard, Michael. 1978. *War and the Liberal Conscience*. New Brunswick: Rutgers University Press.

———. 1984. *The Causes of Wars and Other Essays,* 2nd ed. Cambridge: Harvard University Press.

———. 1991. *The Lessons of History*. New Haven: Yale University Press.

Howarth, David. 1968. *Waterloo: Day of Battle*. New York: Atheneum.

Hudson, G.F., Richard Lowenthal, and Roderick MacFarquhar, eds. 1961. *The Sino-Soviet Dispute*. New York: Praeger.

Huntington, Samuel P. 1961. *The Common Defense*. New York: Columbia University Press.

————. 1984. Will More Countries Become Democratic? *Political Science Quarterly* 99 (2, Summer): 193–218.

————. 1989. No Exit: The Errors of Endism. *National Interest,* Fall, 3–11.

————. 1991a. America's Changing Strategic Interests. *Survival,* January/February, 3–17.

————. 1991b. *The Third Wave: Democratization in the Late Twentieth Century.* Norman: University of Oklahoma Press.

————. 1993a. Why International Primacy Matters. *International Security* 17 (4, Spring): 68–83.

————. 1993b. The Clash of Civilizations? *Foreign Affairs* 72 (3, Summer): 22–49.

————. 1993c. If Not Civilizations, What? Paradigms of the Post-Cold War World. *Foreign Affairs* 72 (5, November/December): 186–194.

Huth, Paul, and Bruce Russett. 1990. Testing Deterrence Theory: Rigor Makes a Difference. *World Politics* 42 (4, July): 466–501.

Ike, Nobutaka. 1967. *Japan's Decision for War: Records of the 1941 Policy Conferences.* Stanford: Stanford University Press.

Inge, William Ralph. 1919. *Outspoken Essays.* London: Longmans, Green.

James, William. 1911. *Memories and Studies.* New York: Longmans, Green.

Jefferson, Thomas. 1939. *Democracy.* Ed. Saul K. Padover. New York: Appleton-Century.

Jervis, Robert. 1979. Deterrence Theory Revisited. *World Politics* 31 (2, January): 289–324.

————. 1980. The Impact of the Korean War on the Cold War. *Journal of Conflict Resolution* 24 (4, December): 563–592.

————. 1984. *The Illogic of American Nuclear Strategy.* Ithaca: Cornell University Press.

————. 1985. Introduction. In *Psychology and Deterrence,* ed. Robert Jervis, Richard Ned Lebow, and Janice Gross Stein, 1–12. Baltimore: Johns Hopkins University Press.

————. 1988. The Political Effects of Nuclear Weapons. *International Security* 13 (2, Fall): 28–38.

————. 1993. International Primacy: Is the Game Worth the Candle? *International Security* 17 (4, Spring): 52–67.

Johnson, James Turner. 1987. *The Quest for Peace: Three Moral Traditions in Western Cultural History.* Princeton: Princeton University Press.

Jones, Robert Huhn. 1969. *The Roads to Russia.* Norman: University of Oklahoma Press.

Jordan, David Starr. 1913. *War and Waste.* Garden City: Doubleday, Page.

Josephus. 1982 ed. *The Jewish War.* Ed. Gaalya Cornfeld. Grand Rapids, Mich.: Zondervan.

Kaeuper, Richard W. 1988. *War, Justice, and Public Order: England and France in the Later Middle Ages.* New York: Oxford University Press.

Kagan, Donald. 1987. World War I, World War II, World War III. *Commentary,* March, 21–40.

Kahn, Herman. 1961. *On Thermonuclear War.* Princeton: Princeton University Press.

Kant, Immanuel. 1957. *Perpetual Peace.* Indianapolis: Bobbs-Merrill.

Kaplan, Morton A. 1957. *System and Process in International Politics.* New York: Wiley.

Katzenstein, Peter J., and Nobuo Okawara. 1993. Japan's National Security: Structures, Norms, and Policies. *International Security* 17 (4, Spring): 84–118.

Kaysen, Carl. 1990. Is War Obsolete? *International Security* 14 (4, Spring): 42–64.

Kaysen, Carl, Robert S. McNamara, and George W. Rathjens. 1991. Nuclear Weapons After the Cold War. *Foreign Affairs* 70 (4, Fall): 95–110.

Keatley, Robert. 1989. Gorbachev Peace Offensive Jars the West. *Wall Street Journal,* 20 January, A18.

Keegan, John. 1976. *The Face of Battle.* London: Penguin.

————. 1982. *Six Armies in Normandy.* New York: Penguin.

————. 1987. The Evolution of Battle and the Prospects of Peace. In *Arms at Rest: Peacemaking and Peacekeeping in American History,* ed. John R. Challinor and Robert L. Beisner, 189–201. New York: Greenwood.

————. 1990. Defeat: A Neglected Subject. *National Interest,* Fall, 75–80.

————. 1993. *A History of Warfare.* New York: Knopf.

Keller, Bill. 1987. Russians Urging U.N. Be Given Greater Powers. *New York Times,* 3 October, A1.

————. 1988. New Soviet Ideologist Rejects Idea of World Struggle Against West. *New York Times,* 6 October, A1.

Kellet, Anthony. 1982. *Combat Motivation.* Boston: Kluwer-Nijhoff.

Kennan, George F. 1947. The Sources of Soviet Conduct. *Foreign Affairs* 25 (4, July): 566–582.

————. 1961. *Russia and the West Under Lenin and Stalin.* Boston: Little Brown.

————. 1987. Containment Then and Now. *Foreign Affairs* 65 (4, Spring): 885–890.

————. 1989. This Is No Time for Talk Of German Reunification. *Washington Post,* 12 November, D1.

Kennedy, John F. 1964. *Public Papers of the Presidents of the United States: John F. Kennedy, 1963.* Washington, DC: United States Government Printing Office.

Kennedy, Paul. 1983. *Strategy and Diplomacy: 1870–1945.* London: Allen and Unwin.

————. 1987. *The Rise and Fall of the Great Powers.* New York: Random House.

————. 1993. *Preparing for the Twenty-First Century.* New York: Random House.

Kennedy, Robert F. 1971. *Thirteen Days: A Memoir of the Cuban Missile Crisis.* New York: Norton.

Kershaw, Ian. 1987. *The 'Hitler Myth': Image and Reality in the Third Reich.* New York: Oxford University Press.

Khrushchev, Nikita. 1970. *Khrushchev Remembers.* Ed. Edward Crankshaw and Strobe Talbott. Boston: Little, Brown.

————. 1974. *Khrushchev Remembers: The Last Testament.* Ed. Strobe Talbott. Boston: Little, Brown.

King, Ernest J. 1946. *U.S. Navy at War, 1941–1945.* Washington, DC: U.S. Office of Naval Operations, United States Navy Department.

Kissinger, Henry A. 1977. *American Foreign Policy,* 3rd ed. New York: Norton.

————. 1979. *White House Years.* Boston: Little, Brown.

Knorr, Klaus. 1985. Controlling Nuclear War. *International Security* 9 (4, Spring): 79–98.

Knox, R. Buick. 1967. *James Ussher: Archbishop of Armagh.* Cardiff: University of Wales Press.

Knox, MacGregor. 1984. Conquest, Foreign and Domestic, in Fascist Italy and Nazi Germany. *Journal of Modern History* 56 (March): 1–57.

————. 1990. After the Cold War: Notes of a Pessimist. Rochester, N.Y.: Department of History, University of Rochester, 20 September.

Kramer, Marguerite, and Bruce Russett. 1984. Images of World Futures. *Journal of Peace Research* 21 (1): 317–336.

Kraus, Sidney, ed. 1962. *The Great Debates: Kennedy vs. Nixon, 1960.* Bloomington, IN: University of Indiana Press.

Krauthammer, Charles. 1991. The Unipolar Moment. *Foreign Affairs: America and the World 1990/91* 70 (1): 23–33.

Kuehl, Warren F. 1969. *Seeking World Order: The United States and International Organization to 1920.* Nashville: Vanderbilt University Press.

Lambeth, Benjamin S. 1972. Deterrence in the MIRV Era. *World Politics* 24 (2, January): 221–241.

Layne, Christopher. 1993. The Unipolar Illusion: Why New Great Powers Will Rise. *International Security* 17 (4, Spring): 5–51.

Lea, Homer. 1909. *The Valor of Ignorance.* New York: Harper.

Lebow, Richard Ned. 1981. *Between Peace and War: The Nature of International Crisis.* Baltimore: Johns Hopkins University Press.

———. 1984. Windows of Opportunity: Do States Jump Through Them? *International Security* 9 (1, Summer): 147–186.

———. 1985. The Deterrence Deadlock: Is There a Way Out? and Conclusions. In *Psychology and Deterrence,* ed. Robert Jervis, Richard Ned Lebow and Janice Gross Stein, 153–232. Baltimore: Johns Hopkins University Press.

Levy, Jack S. 1983. *War in the Modern Great Power System, 1495–1975.* Lexington: University Press of Kentucky.

———. 1989a. The Causes of War: A Review of Theories and Evidence. In *Behavior, Society, and Nuclear War,* vol. 1, ed. Philip E. Tetlock, Jo L. Husbands, Robert Jervis, Paul C. Stern and Charles Tilly, 209–333. New York: Oxford University Press.

———. 1989b. Quantitative Studies of Deterrence Success and Failure. In *Perspectives on Deterrence,* ed. Paul C. Stern, Robert Axelrod, Robert Jervis and Roy Radner, 98–133. New York: Oxford University Press.

———. 1991. Long Cycles, Hegemonic Transitions, and the Long Peace. In *The Long Postwar Peace: Contending Explanations and Projections,* ed. Charles W. Kegley, Jr., 147–176. New York: HarperCollins.

Lewis, Paul. 1987. New Soviet Interest in U.N. Broadens. *New York Times,* 25 September, A8.

———. 1989. Greater U.N. Role Urged by Soviets. *New York Times,* 5 October, A20.

———. 1993. Ex-Foes Trade Stories From Cold War Trenches. *New York Times,* 1 March, A7.

Lid, Nils. 1956. Berserk. Trans. Robert Pahre. In *Kulturhistoriskt Lexikon for Nordisk Medeltid, Band 1,* 499–500. Malmo, Sweden: Allhems Forlag.

Lienesch, Michael. 1992. Wo(e)begon(e) Democracy. *American Journal of Political Science* 36 (4, November): 1004–1014.

Lightfoot, John. 1989. *A Commentary on the New Testament from the Talmud and Hebraica.* Peabody, Mass: Hendrickson.

Lindblom, Charles E. 1977. *Politics and Markets: The World's Political-Economic Systems.* New York: Basic Books.

Linderman, Gerald F. 1987. *Embattled Courage: The Experience of Combat in the Civil War.* New York: Free Press.

Lingeman, Richard R. 1970. *Don't You Know There's A War On? The American Home Front, 1941–1945.* New York: Putnam's Sons.

Link, Arthur S. 1957. *Wilson, the Diplomatist: A Look at his Major Foreign Policies.* Baltimore: Johns Hopkins Press.

Linz, Juan J. 1978. *The Breakdown of Democratic Regimes: Crisis, Breakdown, and Reequilibration.* Baltimore: Johns Hopkins University Press.

Lloyd George, David. 1933. *War Memoirs.* London: Ivor Nicholson & Watson.

———. 1938. *The Truth About the Peace Treaties.* London: Victor Gollancz.

Locke, John. 1970. *Two Treatises of Government.* Ed. Peter Laslett. Cambridge: Cambridge University Press.

Lorch, Donatella. 1993. G.I.'s Storm the Beach to Get Away From It All. *New York Times,* 12 March, A4.

Lord, Walter. 1957. *Day of Infamy.* New York: Holt.

Lorenz, Konrad. 1966. *On Aggression.* New York: Bantam.

Luard, Evan. 1986. *War in International Society.* New Haven: Yale University Press.

Luttwak, Edward N. 1983a. *The Grand Strategy of the Soviet Union.* New York: St. Martin's.

———. 1983b. Of Bombs and Men. *Commentary,* August, 77–82.

Machiavelli, Niccolò. [1532 and 1531] 1950. *The Prince and The Discourses.* Trans. Luigi Ricci. New York: Modern Library.

Maddison, Angus. 1983. A Comparison of Levels of GDP Per Capita in Developed and Developing Countries, 1700–1980. *Journal of Economic History,* 43 (1, March): 27–41.

Manchester, William. 1989. *The Last Lion, Winston Spencer Churchill: Alone, 1932–1940.* Boston: Little, Brown.

Mandelbaum, Michael. 1981. *The Nuclear Revolution.* Cambridge: Cambridge University Press.

Mansfield, Sue. 1982. *The Gestalts of War.* New York: Dial.

May, Ernest R. 1984. The Cold War. In *The Making of America's Soviet Policy,* ed. Joseph S. Nye, Jr., 209–230. New Haven: Yale University Press.

May, Michael. 1985. The U.S.-Soviet Approach to Nuclear Weapons. *International Security* 9 (4, Spring).

Mayer, Arno. 1959. *Political Origins of the New Diplomacy, 1917–1918.* New Haven: Yale University Press.

McGwire, Michael. 1985. Deterrence: The Problem, Not the Solution. *SAIS Review* 5 (2, Summer-Fall): 105–124.

McEvedy, Colin, and Richard Jones. 1978. *Atlas of World Population History.* New York: Penguin.

McNaugher, Thomas L. 1990. Ballistic Missiles and Chemical Weapons: The Legacy of the Iran-Iraq War. *International Security* 15 (2, Fall).

McNeill, William H. 1982. *The Pursuit of Power: Technology, Armed Force, and Society since A.D. 1000.* Chicago: University of Chicago Press.

———. 1990. Book review: Retreat from Doomsday. *Technology and Change* 31 (1, January): 191–192.

Mead, Margaret. 1964. Warfare Is Only an Invention—Not a Biological Necessity. In *War: Studies from Psychology, Sociology, Anthropology,* ed. Leon Bramson and George W. Goethals, 269–274. New York: Basic Books.

Mearsheimer, John J. 1983. *Conventional Deterrence.* Ithaca: Cornell University Press.

———. 1984/85. Nuclear Weapons and Deterrence in Europe. *International Security* 9 (3, Winter): 19–47.

———. 1988. *Liddell Hart and the Weight of History.* Ithaca, NY: Cornell University Press.

———. 1990. Back to the Future: Instability in Europe After the Cold War. *International Security* 15 (1, Summer): 5–56.

Medvedev, Roy. 1983. *Khrushchev.* Garden City, NY: Doubleday.

———. 1986. *China and the Superpowers.* New York: Basil Blackwell.

Meisner, Maurice. 1986. *Mao's China and After.* New York: Free Press.

Melosi, Martin V. 1977. *The Shadow of Pearl Harbor: Political Controversy over the Surprise Attack, 1941–1946.* College Station: Texas A&M University Press.

Mencken, H.L. 1920a. *A Book of Burlesques.* New York: Knopf.

———. 1920b. *Prejudices: Second Series.* New York: Knopf.

Messenger, Charles. 1989. *The Chronological Atlas of World War Two.* New York: Macmillan.

Meyer, Stephen M. 1984. *The Dynamics of Nuclear Proliferation.* Chicago: University of Chicago Press.

Mikoyan, Sergo. 1992. Stop Treating Russia Like a Loser. *New York Times,* 25 March, A23.

Milburn, Thomas W. 1959. What Constitutes Effective U.S. Deterrence? *Journal of Conflict Resolution* 3 (2, June): 138–145.

Millet, Allan R., and William B. Moreland. 1976. What Happened? The Problem of Causation in International Affairs. In *Historical Dimensions of National Security Problems,* ed. Klaus Knorr, 5–37. Lawrence: University Press of Kansas.

Millis, Walter, ed. 1951. *The Forrestal Diaries.* New York: Viking.

Milner, Helen. 1991. The Assumption of Anarchy in International Relations Theory: A Critique. *Review of International Studies* 17: 67–85.

Milward, Alan S. 1977. *War, Economy and Society, 1939–1945.* Berkeley: University of California Press.

Mitgang, Herbert. 1991. Looking at History with a Military Slant. *New York Times,* 3 April, 17A.

Montross, Lynn. 1944. *War Through the Ages.* New York: Harper.

Moore, Barrington. 1966. *Social Origins of Dictatorship and Democracy.* New York: Basic Books.

Morgan, Edmund S. 1988. *Inventing the People: The Rise of Popular Sovereignty in England and America.* New York: Norton.

Morgan, Patrick. 1977. *Deterrence: A Conceptual Analysis.* Bevery Hills, CA: Sage.

Morgenthau, Hans J. 1948. *Politics Among Nations: The Struggle for Power and Peace.* New York: Knopf.

Morison, Samuel Eliot. 1948. *The Rising Sun in the Pacific: 1931–April 1942.* Boston: Little, Brown.

———. 1963. *The Two-Ocean War: A Short History of the United States Navy in the Second World War.* Boston: Little, Brown.

Morton, Louis. 1962. *The United States Army in World War II: The War in the Pacific, Vol. 10: Strategy and Command: The First Two Years.* Washington, DC: Department of the Army, Office of the Chief of Military History.

Mosher, Stacy. 1991. Hong Kong: The governor's men. *Far Eastern Economic Review,* (3 October): 11–13.

Moynihan, Daniel Patrick. 1975. The American Experiment. *Public Interest* (41, Fall): 4–8.

———. 1992. End the "Torment of Secrecy". *National Interest,* Spring, 18–21.

Mueller, John. 1967. Incentives for Restraint: Canada as a Nonnuclear Power. *Orbis* 11 (3, Fall): 864–884.

———. 1968. *Deterrence, Numbers, and History.* Los Angeles: Security Studies Project, UCLA.

———. 1973. *War, Presidents and Public Opinion.* New York: Wiley. (Reprinted 1985 by University Press of America, Lanham, Md.).

———. 1985. The Bomb's Pretense as Peacemaker. *Wall Street Journal,* 4 June, 32.

———. 1986. Containment and the Decline of the Soviet Empire: Some Tentative Reflections on the End of the World as We Know It. Paper given at the National Convention of the International Studies Association. Anaheim, Calif., 25–29 March.

———.1988a. Trends in Political Tolerance. *Public Opinion Quarterly* 52 (1, Spring): 1–25.

———. 1988b. The Essential Irrelevance of Nuclear Weapons: Stability in the Postwar World. *International Security* 13 (2, Fall): 55–79.

———. 1989a. *Retreat from Doomsday: The Obsolescence of Major War.* New York: Basic Books.

————. 1989b. Enough Rope: The Cold War Was Lost, Not Won. *New Republic,* 3 July, 14–16.

————. 1989c. Democracy: All They Need to Do Is Catch the Bug. *Los Angeles Times,* 19 November, M7.

————. 1989–90. A New Concert of Europe. *Foreign Policy* (77, Winter): 3–16.

————. 1990. Democratization as a Marketing Phenomenon. Paper presented at the Conference on Global Trends of Democratization. Skidmore College, Saratoga Springs, New York, 3–4 November.

————. 1991a. Taking Peace Seriously: Two Proposals. In *Soviet-American Relations After the Cold War,* ed. Robert Jervis and Seweryn Bialer, 262–275. Durham: Duke University Press.

————. 1991b. Changing Attitudes Towards War: The Impact of the First World War. *British Journal of Political Science* 21 (1, January): 1–28.

————. 1991c. Deterrence, Nuclear Weapons, Morality, and War. In *After the Cold War: Questioning the Morality of Nuclear Deterrence,* ed. Charles W. Kegley, Jr. and Kenneth L. Schwab, 69–97. Boulder, Colo.: Westview Press.

————. 1991d. Is War Still Becoming Obsolete? Paper given at the Annual Meeting of the American Political Science Association. Washington, DC, 29 August–1 September.

————. 1991e. War: Natural, But Not Necessary. In *The Institution of War,* ed. Robert A. Hinde, 13–29. London: Macmillan.

————. 1991/92. Pearl Harbor: Military Inconvenience, Political Disaster. *International Security* 16(3, Winter): 172–203.

————. 1992a. Quiet Cataclysm: Some Afterthoughts About World War III. *Diplomatic History* 19 (1, Winter): 66–75.

————. 1992b. Democracy and Ralph's Pretty Good Grocery: Elections, Inequality, and the Minimal Human Being. *American Journal of Political Science* 36 (4, November): 983–1003.

————. 1992c. Theory and Democracy: A Reply to Michael Lienesch. *American Journal of Political Science* 36 (4, November): 1015–1022.

————. 1993. The Impact of Ideas on Grand Strategy. In *The Domestic Bases of Grand Strategy,* ed. Richard Rosecrance and Arthur Stein, 48–62. Ithaca: Cornell University Press.

————. 1994a. *Policy and Opinion in the Gulf War.* Chicago: University of Chicago Press.

————. 1994b. *The Perfect Enemy: Assessing the Gulf War.* Rochester, N.Y.: Department of Political Science, University of Rochester.

————. 1994c. The Catastrophe Quota: Trouble After the Cold War. *Journal of Conflict Resolution* 38 (3, September).

Mueller, Karl P. 1991. *Strategy, Asymmetric Deterrence, and Accommodation: Middle Powers and Security in Modern Europe.* Dissertation, Princeton University.

Muir, Malcolm. 1990. Reevaluating Major Naval Combatants of World War II. In *The United States Navy in World War II: An Assessment,* ed. James J. Sadkovich. Westport, Conn.: Greenwood.

Muravchik, Joshua. 1992. *Exporting Democracy: Fulfilling America's Destiny.* Washington, DC: AEI Press.

Nadelmann, Ethan A. 1990. Global Prohibition Regimes: The Evolutiion of Norms in International Society. *International Organization* 44 (4, Autumn): 479–526.

Nakamura, Takafusa. 1983. *Economic Growth in Prewar Japan.* New Haven: Yale University Press.

National Planning Association. 1958. *1970 Without Arms Control.* Washington, DC: National Planning Association.

Nevins, Allan. 1946. How We Felt About the War. In *While You Were Gone: A Report on Wartime Life in the United States,* ed. Jack Goodman, 3–27. New York: Simon and Schuster.

Nobel, Alfred. 1925. How Wars Will Come to an End. *The Forum (New York)* 74 (1, July): 194–198. As recorded from notes made in 1890 by E. Schneider-Bonnet.

Notestein, Wallace, and Elmer E. Stoll, eds. 1917. *Conquest and Kultur: Aims of the Germans in Their Own Words.* Washington, DC: U.S. Government, Committee on Public Information.

Nye, Joseph S., Jr. 1987. Nuclear Learning and U.S.-Soviet Security Regimes. *International Organization* 41 (3, Summer): 371–402.

Oberdorfer, Don. 1992. *The Turn: From the Cold War to a New Era.* New York: Touchstone.

Office of the Chief of Military History. 1952. *The U.S. Army in World War II. Pictorial Record: The War Against Japan.* Washington, DC: Department of the Army.

Organski, A.F.K., and Jacek Kugler. 1980. *The War Ledger.* Chicago: University of Chicago Press.

Osgood, Charles E. 1962. *An Alternative to War or Surrender.* Urbana: University of Illinois Press.

Overy, R.J. 1982a. Hitler's War and the German Economy: A Reinterpretation. *Economic History Review* 35 (2, May): 272–291.

———. 1982b. *The Nazi Economic Recovery 1932–1938.* London: Macmillan.

Park, Robert E. 1964. The Social Function of War. In *War: Studies from Psychology, Sociology, Anthropology,* ed. Leon Bramson and George W. Goethals, 230–244. New York: Basic Books.

Parker, Geoffrey. 1984. *The Thirty Years War.* London: Routledge and Kegan Paul.

Patterson, David S. 1976. *Toward a Warless World: The Travail of the American Peace Movement, 1887–1914.* Bloomington: Indiana University Press.

Pear, Robert. 1990. Soviet Experts Say Their Economy Is Worse Than U.S. Has Estimated. *New York Times,* 24 April, A14.

Perry, James M. 1986. They May Poke Fun at the Swiss Navy, But Not at the Army. *Wall Street Journal,* 8 December, 1.

Pessen, Edward. 1984. *The Log Cabin Myth: The Social Backgrounds of the Presidents.* New Haven: Yale University Press.

Pipes, Richard. 1984. *Survival Is Not Enough.* New York: Simon and Schuster.

Plato. 1957 ed. *The Republic.* Trans. A. D. Lindsay. New York: Dutton.

Pogge von Strandmann, Hartmut. 1988. Germany and the Coming of War. In *The Coming of the First World War,* ed. R.J.W. Evans and Hartmut Pogge von Strandmann. Oxford: Clarendon.

Pollack, Jonathan D. 1984. China and the Global Strategic Balance. In *China's Foreign Relations in the 1980s,* ed. Harry Harding, 146–176. New Haven: Yale University Press.

Popkin, Samuel L. 1991. *The Reasoning Voter: Communication and Persuasion in Presidential Campaigns.* Chicago: University of Chicago Press.

Posen, Barry R. 1984/85. Measuring the European Conventional Balance. *International Security* 9 (3, Winter): 47–88.

———. 1993. Nationalism, the Mass Army, and Military Power. *International Security* 18 (2, Fall): 80–124.

Prange, Gordon W., with Donald M. Goldstein, and Katherine V. Dillon. 1981. *At Dawn We Slept: The Untold Story of Pearl Harbor.* New York: McGraw-Hill.

———. 1982. *Miracle at Midway.* New York: McGraw-Hill.

———. 1986. *Pearl Harbor: The Verdict of History.* New York: McGraw-Hill.

———. 1988. *December 7, 1941: The Day the Japanese Attacked Pearl Harbor.* New York: McGraw-Hill.

Preston, Richard A. 1977. *The Defense of the Undefended Border.* Montreal: McGill-Queens University Press.

Prial, Frank J. 1992. U.N. Seeks Signal on Troop Notice. *New York Times,* 30 October, A11.

Puleston, William D. 1947. *The Influence of Sea Power in World War II.* New Haven: Yale University Press.

Queller, Donald E. 1977. *The Fourth Crusade: The Conquest of Constantinople 1201–1204.* Philadelphia: University of Pennsylvania Press.

Quester, George H. 1977. *Offense and Defense in the International System.* New York: Wiley.

Rapoport, Anatol. 1992. *Peace. An Idea Whose Time Has Come.* Ann Arbor: University of Michigan Press.

Rappard, William E. 1940. *The Quest for Peace Since the World War.* Cambridge: Harvard University Press.

Ray, James Lee. 1989. The Abolition of Slavery and the End of International War. *International Organization* 43 (Summer): 405–439.

Reeves, Richard. 1993. *President Kennedy: Profile of Power.* New York: Simon & Schuster.

Rich, Norman. 1973. *Hitler's War Aims: Ideology, the Nazi State, and the Course of Expansion.* New York: Norton.

Richardson, James O. 1973. *On the Treadmill to Pearl Harbor.* Washington, DC: Department of the Navy, Naval History Division.

Riker, William H. 1964. Some Ambiguities in the Notion of Power. *American Political Science Review* 58 (2, June): 341–349.

———. 1965. *Democracy in the United States.* 2nd ed. New York: Macmillan.

———. 1982. *Liberalism Against Populism.* San Francisco: Freeman.

Roazen, Paul. 1968. *Freud: Political and Social Thought.* New York: Knopf.

Robbins, Keith. 1976. *The Abolition of War: The "Peace Movement" in Britain, 1914–1919.* Cardiff: University of Wales Press.

Rosebery, Mercedes. 1944. *This Day's Madness.* New York: Macmillan.

Rosecrance, Richard. 1975. *Strategic Deterrence Reconsidered.* London: International Institute for Strategic Studies, Adelphi Paper No. 116 (Spring).

———. 1986. *The Rise of the Trading State: Conquest and Commerce in the Modern World.* New York: Basic Books.

———. 1992. A New Concert of Powers. *Foreign Affairs* 71 (2, Spring): 64–82.

Rosen, Stephen Peter. 1988. New Ways of War: Understanding Military Innovation. *International Security* 13 (1, Summer): 134–168.

Rothgeb, John M., Jr. 1993. *Defining Power: Influence and Force in the Contemporary International System.* New York: St. Martin's.

Rush, Myron. 1993. Fortune and Fate. *National Interest,* Spring, 19–25.

Russell, Bertrand. 1953. *The Impact of Science on Society.* New York: Simon and Schuster.

Russett, Bruce. 1972. *No Clear and Present Danger: A Skeptical View of the United States' Entry into World War II.* New York: Harper and Row.

———. 1983. *The Prisoners of Insecurity.* San Francisco: Freeman.

———. 1990. *Controlling the Sword: The Democratic Governance of National Security.* Cambridge: Harvard University Press.

Rustow, Dankwart A. 1970. Transitions to Democracy: Toward a Dynamic Model. *Comparative Politics* 2 (3, April): 337–363.

Ryder, H.I.D. 1899. The Ethics of War. *The Nineteenth Century* 45 (May): 716–728.

Safire, William. 1991. Optimists Are the Realists. *New York Times,* 26 December, A25.

———. 1993. Depart With Honor. *New York Times,* 7 October, A29.

Sagan, Carl. 1983/84. Nuclear War and Climatic Catastrophe: Some Policy Implications. *Foreign Affairs* 62 (2, Winter): 257–292.

Sagan, Scott. 1988. Origins of the Pacific War. *Journal of Interdisciplinary History* 18 (4, Spring): 893–922.

Saxon, A.H. 1989. *P.T. Barnum: The Legend and the Man.* New York: Columbia University Press.

Schell, Jonathan. 1982. *The Fate of the Earth.* New York: Knopf.

Schelling, Thomas C. 1966. *Arms and Influence.* New Haven: Yale University Press.

Schilling, Warner R. 1961. The H-Bomb Decision. *Political Science Quarterly* 76 (1, March): 24–46.

———. 1965. Surprise Attack, Death, and War. *Journal of Conflict Resolution* 9 (3, September): 285–290.

Schlesinger, James. 1967. *On Relating Non-technical Elements to Systems Studies.* Santa Monica, Calif.: RAND Corporation, P-3545 (February).

Schmitt, Eric. 1993. Arms Sales to Third World, Especially by Russians, Drop. *New York Times,* 20 July, A2.

Schroeder, Paul W. 1958. *The Axis Alliance and Japanese-American Relations, 1941.* Ithaca: Cornell University Press.

———. 1985. Does Murphy's Law Apply to History. *Wilson Quarterly,* New Year's, 84–93.

———. 1990. The Neo-Realist Theory of International Politics: An Historian's View. Paper presented at AAAS/University of Rochester Conference. Rochester, N.Y., 19–20 October.

Scott, Ian. 1989. *Political Change and the Crisis of Legitimacy in Hong Kong.* Honolulu: University of Hawaii Press.

Scrugham, Mary. 1921. *The Peaceable Americans of 1860–1861: A Study of Public Opinion.* New York: Columbia University Press.

Seitz, Don C. 1929. *Famous American Duels.* New York: Crowell.

Seward, Desmond. 1991. *Metternich: The First European.* New York: Viking.

Shafir, Michael. 1993. Growing Political Extremism in Romania. *RFE/RL Research Report,* April, 18–22.

Sharp, Gene. 1973. *The Politics of Nonviolent Action.* Boston: Porter Sargent.

Sherman, Frederick. 1950. *Combat Command: The American Aircraft Carriers in the Pacific War.* New York: Dutton.

Shevchenko, Arkady N. 1985. *Breaking with Moscow.* New York: Knopf.

Shiller, Robert J., Maxim Boychko, and Vladimir Korobov. 1991. Popular Attitudes Toward Free Markets: The Soviet Union and the United States Compared. *American Economic Review* 81 (3, June): 385–400.

Shlaes, Amity. 1988. Talk Turns to Triple Zero in West Germany. *Wall Street Journal,* 9 December, A22.

Shulman, Marshall D. 1963. *Stalin's Foreign Policy Reappraised.* New York: Atheneum.

Singer, J. David. 1962. *Deterrence, Arms Control, and Disarmament.* Columbus: Ohio State University Press.

Singer, J. David, and Melvin Small. 1972. *The Wages of War 1816–1965: A Statistical Handbook.* New York: Wiley.

Singer, J. David. 1991. Peace in the Global System: Displacement, Interregnum, or Transformation? In *The Long Postwar Peace: Contending Explanations and Projections,* ed. Charles W. Kegley, Jr. New York: HarperCollins.

Singer, Max, and Aaron Wildavsky. 1993. *The Real World Order: Zones of Peace, Zones of Conflict.* Chatham, N.J.: Chatham House.

Sivard, Ruth Leger. 1987. *World Military and Social Expenditures 1987/88.* Washington, DC: World Priorities.

Siverson, Randolph. 1990. Review of "Retreat from Doomsday". *American Political Science Review* 84 (3, September): 1062–1063.

Slackman, Michael. 1990. *Target: Pearl Harbor.* Honolulu: University of Hawaii Press.

Small, Melvin. 1980. *Was War Necessary? National Security and U.S. Entry into War.* Beverly Hills, Calif.: Sage.

Small, Melvin, and J. David Singer. 1982. *Resort to Arms: International Civil Wars, 1816–1980.* Beverly Hills, Calif.: Sage.

Smith, M. Brewster. 1949. Combat Motivations Among Ground Troops. In *The American Soldier: Combat and Its Aftermath,* ed. Samuel A. Stouffer, 105–191. Princeton: Princeton University Press.

Smith, Sydney. 1956 ed. *Selected Writings of Sydney Smith.* Ed. W.H. Auden. New York: Farrar, Straus and Cudahy.

Smith, R. Elberton. 1959. *The United States Army in World War II: The War Department, Vol. 5: The Army and Economic Mobilization.* Washington, DC: Department of the Army, Office of the Chief of Military History.

Smoke, Richard. 1987. *National Security and the Nuclear Dilemma: An Introduction to the American Experience.* New York: Random House.

Snorri, Sturluson. 1966. *King Harald's Saga.* Baltimore, Md.: Penguin.

Snow, C.P. 1961. The Moral Un-Neutrality of Science. *Science,* 27 January, 255–259.

Snyder, Glenn H. 1961. *Deterrence and Defense.* Princeton: Princeton University Press.

Snyder, Jack. 1984. *The Ideology of the Offensive.* Ithaca: Cornell University Press.

———. 1987/88. The Gorbachev Revolution: A Waning of Soviet Expansionism? *International Security* 12 (3, Winter): 93–131.

Snyder, Louis L. 1982. *Louis L. Snyder's Historical Guide to World War II.* Westport, Conn.: Greenwood.

Solzhenitsyn, Aleksandr I. 1981. *The Mortal Danger: How Misconceptions About Russia Imperil America.* New York: Harper and Row.

Sorensen, Theodore C. 1965. *Kennedy.* New York: Harper and Row.

Spector, Ronald H. 1985. *Eagle Against the Sun: The American War with Japan.* New York: Vintage.

Squires, James Duane. 1935. *British Propaganda at Home and in the United States From 1914 to 1917.* Cambridge: Harvard University Press.

Squires, Jim. 1990. Television's Civil War. *Wall Street Journal,* 8 October, A12.

Stacey, C.P. 1955. *The Undefended Border: The Myth and the Reality.* Ottawa: Canadian Historical Association.

Stein, Janice Gross. 1985. Calculation, Miscalculation, and Conventional Deterrence: The View from Cairo. In *Psychology and Deterrence,* ed. Robert Jervis, Richard Ned Lebow and Janice Gross Stein, 34–59. Baltimore, Md: Johns Hopkins.

Stephan, John J. 1984. *Hawaii Under the Rising Sun: Japan's Plans for Conquest After Pearl Harbor.* Honolulu: University of Hawaii Press.

Stern, Paul C., Robert Axelrod, Robert Jervis, and Roy Radner. 1989. Deterrence in the Nuclear Age: The Search for Evidence. In *Perspectives on Deterrence,* ed. Paul C. Stern, Robert Axelrod, Robert Jervis, and Roy Radner, 3–24. New York: Oxford University Press.

Stevens, William Oliver. 1940. *Pistols at Ten Paces: The Story of the Code of Honor in America.* Boston: Houghton Mifflin.

Stillwell, Paul, ed. 1981. *Air Raid: Pearl Harbor! Reflections on a Day of Infamy.* Annapolis, Md.: Naval Institute Press.

Stockton, Richard. 1932. *Inevitable War.* New York: Perth.

Stowe, Steven M. 1987. *Intimacy and Power in the Old South: Ritual in the Lives of the Planters.* Baltimore: Johns Hopkins University Press.

Streit, Clarence. 1939. *Union Now: A Proposal for a Federal Union of Democracies.* New York: Harper.

Stromberg, Roland N. 1982. *Redemption by War: The Intellectuals and 1914.* Lawrence, Kans.: Regents Press of Kansas.

Stuart, Reginald G. 1987. United States Expansionism and the British North American Provinces, 1783–1871. In *Arms at Rest: Peacemaking and Peacekeeping in American History,* ed. Joan R. Challinor and Robert L. Beisner, 101–132. Westport, Conn.: Greenwood.

Sumner, William Graham. 1924. War. In *Selected Essays of William Graham Sumner,* ed. Albert Galloway Keller and Maurice Rea Davie, 310–341. New Haven: Yale University Press.

Talbott, Strobe. 1981. The Strategic Dimension of the Sino-American Relationship. In *The China Factor,* ed. Richard H. Solomon, 81–113. Englewood Cliffs, N.J.: Prentice-Hall.

Taubman, William. 1982. *Stalin's American Policy.* New York: Norton.

Thomas, Hugh. 1987. *Armed Truce: The Beginnings of the Cold War, 1945–46.* New York: Atheneum.

Thorpe, James A. 1978. Truman's Ultimatum to Stalin on the 1946 Azerbaijan Crisis: The Making of a Myth. *Journal of Politics* 40 (1, February): 188–195.

Thucydides. 1934. *The Pelopennesian War.* New York: Modern Library.

Thursfield, H.G., ed. 1943. *Brassey's Naval Annual 1943.* New York: Macmillan.

Tocqueville, Alexis de. [1835–40] 1990. *Democracy in America.* Trans. Henry Reeve. New York: Vintage.

Toland, John. 1961. *But Not in Shame: The Six Months After Pearl Harbor.* New York: Random House.

———. 1970. *The Rising Sun: The Decline and Fall of the Japanese Empire, 1936–1945.* New York: Random House.

Tolstoy, Leo. 1904. *Bethink Yourselves!.* New York: T.Y. Crowell.

———. [1862–69] 1966. *War and Peace.* New York: Norton.

Toynbee, Arnold J. 1950. *War and Civilization.* New York: Oxford University Press.

———. 1969. *Experiences.* New York: Oxford University Press.

Trachtenberg, Marc. 1985. Nuclear Weapons and the Cuban Missile Crisis. *International Security* 10 (1, Summer): 156–163.

———. 1991. The Future of War. *Diplomatic History* 15 (2, Spring): 287–290.

Treitschke, Heinrich von. 1916. *Politics.* New York: Macmillan.

Truman, Harry S. 1966. *Public Papers of the Presidents of the United States: Harry S. Truman, 1952–1953.* Washington, DC: United States Government Printing Office.

Tsouras, Peter, and Elmo C. Wright, Jr. 1991. The Ground War. In *Military Lessons of the Gulf War,* ed. Bruce W. Watson, Bruce George, Peter Tsouras, and B.L. Cyr, 81–120. Novato, Calif.: Presidio Press.

Tucker, Robert W., and David C. Hendrickson. 1992. *The Imperial Temptation: The New World Order and America's Purpose.* New York: Council on Foreign Relations Press.

U.S. Army, Manhattan Engineer District. 1946. *The Atomic Bombings of Hiroshima and Nagasaki.* Washington, DC: United States Army.

U.S. Congress, Joint Committee on the Investigation of the Pearl Harbor Attack. 1946a. *Hearings.* Washington, DC: United States Government Printing Office.

———. 1946b. *Report.* Washington, DC: United States Government Printing Office.

Ulam, Adam S. 1968. *Expansion and Coexistence.* New York: Praeger.

———. 1971. *The Rivals: America and Russia Since World War II.* New York: Penguin.

United States Strategic Bombing Survey (USSBS). 1946. *Japan's Struggle to End the War.* New York: Garland.

Ure, Andrew. 1835. *The Philosophy of Manufactures: Or, An Exposition of the Scientific, Moral, and Commercial Economy of the Factory System of Great Britain.* London: Charles Knight, Ludgate-Street.

Urquhart, Brian. 1993. For a UN Volunteer Military Force. *New York Review of Books,* 10 June, 3–4.

Utley, Jonathan G. 1985. *Going to War with Japan, 1937–1941.* Knoxville: University of Tennessee Press.

Vale, Malcolm. 1981. *War and Chivalry.* Athens: University of Georgia Press.

Van Evera, Stephen. 1984. The Cult of the Offensive and the Origins of the First World War. *International Security* 9 (1, Summer): 58–107.

———. 1990/91. Primed for Peace: Europe After the Cold War. *International Security* 15 (3, Winter): 7–57.

Vasquez, John A. 1991. The Deterrence Myth: Nuclear Weapons and the Prevention of Nuclear War. In *The Long Postwar Peace: Contending Explanations and Projections,* ed. Charles W. Kegley, Jr., 205–223. New York: HarperCollins.

Voslensky, Michael. 1984. *Nomenklatura: The New Soviet Ruling Class.* Garden City, N.Y.: Doubleday.

Wallin, Homer N. 1946. Rejuvenation at Pearl Harbor. *U.S. Naval Institute Proceedings* 72 (12, December): 1521–1547.

———. 1968. *Pearl Harbor: Why, How, Fleet Salvage and Final Appraisal.* Washington, DC: United States Navy, Naval History Division.

Waltz, Kenneth N. 1959. *Man, the State and War.* New York: Columbia University Press.

———. 1979. *Theory of International Politics.* Reading, Mass.: Addison-Wesley.

———. 1988. The Origins of War in Neorealist Theory. *Journal of Interdisciplinary History* 18 (4, Spring): 615–628.

———. 1990. Nuclear Myths and Political Realities. *American Political Science Review* 84 (3, September): 731–745.

Wank, Solomon. 1988. The Austrian Peace Movement and the Habsburg Ruling Elite, 1906–1914. In *Peace Movements and Political Cultures,* ed. Charles Chatfield and Peter van den Dungen, 40–63. Knoxville: University of Tennessee Press.

Wedgwood, C.V. 1938. *The Thirty Years War.* London: Jonathan Cape.

Weigley, Russell F. 1973. *The American Way of War: A History of United States Military Strategy and Policy.* New York: Macmillan.

———. 1976. Military and Civilian Leadership. In *Historical Dimensions of National Security Problems,* ed. Klaus Knorr, 38–77. Lawrence: University Press of Kansas.

Wells, H.G. 1914. *The War That Will End War.* New York: Duffield.

———. 1968. *The Last Books of H.G. Wells.* London: H.G. Wells Society.

Werth, Alexander. 1964. *Russia at War, 1941–1945.* New York: Dutton.

West, Rebecca. 1941. *Black Lamb and Grey Falcon: A Journey through Yugoslavia.* New York: Viking.

Williams, Lena. 1990. Free Choice: When Too Much Is Too Much. *New York Times,* 14 February, C1.

Williams, Mary Wilhelmine. 1920. *Social Scandinavia in the Viking Age.* New York: Macmillan.

Willmott, H.P. 1982. *Empires in the Balance.* Annapolis, Md.: Naval Institute Press.

———. 1983. *The Barrier and the Javelin: Japanese and Allied Pacific Strategies, February to June 1942.* Annapolis, Md.: Naval Institute Press.

Wilson, Edmund. 1962. *Patriotic Gore.* New York: Oxford University Press.

Winter, J.M. 1989. Causes of War. In *Aggression and War: Their Biological and Social Bases,* ed. Jo Groebel and Robert A. Hinde, 194–201. Cambridge: Cambridge University Press.

———. 1989. *The Experience of World War I.* New York: Oxford University Press.

Wohlstetter, Albert. 1959. The Delicate Balance of Terror. *Foreign Affairs* 27 (2, January): 211–234.

Wohlstetter, Roberta. 1962. *Pearl Harbor: Warning and Decision.* Stanford, Calif.: Stanford University Press.

Woldman, Albert A. 1950. Lincoln Never Said That. *Harper's,* May, 70–74.

Wolf, Charles, Jr., K.C. Yeh, Edmund Brunner, Jr., Aaron Gurwitz, and Marilee Lawrence. 1983. *The Costs of the Soviet Empire.* Santa Monica, Calif.: Rand Corporation.

Woodward, Bob. 1991. *The Commanders.* New York: Simon and Schuster.

Woolsey, R. James, Jr. 1993. Testimony before the Senate Intelligence Committee. 2 February.

Wright, Quincy. 1942. *A Study of War.* Chicago: University of Chicago Press.

Wright, Robin. 1993. Shifting Battle Lines in Arms Race. *Los Angeles Times,* 17 August, H1.

WuDunn, Sheryl. 1993. Beijing Goes All Out to Get Olympics in 2000. *New York Times,* 11 March, A12.

Wyatt, Harold F. 1911. God's Test By War. *Nineteenth Century* 69 (April): 591–606.

Young, Davis A. 1982. *Christianity and the Age of the Earth.* Grand Rapids, Mich.: Zondervan.

INDEX